GAME DEVELOPMENT ESSENTIALS

GAME ARTIFICIAL INTELLIGENCE

John Ahlquist

Jeannie Novak

THOMSON

★

DELMAR LEARNING ™

Australia   Canada   Mexico   Singapore   Spain   United Kingdom   United States

THOMSON

™

DELMAR LEARNING

Game Development Essentials: Game Artificial Intelligence

John Ahlquist & Jeannie Novak

Vice President, Technology and Trades ABU:
David Garza

Director of Learning Solutions:
Sandy Clark

Managing Editor:
Larry Main

Acquisitions Editor:
James Gish

Product Manager:
Sharon Chambliss

Marketing Director
Deborah Yarnell

Marketing Specialist:
Victoria Ortiz

Director of Production:
Patty Stephan

Production Manager:
Stacy Masucci

Content Project Manager:
Michael Tubbert

Technology Project Manager:
Kevin Smith

Editorial Assistant:
Sarah Timm

Cover: *Civilization IV* courtesy of Firaxis Games Inc.

For more information contact Thomson Delmar Learning Executive Woods
5 Maxwell Drive, PO Box 8007, Clifton Park, NY 12065-8007
Or find us on the World Wide Web at www.delmarlearning.com

Library of Congress Cataloging-in-Publication Data
Ahlquist, John.
   Game development essentials : game artificial intelligence / John Ahlquist & Jeannie Novak.
      p. cm.
   Includes index.
ISBN-13: 978-1-4180-3857-1
ISBN-10: 1-4180-3857-1
1. Computer games—Programming. I. Novak, Jeannie, 1966- II. Title.
QA76.76.C672A425 2007
794.8'1526—dc22
      2007018642

NOTICE TO THE READER

CONTENTS

Chapter 2   AI Agents: creating behavior using a finite state machine.....39

Introduction

Game Artificial Intelligence:
creating intelligent opponents & allies

Imagine being surrounded by enemy characters in an action game and wondering how you're going to get out of this dilemma. You attempt to fight the enemies off—but you soon realize that they don't respond to your defensive attacks. One by one, each of the characters collapse to the ground without a fight—or, worse yet, they just stand around doing nothing. Your sense of immersion just went out the window, not to mention any feeling of dramatic tension or challenge. This is an extreme example of ineffective game artificial intelligence (AI)—but it shows how central AI is to the player experience.

This book will provide you with the tools you need to create game AI that will bring enemy and ally characters to life. The path to great game AI is creating opponents and allies that have an appropriate level of intelligence. Allies need to support, and not impede the player. Unintelligent enemies are easy to kill but irritating—but opponents that always defeat the player are no fun at all. The key is to create enemies with behaviors that are possible to defeat—yet challenging enough that the player has a feeling of accomplishment when the enemies are defeated.

This book discusses the difference between game and computer science AI; the collaboration between design and programming in the game AI creation process; methods of creating game AI (including finite state machines, scripting, pathfinding, and hierarchical systems); and maximizing the appearance of intelligence—both by making intelligence behavior visible to the player, and by using "smoke and mirrors" to provide the appearance of intelligent behavior. Game AI differs from computer science AI in that it only has to provide the appearance of being intelligent. In some cases, we achieve this by having intelligent behaviors. In other cases, we can produce the appearance of intelligent behavior by limiting the environment so that only one behavior is appropriate, and then scripting the enemy to perform that behavior. Where appropriate, a pre-scripted sequence can give the impression of a sophisticated enemy.

Ideally, game designers and programmers should collaborate on the creation and implementation of game AI. The designer will specify desired gameplay and behaviors, and the programmer will create the systems to produce the desired behaviors. This book is intended for programmers, designers, and those interested in either role. The programmer produces systems that are appropriate for the game design—while the designer must understand why certain behaviors are easier to produce, and how to use the tools provided by the programmer. Programmers create AI systems and make their features available to designers, while designers must understand how these systems work and have the opportunity to customize and tune working examples of these systems.

Player expectations and game technology will continue to become more sophisticated. The complexity of game AI will only increase, and those involved in creating it will be in high demand. This book will give you the foundation necessary to enter the field of game AI or hone your skills in this essential area of game development.

John Ahlquist
Warrenton, MO

Jeannie Novak
Santa Monica, CA

About the *Game Development Essentials* Series

The *Game Development Essentials* series was created to fulfill a need: to provide students and creative professionals alike with a complete education in all aspects of the game industry. As more creative professionals migrate to the game industry, and as more game degree and certificate programs are launched, the books in this series will become even more essential to game education and career development.

Not limited to the education market, this series is also appropriate for the trade market and for those who have a general interest in the game industry. Books in the series contain several unique features. All are in full-color and contain hundreds of images—including original illustrations, diagrams, game screenshots, and photos of industry professionals. They also contain a great deal of profiles, tips and case studies from professionals in the industry who are actively developing games. Starting with an overview of all aspects of the industry—*Game Development Essentials: An Introduction*—this series focuses on topics as varied as story & character development, interface design, artificial intelligence, gameplay mechanics, level design, online game development, simulation development, and audio.

Jeannie Novak
Lead Author & Series Editor

About *Game Development Essentials: Game Artificial Intelligence*

This book provides an overview of the game artificial intelligence creation and implementation process—complete with a historical framework, basic concepts, behavior control strategies, advanced topics, and future predictions.

This book contains the following unique features:

- Key chapter questions that are clearly stated at the beginning of each chapter
- Coverage that surveys the topics of game artificial intelligence agents, finite and hierarchical state machines, customization, expert systems, and pathfinding

- Thought-provoking review and study questions at the end of each chapter that are suitable for students and professionals alike to help promote critical thinking and problem-solving skills
- Case studies, quotations from leading professionals, and profiles of game developers that feature concise tips and problem-solving exercises to help readers focus in on issues specific to game artificial intelligence
- An abundance of full-color images throughout that help illustrate the concepts and techniques discussed in the book

There are several general themes associated with this book that are emphasized throughout, including:

- Creating and controlling agent behaviors using hierarchical finite state machines
- Collaboration between programmers and designers on conceptualizing and implementing game artificial intelligence systems
- Distinguishing between and combining data-driven and rule-based game artificial intelligence systems
- Understanding features of pathfinding—including planning, searching, and following
- Techniques for maximizing player perception of intelligence

Who Should Read This Book?

This book is not limited to the education market. If you found this book on a shelf at the bookstore and picked it up out of curiosity, this book is for you, too! The audience for this book includes students, industry professionals, and the general interest consumer market. The style is informal and accessible with a concentration on theory and practice—geared toward both students and professionals.

Students that might benefit from this book include:

- College students in game development, design, programming, and engineering degree programs
- Engineering and programming students who are taking game development courses
- Professional students in college-level programs who are taking game development courses
- First-year game development students at universities

The audience of industry professionals for this book include:

- Scripters, engineers, and programmers who are interested in becoming game programmers and designers
- Professionals in other technical careers and entertainment media—including software development, Web development, film, television, and music—who are interested in transferring their skills to the game development industry

How Is This Book Organized?

This book consists of three parts—focusing on industry background, content creation, and production/business cycles.

Part I Creating Behaviors—Focuses on providing a historical and structural context to game artificial intelligence. Chapters in this section include:

- **Chapter 1 History & Concepts: how did we get here (and where is *here* anyway?)**—discusses the history of game artificial intelligence, distinction between game and computer science AI, and an introduction to intelligent agents
- **Chapter 2 AI Agents: creating and controlling behavior using a finite state machine**—explores finite state machines, transitions, and data-driven modular design
- **Chapter 3 Handling Complexity & Broad Scope: multiple states and hierarchical state machines**—reviews the advantages of hierarchical finite state machines, procedural transition generation, and multiple states

Part II Controlling Behaviors—Focuses on customization, expert systems, and pathfinding. Chapters in this section include:

- **Chapter 4 Customizing AI Systems: allowing others to modify and implement the AI**—focuses on black vs. white box systems, scripting languages, and the relationship between designers and programmers
- **Chapter 5 Expert Systems: creating high-level knowledge and improving behavioral control**—explores knowledge bases, inference engines, and rule-based systems
- **Chapter 6 Pathfinding: allowing agents to properly find and follow paths**—introduces path networks, table lookup vs. search algorithms, and path following techniques

Part III: Advanced Topics & Applications—Focuses on exploring advanced path-finding techniques, maximizing the perception of intelligence, and implementing a hypothetical game AI case study. Chapters in this section include:

- **Chapter 7 Advanced Pathfinding Techniques: improving performance and quality**—highlights group vs. single agent operations, short vs. long path searches, and simpified path network hierarchies
- **Chapter 8 Looking Smart: maximizing the player's perception of intelligence**—outlines the use of cues, variety and optimization in conveying the appearance of intelligence
- **Chapter 9 Putting It All Together: designing and building quality game artificial intelligence**—steps in the process of game AI development, career paths of game AI programmers and designers, and the future of game AI

The book also contains a **Resources** section, which includes a list of game development news sources, guides, directories, conferences, articles, and books related to topics discussed in this text.

How to Use This Text

The sections that follow describe text elements found throughout the book and how they are intended to be used.

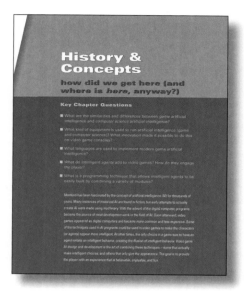

key chapter questions

Key chapter questions are learning objectives in the form of overview questions that start off each chapter. Readers should be able to answer the questions upon understanding the chapter material.

notes

Notes contain thought-provoking ideas provided by the authors that are intended to help the readers think critically about the book's topics.

sidebars

Sidebars offer in-depth information from the authors on specific topics—accompanied by associated images.

quotes

Quotes contain short, insightful thoughts from players, students, and industry observers.

tips

Tips provide advice and inspiration from industry professionals and educators, as well as practical techniques and tips of the trade.

case studies

Case studies contain anecdotes from industry professionals (accompanied by game screenshots) on their experiences developing specific game titles.

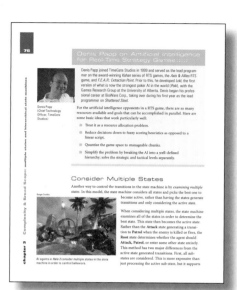

profiles

Profiles provide bios, photos and in-depth commentary from industry professionals and educators.

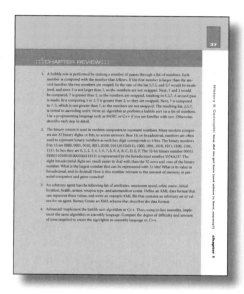

chapter review

A *chapter review* section at the end of each chapter contains a combination of questions and exercises, which allow readers to apply what they've learned. Annotations and answers are included in the instructor's guide, available separately (see next page).

About the Companion DVD

The companion DVD contains the following media:

- Game engines: *Torque* (Windows and Mac versions 1.5.1) and *Game Maker* (version 7)
- 3D modeling and animation software: *3ds Max* (version 9) and *Maya* (version 8.5 PLE)
- Game artificial intelligence programming examples associated with the review exercises in Chapters 2-8
- Game design documentation: GDD template (Chris Taylor/Gas Powered Games), *Sub Hunter* GDD (Michael Black/Torn Space), and *Uncivilized: The Goblin Game* [code name: Salmon] call for game design/submission (Wizards of the Coast)
- Game design articles: Harvey Smith/Witchboy's Cauldron and Barrie Ellis/One Switch Games

- Game concept art: *Tabula Rasa*, *Viewtiful Joe 2*, *Resident Evil 4*
- Game demos/trial versions: 2K Games (*Prey*), Blizzard (*Diablo II*), Firaxis (*Sid Meier's Railroads!*), Stardock (*Galactic Civilizations II: Dread Lords*), THQ (*Company of Heroes*), Enemy Technology (*I of the Enemy: Ril'Cerat*), Star Mountain Studios (*Bergman*, *Weird Helmet*, *Frozen*, *Findella*), and GarageGames (*Dark Horizons: Lore Invasion*, *Gish*, *Marble Blast: Gold*, *Rocket Bowl Plus*, *Zap!*, *Tube Twist*, *Orbz*, *Think Tanks*)

About the Instructor's Guide

The instructor's guide (e-resource, available separately on DVD) was developed to assist instructors in planning and implementing their instructional programs. It includes sample syllabi, test questions, assignments, projects, PowerPoint files, and other valuable instructional resources.

Order Number: 1-4180-4209-9

About the Authors

John Ahlquist developed the tools and engine for Electronic Arts' *Command & Conquer: Generals - Zero Hour* and *The Lord of the Rings: Battle for Middle-Earth*. This included AI and pathfinding systems, as well as creating the level editor, Worldbuilder. After a four-year stint at EA, John now runs Ahlquist Software—developing cutting edge game software for a variety of clients on PC, Xbox 360 and PS3. John previously worked for Altsys/Macromedia on Aldus FreeHand and was one of the creators of Macromedia Fireworks. Prior to Macromedia, John spent seven years working at Texas Instruments, programming Integrated Circuit CAD tools in the Design Automation Department. He has shipped 15 games and major commercial applications over the past 20 years. John is a second-degree black belt in Tae Kwon Do, enjoys mountain biking, and has been playing video games since *Pong*.

Photo credit: Luis Levy

Jeannie Novak is the founder of Indiespace—one of the first companies to promote and distribute interactive entertainment online—where she consults with creative professionals in the music, film, and television industries to help them migrate to the game industry. In addition to being lead author and series editor of the *Game Development Essentials* series, Jeannie is the co-author of three pioneering books on the interactive entertainment industry—including *Creating Internet Entertainment*. Jeannie is the Academic Program Director for the Game Art & Design and Media Arts & Animation programs at the Art Institute Online, where she is also producer and lead designer on a "serious game" that is being built within the *Second Life* environment. She has also been a game instructor and curriculum development expert at UCLA Extension, Art Center College of Design, Academy of Entertainment and Technology at Santa Monica College, DeVry University, Westwood College, and ITT Technical Institute—and she has consulted for the UC Berkeley Center for New Media. Jeannie has developed or participated in game workshops and panels in association with the British Academy of Television Arts & Sciences (BAFTA), Macworld, Digital Hollywood, and iHollywood Forum. She is a member of the International Game Developers Association (IGDA) and has served on selection committees for the Academy of Interactive Arts & Sciences (AIAS). Jeannie was chosen as one of the 100 most influential people in high-technology by *MicroTimes* magazine—and she has been profiled by CNN, *Billboard Magazine,* Sundance Channel, *Daily Variety,* and the *Los Angeles Times.* She received an M.A. in Communication Management from the University of Southern California (USC), where she focused on games in online distance learning. She received a B.A. in Mass Communication from the University of California, Los Angeles (UCLA)—graduating summa cum laude and Phi Beta Kappa. When she isn't writing and teaching, Jeannie spends most of her time recording, performing, and composing music. More information on the author can be found at *http://jeannie.com* and *http://indiespace.com.*

Acknowledgements

The authors would like to thank the following people for their hard work and dedication to this project:

Jim Gish (Acquisitions Editor, Thomson/Delmar), for making this series happen.

Sharon Chambliss (Product Manager, Thomson/Delmar), for moving this project along and always maintaining a professional demeanor.

Michael Tubbert (Content Project Manager, Thomson/Delmar), for his helpful pair of eyes and consistent responsiveness during production crunch time.

Ralph Lagnado & David Ladyman (Image Research & Permissions Specialists), for clearing the many images in this book.

Jason Bramble, for his efforts in tracking, capturing and researching the many images for this book.

Sarah Timm (Editorial Assistant, Thomson/Delmar), for her ongoing assistance throughout the series.

Gina Dishman (Project Manager, GEX Publishing Services), for her diligent work and prompt response during the layout and compositing phase.

Per Olin, for his organized and aesthetically pleasing diagrams.

David Koontz (Publisher, Chilton), for starting it all by introducing Jeannie Novak to Jim Gish.

A big thanks also goes out to the people who contributed their thoughts and ideas to this book:

Chris Taylor (Gas Powered Games)

David Javelosa (Academy of Entertainment & Technology at Santa Monica College)

Denis Papp (TimeGate Studios)

Don Daglow (Stormfront Studios)

Dustin Browder (Blizzard Entertainment)

Frank Gilson (Wizards of the Coast)

Harvey Smith (Midway)

Jeffrey Brown (THQ)

John Comes (Gas Powered Games)

Mark Skaggs (Blue Nitro Studios)

Michael Black (Torn Space)

Stephen Superville (Epic Games)

Thanks to the following people and companies for their tremendous help with referrals and in securing permissions, images, and demos:

Aaron Grant (Activision)

Ai Hasegawa & Hideki Yoshimoto (Namco Bandai Games America Inc.)

Alta Hartmann & Brian Jarrard (Bungie Studios)

Brian Hupp (Electronic Arts)

Briar Lee Mitchell (Star Mountain Studios)

Chris Glover (Eidos)

Chris Taylor & Sabrina Roberts (Gas Powered Games)

Christine Kalb & Annie Ballenger (Autodesk Media & Entertainment)

David Greenspan & Lin Leng (THQ)

David Swofford (NCsoft)

Dennis Shirk & Stephen Martin (Firaxis)

Don McGowan (Microsoft Corporation)

EarlyOfficeMuseum.com

Eric Fritz (GarageGames)

Erik Einsiedel & Teresa Cotesta (BioWare)

Frank Gilson (Wizards of the Coast)

Gabe Newell, Doug Lombardi & Jason Holtman (Valve)

Joe Steinsky

Kathryn Butters (Atari Interactive, Inc.)

Kristin Hatcher (Stardock Entertainment)

Liz Buckley (Majesco Entertainment)

London Science Museum

Mark Beaumont, Estela Lemus, Tamela Craft-Molarahima & Michiko Morita (Capcom)

Mark Rein (Epic Games)

Mark Temple (Enemy Technology)

Michael Black (Torn Space)

Noriko Kato (Taito Corporation)

Paul Crockett (2K Games)

Paul W. Sams, Denise Lopez & Brianna Messina (Blizzard)

Reilly Brennan, Harvey Smith & Tim DaRosa (Midway)

Sophie Jakubowicz & Jocelyn Portacio (Ubisoft)

Sophie Russell & Mark Overmars (YoYo Games)

Steve Biles (IBM)

Todd Hollenshead (id Software)

University of Evansville

University of Washington Design Machine Group

Wendy Zaas (Rogers & Cowan)

Zicel Maymudes (Mattel)

Delmar Learning and the authors would also like to thank the following reviewers for their valuable suggestions and technical expertise:

John Comes
    Gas Powered Games
    Redmond, VA

Ron Hightower
    Westwood College
    Denver, CO

Denis Papp
    TimeGate Studios
    Houston, TX

Questions and Feedback

We welcome your questions and feedback. If you have suggestions that you think others would benefit from, please let us know and we will try to include them in the next edition.

To send us your questions and/or feedback, you can contact the publisher at:

Delmar Learning
Executive Woods
5 Maxwell Drive
Clifton Park, NY 12065
Attn: Graphic Arts Team
(800) 998-7498

Or the series editor at:

Jeannie Novak
Founder & CEO
INDIESPACE
P.O. Box 5458
Santa Monica, CA 90409
jeannie@indiespace.com

DEDICATION

To my wonderful wife Karen who put up with my periodic absences, and to JMS for getting me started in this wonderful mess that is video game development.

—*John*

To Luis, my closest ally. Thanks for sharing the path with me.

—*Jeannie*

Part I:
Creating
Behaviors

History & Concepts

how did we get here (and where is *here*, anyway?)

Key Chapter Questions

- What are the similarities and differences between *game* artificial intelligence and *computer science* artificial intelligence?

- What kind of equipment is used to run artificial intelligence (game and computer science)? What innovation made it possible to do this on video game consoles?

- What languages are used to implement modern game artificial intelligence?

- What do *intelligent agents* add to video games? How do they engage the player?

- What is a programming technique that allows intelligent agents to be easily built by combining a variety of modules?

Mankind has been fascinated by the concept of artificial intelligence (AI) for thousands of years. Many instances of historical AI are found in fiction, but early attempts to actually create AI were made using machinery. With the advent of the digital computer, programs became the source of most development work in the field of AI. Soon afterward, video games appeared as digital computers and became more common and less expensive. Some of the techniques used in AI programs could be used in video games to make the characters (or agents) appear more intelligent. At other times, the only choice in a game was to have an agent imitate an intelligent behavior, creating the illusion of intelligent behavior. Video game AI design and development is the art of combining these techniques—some that actually make intelligent choices, and others that only give the appearance. The goal is to provide the player with an experience that is believable, enjoyable, and fun.

Game AI vs. Computer Science AI

When people refer to *artificial intelligence (AI)*, they are generally referring to AI as it is used in computer science. Game AI and computer science AI, however, are only distantly related. Computer science AI is defined as intelligence that is exhibited by an artificial entity (usually assumed to be a computer). Although AI has a science fiction connotation, it forms a vital branch of computer science, dealing with intelligent behavior, learning, and adaptation in machines. Research in AI is concerned with producing machines to automate tasks requiring intelligent behavior. In contrast, game AI is concerned with the creation of behaviors in a video game that give the impression of intelligent behavior on the part of the game's player.

Computer science AI is about substance. The goal is to actually solve problems that require intelligence. Game AI is about appearances. The goal in a video game is for the characters in the game, and any "computer-controlled players," to appear to behave and play intelligently.

In some cases, the two fields overlap. One way to give the impression of intelligent behavior is to actually create intelligent behaviors. Often AI techniques, such as *expert systems,* are used in video games to create intelligent-appearing behaviors. An expert system is a database and logic engine that stores information (knowledge) from a human expert and uses it to answer questions or control a process—in this case, a game. In other cases a combination of scripting, triggers, and animations are combined to give the appearance of intelligent behavior when in fact no actual AI algorithms are remotely involved. The game designer creating the behavior, rather than an algorithm, is the source of the intelligence. The information from an expert system is captured from one or more human experts and a computer program that combines known facts with the information to solve problems or answer questions.

Good game AI consists of a well thought-out fusion of AI algorithms, scripting, and hooks for game designer control of behaviors. This allows for the creation of the behaviors that the player expects from an intelligent character or opponent in a video game.

A Brief Overview of Computer Science AI

Mankind has been fascinated with artificial intelligence as long as people have been making machines, both in fact and in fiction. Prior to the advent of electronic computers in the mid-20th century, working examples were mechanical and the fiction was often biological in nature. The golem was an early example of a fictitious AI, and the Frankenstein story was a cautionary tale concerning the creation of an artificial intelligence. However, mechanical automata were extremely limited, and AI was much more capable in fiction than in fact. Computers gave people tools that could perform logic and reasoning tasks, and suddenly the science of "artificial intelligence" was possible.

Mechanical Automata

An automaton is a machine that controls itself. A cuckoo clock is a simple automaton. Early *automata* were mechanical. In the first century AD, Heron of Alexandria built a variety of machines, including the first documented steam engine. He is also credited with creating the first analog programming system. This consisted of a series of geared spindles connected to weights. The weights consisted of sand that drained out over time. This system was used to control effects in his automatic theatre such as the opening and closing of doors, movement of figures in the background, and lighting changes. Mechanical calculators were created starting in the 1600s and continued to be built through the 1970s. William Schickard created the first mechanical calculator in 1623. It used gears and cogs normally used in making clocks.

EarlyOfficeMuseum.com

The Schickard Calculator was an early mechanical calculator.

Blaise Pascal's Pascaline

Blaise Pascal created a mechanical calculator in 1642 called the Pascaline, which performed addition and subtraction on decimal numbers. Later versions were able to handle numbers up to 9,999,999.

While the binary number system was described in detail by Gottfried Leibniz in the 17th century and Boolean logic was developed in 1800, mechanical calculators continued to use the decimal system, as well as some early electronic computers, such as the *ENIAC* in 1945. *Boolean logic* is the complete set of logical operations for the operators AND, OR, and NOT. Boolean logic can be used with two values—0 or false, and 1 or true. Numbers can be represented by a series of Boolean values as well using binary representation. It turns out that it is relatively straightforward to represent Boolean values in a digital electronic circuit with a high voltage value (or on, representing 1) and a low voltage value (or off, representing 0). ENIAC was the first large scale reprogrammable general purpose electronic digital computer, completed in February, 1946. Several computing systems were developed in the early 1940s, but ENIAC was the first to combine all of their features. Modern digital computers operate on the same principles as ENIAC, with integrated circuitry replacing vacuum tubes and wires.

Programmable Systems

Charles Babbage designed a series of mechanical calculators, starting in 1822. The first was called the *difference engine* and was intended to compute the value of polynomial functions. Although he started construction, Babbage was never able to complete the difference engine. Instead, after he abandoned the difference engine's construction, Babbage designed the *analytical engine*—the first mechanical calculator that was to be programmed using a series of punch cards. Although the analytical engine was never constructed, the Science Museum of London used Babbage's plans for *Difference Engine No. 2* and built a working engine from 1985 to 1991. The engine weighs 2.6 tons and consists of 4,000 moving parts. It correctly generated its result to 31 decimal digits of accuracy. Unfortunately, programmable mechanical calculators proved to be a dead end.

Joe Steinsky

The London Science Museum

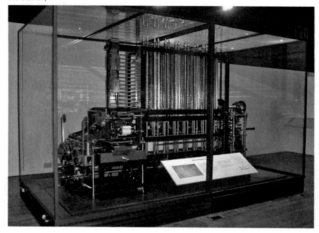 

Charles Babbage's difference engine (left) and analytical engine (right) were two of the most complex mechanical calculating machines.

Programmable electronic computers were developed in the 1940s. The Mark I was brought online at Manchester University in 1949. Alan Turing attempted to program it to play chess. The program was too large to actually run on the Mark I, so Turing hand simulated the program, playing several games against different opponents. The program played a mediocre game of chess, similar to Turing himself. The program lost most of the games it played.

The *Turing Test* is a test of a machine's ability to perform human-like conversation proposed in 1950 by Alan Turing. It involves a human judge taking part in a conversation with two other parties—one a person, the other the machine. Both parties attempt to appear human. If the judge cannot reliably determine which is which, the machine passes the test. Turing proposed the test to replace the question, "Can a machine think?" No machine has passed the Turing test as of 2007. Conversational programs such as ELIZA have made people believe that they were conversing with another human, but this has only occurred in situations where the person thought that the other party was also human, and was not trying to determine whether or not it was a machine.

The microprocessor was developed in the 1970s and led to both personal computer systems and programmable video game consoles. Prior to the microprocessor, even the simplest computers required several large printed circuit boards and a number of electronic components. Minicomputers, such as PDP-8 and LINC, were still the size of refrigerators and cost tens of thousands of dollars. With the advent of microprocessors, it was possible to build business systems smaller than a typewriter that cost only a few thousand dollars. This led to the creation of the Apple II, IBM PC, and a host of other personal computers.

The microprocessor itself was so small and inexpensive that Atari could build the 2600 in 1977 with a fully functional computer consisting of a microprocessor and a small amount of memory and sell the system for less than $200. Before the microprocessor, the cost and size of a video game system with a fully functional computer was prohibitive.

AI Development

In 1949, Arthur Samuel began work on a checkers-playing machine that learned from experience. The first program was developed on an IBM 701 computer. The program used heuristic search methods to determine the depth of search and a board evaluation function to evaluate a given board position. It used a rote learning mechanism that remembered previous board positions and the results of the evaluation. Over time, the program learned to play a decent, but not expert, game of checkers.

IBM

The IBM 701 was used to develop one of the early checkers-playing programs.

University of Evansville

The General Problem Solver was able to solve puzzles such as the Tower of Hanoi (pictured).

Allen Newell, J.C. Shaw, and Herbert Simon implemented the Logic Theorist in 1956. This program was able to discover proofs of geometric theorems. The General Problem Solver was developed in 1957. It applied several symbolic reasoning techniques: means/end analysis, planning, and selective trial and error. It was able to solve a variety of tasks, including logic problems and puzzles, such as the Tower of Hanoi.

Fuzzy logic was developed in 1965 by Lotfi Zadeh. Traditional Boolean logic deals with facts that are true or false, while fuzzy logic techniques allow reasoning with facts that are not strictly true or false. For example, the level of gasoline in a tank, ranging from 0 to 100%full, can be used in fuzzy logic reasoning.

The ELIZA Effect

In 1964, Joseph Weizenbaum implemented ELIZA—a program that performed text analysis and successfully simulated a conversation (known as the "ELIZA effect.") This development was more useful for game AI, since it demonstrated a case where the appearance of intelligence was much greater than the reality. The ELIZA effect is discussed in more detail in Chapter 7.

Fuzzy Logic

Many AI problems are amenable to Boolean logic, which has two values. Whether the AI should attack or whether it should retreat can be stored in a single Boolean value. Whether its gun has ammunition is a true or false value. The following test uses Boolean logic values and operations: If the gun has ammunition and we should attack, then fire the gun.

By adding more Boolean values and tests, a wide variety of conditions can be represented and acted upon. Many games rely exclusively on these kinds of tests and values, using a large number of them to achieve complex behaviors.

Other AI problems do not fit well into the Boolean logic model. Consider a racing car game where cars race around a track in small groups. One task for the AI is steering cars around the track. The steering control is not a two valued control. There are a multitude of positions between straight ahead and a hard left turn. Thus, Boolean logic does not provide a direct way to control a steering wheel.

Fuzzy logic values consist of numbers. A common range is between 0 and 1. Values from the game are mapped into values in this range, and results are also numbers in this range. One value could be the position of the car in the street, from left to right. On the left curb the value is 0, on the right curb the value is 1. In the middle of the street the value is 0.5. We can call this example LRPos. The steering is set up so that a value of 0 is a hard left turn, a value of 0.5 is straight ahead, and a value of 1 is a hard right turn. If we apply the LRPos directly to the steering, we get a broken behavior; if the car is on the right side of the road, it makes a hard right turn and drives off of the road.

We can use the Fuzzy logic operator "NOT" to correct this. The value of NOT(VALUE) is 1.0 – VALUE. So we can use:

Steering = NOT(LRPos)

When the car is on the left side, LRPos is 0, NOT(LRpos) is 1, and the car will make a hard right turn toward the center of the road. As the car approaches the center, LRPos will increase toward 0.5, the steering value will decrease from 1 toward 0.5, and the car will straighten. If the car overshoots the center, it will turn the steering to the left.

Other values, such as the presence of a car on the left or right side can be calculated as well. Fuzzy logic operators AND and OR can be used to create complex fuzzy logic formulas, taking many conditions into account. The AI can then use the steering to keep the car on the road while avoiding other vehicles.

Knowledge-Based and Expert Systems

Knowledge-based systems appeared in the late 1960s. It became apparent to researchers in a number of areas that detailed knowledge about the world may be necessary to perform AI tasks. Natural language processing was more effective if the program had knowledge about the world to resolve ambiguities. Visual analysis of scenes, determining edges and objects, was more effective if the program had knowledge of how objects appear; if you see part of an object adjacent to another object, it is likely that the partial object is behind the other object. Rules such as these embedded in the AI processing resulted in more effective AI systems. There was some question regarding whether this was really AI, since the programmer and system designer were responsible for collecting the knowledge for the system. The knowledge-based systems turned out to be useful in real-life situations, so they represent an AI technique commonly used today in business and industry.

Diagram by Per Olin

DENDRAL was an AI system designed to analyze the results of a mass spectrograph. A mass spectrograph is used to perform chemical analysis by plotting a graph of the mass-to-charge ratio of the sample. Chemists can analyze this graph and determine the chemical composition of the sample. The authors of DENDRAL collected a great deal of information from chemists who were experts in the use of the mass spectrograph. One of the key results was developing a way to represent this knowledge in a large database. DENDRAL was specific to this problem, the analysis of mass spectrograph data, but it led to the more general *expert system*.

MYCIN was developed in 1974. The first expert system used a rule set and inference engine to capture medical knowledge and use that knowledge to diagnose bacterial infections. This system included a general purpose inference engine. The rule set was specific to a given problem, in this case bacterial infections. Additional rule sets were developed to operate in other areas. Expert systems are one of the commonly used AI systems in business and industry. They are used in diverse applications, from detecting credit card fraud to diagnosing problems with personal computers.

The first autonomous vehicle was created in 1979. Hans Moravec developed the Cart, a mobile robot with external visual sensors. The Cart maintained an internal 3D model of its environment, and moved around based on that model. However, it was far from real time. It took a "step" about once every 15 minutes. Rodney Brooks worked to create less expensive robots and created *Allen* in 1985. One of the key innovations he brought was tying sensor inputs directly to actions, rather than trying to interpret the sensor input into a world model and then analyzing the world model. This produced good real-time behaviors. Brooks went on to develop commercial robots, including mine detecting robots for the military, and the Sony AIBO robotic dog.

The Japanese government announced the *Fifth Generation* project in 1981 with significant AI goals. The project developed custom hardware and software to implement parallel inference machines. The system's software was written in a variant of Prolog. The resulting systems were not viable commercially. They could not run existing software, and general purpose computers became faster and much more cost effective. The Fifth Generation project was discontinued in 1992.

Creating an expert chess computer has been a goal for the AI community since the construction of the first programmable electronic computers in the 1940s. In 1988 Feng-hsiung Hsu, Thomas Anantharaman, Mike Brown, Murray Campbell, and Andreas Nowatzyk created a chess playing machine called Deep Thought at Carnegie Mellon University. Deep Thought won the Fredkin Prize that year as the first chess playing computer to play grandmaster-level chess. Hsu moved to IBM, and was the system architect of Deep Blue with C. J. Tan, Murray Campbell, Joseph Hoane, Jerry Brody, and Joel Benjamin. Deep Blue won the match against Gary Kasparov in 1997, becoming the first chess computer to defeat the human world champion.

History of Game AI Agents

Game AI consists of the creation and control of behaviors for autonomous *agents* in video games. Early video games such as *Pong* and *Spacewar!* had no agents and required two players. Arcade owners discovered that it was easier to get one person to feed a game quarters than two, so games were developed for single players, and agents provided the opponents. We will primarily consider two kinds of agents: characters, and virtual players. Characters are visible in the game, and the human player can interact directly with them either by shooting them, or by engaging in conversation and *then* shooting them! Characters perform a variety of functions in current games. They can give the player something to do, such as defending against an attacking character. They can perform interesting behaviors on their own to provide ambience. Civilian characters in *Command & Conquer: Generals* walk around; when they perceive danger, they run and scream—but they do not affect the outcome of the game one way or another. Finally, characters can be used to advance the plot in a story-driven game. Characters in current games have sophisticated animations and models, similar in quality to computer-generated movies. Virtual players take the place of human players. In a computer-based chess game, human players do not actually see the virtual player in the game—but they see the results of the moves that the virtual player makes. Strategy and planning is usually a focus of the virtual player.

Characters

Agents that are present as characters in a game may fulfill a variety of needs. They provide the player with something to do—such as to kill or be killed. They can serve as allies or subordinates, allowing the player to give orders and play cooperatively. Agents might also perform a scripted part, advancing the story is plot. Examples can be as simple as the ghosts in *Pac-Man* and the space ship in *Asteroids*, to the more complex aliens in *Half-Life* and demons in *Doom 3*. Other examples are tanks in real-time strategy (RTS) games such as *Command & Conquer* and *Rise of Nations*—or wizards and trolls in games such as *Warcraft*. *Non-player characters (NPCs)*, such as Jedi Knights and Sith warriors in games from the *Star Wars* universe (including *Knights of the Old Republic*), round out the list.

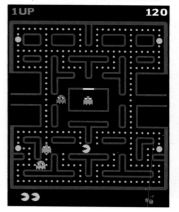 

The ghosts in *Pac-Man* (left) and the alien monsters in *Half-Life 2* (right) both provide a source of danger to the player that can be defeated with skillful play.

The player's opponent is a virtual player in a chess program such as *Chessmasters 10*.

Virtual Player

There is a second type of agent that is not visible in the game but has a presence nonetheless. This is the AI *virtual player* that takes the place of a human opponent in a game. A good example is chess. The human player plays against the AI. The AI player does not have a visual representation, but we know that it is there by the moves that it makes. So unlike a character, we perceive the AI player through the decisions it makes, rather than actually seeing the AI Player.

Using Multiple Agent Types

Some games contain agents that are only characters or virtual players. Board games such as chess and checkers only have a virtual player AI. *Civilization* uses multiple virtual players; the individual units (warriors, settlers, tanks) have little or no intelligence. The opposing civilizations are controlled by AI players that controlled their units' creation and construction. Other games such as *Half-Life* consist of only character AI. The player battles a series of entities, humanoid and otherwise, but there is no sense of an opposing player in the game. The individual characters are supposed to have intelligent behavior.

Electronic Arts

Some games (such as many RTSs) use both types of AI. *Red Alert 2* has agents in the game with a moderate degree of intelligence. Since the player is the commander, they do not show a lot of initiative, but they are good at following orders. Resource collection agents will automatically continue collecting resources. Tanks can be ordered to attack a target; they will pathfind to the target, move into range, and fire until the target is destroyed. In addition, there is a virtual player that issues orders to the enemy units. The virtual player schedules unit construction, builds structures, attacks the human player, and defends its base.

Red Alert 2 has character agents, such as infantry and tanks, in addition to an invisible virtual player that manages the opposing base, unit construction, and battle management.

Early Agents

There were no AI agents in early video games. *Pong* and *Spacewar!* required two players. Vendors quickly discovered that playing against the machine was a good way to get people to spend quarters. They came up with ways to play the games that involved playing against the machine. There were not actually any agents that were played; the games were more like solitaire. An example of this is the *Breakout* game, which is actually similar to *Pong*; but instead of playing against another human, people played against a row of blocks at the top of the screen. The ball would bounce up and remove the blocks, thus giving the player a point for each block and a goal to clear the most blocks. So in games such as this, there are no agents at all and no need for AI. Other subsequent games are similar in that they require no AI. A good example of a popular game in this vein is *Tetris*. The point of the game is to fit the blocks into the pattern and catch them as they come down. The game itself generates the blocks in a random fashion, and players play the game against the computer.

Courtesy of Atari Interactive, Inc.

Courtesy of Atari Interactive, Inc.

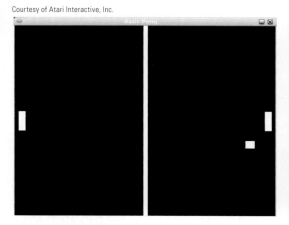 

Early games such as *Pong* (left) and *Breakout* (right) had no AI agents at all. *Pong* required another person for the opponent, and in *Breakout*, the opponent was a motionless wall of colored blocks.

Character Agents

Other games began using *character agents*. Some early examples are the ghosts in *Pac-Man* that moved through a maze. The player's job was to avoid them and collect the dots. The early games ran on very limited microprocessors. As a result, the AI was very simple. It was often not much more intelligent than the falling blocks in *Tetris*. Often, the agents moved in simple, fixed patterns and did not react in any way to the presence of the players' representation. Games of this era, such as *Space Invaders* and *Asteroids*, had very simple agents as well.

Taito Corporation

Courtesy of Atari Interactive, Inc.

 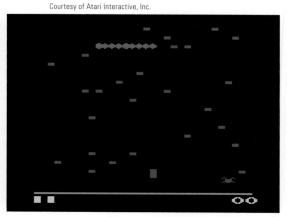

Early agents, such as the aliens in *Space Invaders*, had extremely simple behaviors. Subsequent games such as *Centipede* provided agents with more interesting, though still repetitive, behaviors.

A more interesting game along these lines was *Centipede,* where the agent had a more complex behavior. The centipede bounced off the mushrooms, and the pattern changed as mushrooms were destroyed by the player. Another agent was the spider that would fall down and drop mushrooms. Still, there was very little intelligence associated with the agents. Their behaviors were mechanical and predictable. Part of the fun of the game was figuring out the movement of the centipede and firing correctly with the trackball to destroy the centipede in the most efficient manner possible.

As time went on, however, hardware became more capable and agents became more complex. 3D games became prevalent, the player could see in three dimensions, and agents had to move in a 3D world. In *Doom*, the agents (demons and monsters) would wait until the player came near and then they would move to attack the player. This is still simple, but a more sophisticated behavior than earlier examples. The agents had to be able to track the player in a 3D space, aim and fire at them.

Courtesy of id Software, Inc.   Bungie Studios

Enemy agents in *Doom* (left) performed simple attack behaviors. *Halo* (right) provided agents with more sophisticated attack behaviors that made use of cover.

Character agents have become more complex and can perform tactical behaviors as well as a simple approach the player and attack behaviors. They can use cover and move behind objects to stay out of the way of fire. Games such as *Half-Life* and *Halo* have agents that can use coordinated squad behaviors. They flank the player and perform more sophisticated activities that give the player more of an impression of there being intelligence beyond the agents, perhaps a squad leader directing their movements.

Another way character agents demonstrate intelligent behavior is through reacting to their environment. In games of this genre, hand grenades are a common weapon. In early implementations, the player could throw a hand grenade at an opponent and the AI would not react. This did not appear particularly intelligent. An improvement

Electronic Arts

Agents in *Medal of Honor: Pacific Assault* react to the presence of a hand grenade.

on that in *Medal of Honor: Pacific Assault* was for the agents to recognize that there was a hand grenade and move away from it.

Call of Duty 2 implements this in its squad AI, so if a hand grenade comes, a squad of units will holler that there is a grenade, which is useful for warning the player, and at the same time move away from it, if possible, so they will not get damaged. An additional improvement for *Medal of Honor: Pacific Assault* was to add the behavior that if the grenade was close by, the AI would attempt to reach down, pick up the grenade and throw it back. Sometimes, depending on the timing of the grenade, when the AI attempted to pick it up, it would be successful at throwing it back. Other times, it would blow up and damage the AI—but nonetheless, the behavior appeared much more intelligent to the player than the AI ignoring the hand grenade.

Virtual Player Agents

Early *virtual player agents* were developed for board games, such as chess and checkers. Strategy games also required the creation of virtual players. Early games such as *Empire: Wargame of the Century* pitted the player against one or more enemies controlled by the computer.

In this genre, the human player creates and moves units, and the units resolve combat. The games are *turn-based* and the units themselves are very simple and are not particularly intelligent. The units can be ordered to move, and when the units encounter an enemy unit, there is a combat resolution based on the relative strengths of the units. These units are similar to chess pieces, in that the individual pieces are not intelligent but are moved by an intelligent player.

An excellent example of this is *Civilization*, in which the intelligence appears on the part of the computer player who performs similar operations to those done by the human player. In *Civilization*, the player builds cities and units that can be moved, can occupy territories, and can build improvements. The player can improve cities to produce more advanced units and produce them faster.

The virtual player agent performs the same operations as the player. The way we perceive the presence and intelligence of the virtual player is through the moves it makes and the results of the choices it makes.

Civilization (left) and *Command & Conquer 3: Tiberian Sun* (right) both provide an invisible virtual player that functions as the player's opponent.

RTSs had a similar need for virtual players. *Command & Conquer* provided two modes of play. The first was a scripted series of missions that the player had to beat. These were controlled by the designer, and relied more on scripting than on AI. The game also included a multiplayer mode. In this mode, multiple human players could play an unscripted game using the units and structures provided. The initial version of multiplayer was like *Pong* in that it required a human opponent.

Later RTS games such as *Starcraft* and *Command & Conquer: Tiberian Sun* included a virtual player for multiplayer mode. This mode, called skirmish mode, allowed a human to play an unscripted multiplayer game against one or more computer opponents. This is another example of a virtual player.

History of Game AI Implementation Methods

Electronic games in general and AI in particular have been implemented using a variety of different techniques since electronic games first emerged. These games are programs running on microprocessors—descendants of the first electronic, programmable digital computer, the ENIAC. These programs are a series of machine instructions stored in memory. Each instruction is a number specific to the processor. For example, the instruction to push 32 bits of the B register on the stack on a Pentium processor is 83. The instruction to move 32 bits of register C into register A is 35777. Early computers, such as a PDP8 microcomputer, had switches on the front of the computer so that the initial program could be entered by hand. Determining the sequence of numbers by hand (called hand assembly) was tedious and error prone, so programs called assemblers were written that converted a symbolic assembly language into the machine instructions. Assembly language instructions used mnemonic abbreviations for the instructions. The assembly language instruction to move 32 bits of register C into register A is:

```
MOV   EAX,ECX
```

Although somewhat obscure, it is vastly easier to remember than 35777. And you could probably guess the instruction to move register C into B:

```
MOV   EBX,ECX
```

Design Machine Group, University of Washington

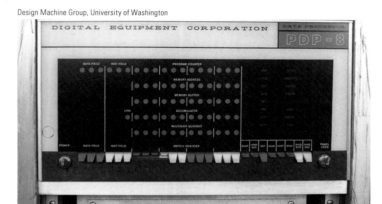

The switches on the control panel of the PDP8 microcomputer could be used to enter the instruction code numbers by hand.

However, it is unlikely that you would guess that the actual instruction is 35801.

Assembly language is much easier to use than machine instructions, but it is still very time-consuming. Early games were written in assembly language because the hardware was too limited in memory and processing power to support high level languages. As game consoles and personal computers became more capable, high level languages, such as C++, allowed programmers to create more complex and capable programs, resulting in more intricate, detailed, and interesting games. Scripting languages have been added to allow designers and mod makers to change game behavior without having to re-compile the game.

Courtesy of Atari Interactive, Inc.

The Atari 2600 VCS required that game code be very small due to memory limitations.

Assembly Language

Initially, games were written in *assembly language* primarily to the limitations of the hardware platforms that they were running on. The advantage to using assembly language is that it is possible, although difficult, to write extremely small code. It is also possible to write very efficient code. The early video game consoles and video game arcade systems had extremely limited memory and microprocessors. An Atari 2600 VCS had only 4K bytes of program memory for an entire game.

Using assembly language to produce small code was critical, and thus, assembly language was a good choice even though it was very difficult to program in assembly language.

This is a sample of Pentium assembly language that calls a function with two arguments: a pointer to an object, and a two-dimensional coordinate:

```
mov     eax,dword ptr [y]
push    eax
mov     ecx,dword ptr [x]
push    ecx
lea     ecx,[ebp-108h]
call    Coord2D::Coord2D (4B38FBh)
push    eax
mov     edx,dword ptr [subGroup]
push    edx
mov     ecx,dword ptr [this]
call    Game::CreateAgent (4BAC5Ah)
```

The corresponding line of C++ code that generated the assembly language appears as:

```
CreateAgent(subGroup, Coord2D(x,y));
```

As you can see, the assembly language is more complicated. It requires 10 lines of assembly language code to implement one line of C++ code. In addition, it requires an extensive knowledge of the computer hardware and the instruction set. It is possible to develop software in high level languages much more quickly than in assembly language. Studies have shown that developing in assembly language is generally 5–10 times slower than developing in a high level language.

Assembly language is not appropriate for the development of sophisticated AI systems. They require a lot of code, and developing that quantity of code in assembly language is prohibitive. In addition, the code to support AI systems requires great deal of memory. The *Lua* scripting system, which is one of the smaller general purpose scripting systems, takes over 100,000 bytes of memory. The memory limitations and the difficulty of writing AI in assembly language forced developers to get by with AI systems that were, at best, very simple.

Although little modern game code is written in assembly language, it is still very useful for a programmer to have a good understanding of assembly language. Assembly language corresponds directly to machine instructions. The high level C++ code, for example, is converted into machine language instructions for execution by the processor. Modern optimizing compilers re-arrange the order of operations to improve performance and keep variables in registers rather than saving them to memory. Debug builds disable these optimizations in order to make debugging easier. However, some bugs only show up in fully optimized builds, and often the QA group is running an optimized build. Crash logs returned from QA often provide only assembly level information. So it is important to be able to examine and understand the assembly language level code when debugging. Almost no AI code in a video game is actually written in assembly language. The code size is no longer an issue; modern games may have 4–8 megabytes of code. On a 512 megabyte console or personal computer there is little value in reducing the code size since 90 percent of the memory is consumed by art assets—textures and models.

Early video games were written in assembly language due to the memory and processor limitations of the hardware. Due to the same limitations, as well as the difficulty of writing complex software in assembly language, early AI code was minimal to nonexistent. Assembly language comprises a very small percentage of the code in modern games, but assembly language programming skills are still valuable when debugging optimized game code.

Courtesy of id Software, Inc.

Doom was created using the high level language C in addition to assembly language.

C and C++

Over time, personal computers and video game consoles were shipped with faster, more capable microprocessors, and more system memory. Authors began to write games in higher level languages, primarily C and C++. *Doom*, for example, was written for the PC in C, although assembly language was also used for parts of the game. In the case of *Doom*, assembly language was used for performance reasons. The 3D rendering system was executed in software. In order to get enough performance to even get a 320 × 240 display rendering in real time, it was necessary to write large chunks of the rendering system in assembly language to get the maximum performance.

However, substantial parts of the game were written in C in areas where performance was not as critical. The AI could be written in a higher-level language, which opened the door for implementing more sophisticated AI techniques.

The drawback of using C++ is that it is a very rich language—requiring a programmer to know a great deal about it and how it can be used, particularly when working within a memory constrained system such as the PlayStation Portable (PSP). In addition, errors in C or C++ can cause the game to crash. This requires very careful development, testing, and QA verification to make sure that the game is stable and robust. The engine code in modern games is sufficiently complex that it can take several minutes or longer to build the application when changes are made to the C++ source code, resulting in a slow develop and test cycle.

Scripting Languages

As game hardware became available with faster processors and more memory another method for implementing game play features and AI became available: the use of an interpreted *text-based* language. This is often called a *scripting* language. The key aspect is that the language is interpreted rather than compiled. Scripting languages are generally layered on top of the C++ engine.

The following are just a few features of scripting languages:

- Scripts can be loaded at runtime. This allows changes to be made and tested more quickly than changes to C++ code.
- Scripts can be specific to a particular level or area in a game. This allows customization that is difficult to maintain in C++ code.
- Scripting implementations can be "bomb proofed" so that errors in scripts are handled gracefully, and do not cause the game to crash.
- Scripting implementations are customized to the game. Game specific features can be added to a scripting environment to make game development faster and easier.

There are a couple of drawbacks to using an interpreted (scripting) language. One is that the interpreted languages are slower to execute than compiled languages like C++, so there is a performance overhead. There is also a memory cost for the code that interprets the script. Additionally, it is necessary to write "glue code" to interface between the script system and the engine so that scripts can do actual work in the game.

As a result, it takes some time to integrate the script engine into a game. Before someone can write AI and control code in an interpreted language, a C++ engineer has to define the interface and implement the glue code so that those features are available to the other programmers or designers using the interpreted language.

Gas Powered Games

Epic Games

AI behaviors are specified with the Lua scripting language in *Supreme Commander* (left), while the AI code that controls the enemy characters shown in *Gears of War* (right) is written in the UnrealScript scripting language.

A wide variety of interpreted languages are used in video game development. Lua is a free open source interpreted language that is used in a variety of games. *PainKiller* uses Lua, as do *Supreme Commander* and *The Lord of the Rings: The Battle for Middle-Earth*. Python is another open source interpreted language that is used in a variety of games such as *Earth and Beyond* and *Civilization IV*. UnrealScript is an interpreted language in the Unreal engine and has been used in a variety of games, such as *SWAT 4*, *Tribes,* and *Gears of War*.

GUI and Graphical Scripting Systems

A more recent method for creating and controlling AI is using a *graphical user interface (GUI)* system that is created specifically for the game. This allows the AI programmers and designers to enter the information necessary to create and control the behaviors of the AI via a graphical user interface.

Self Documenting

The use of a GUI is *self-documenting*, and it serves as an educational tool and a reminder. *Command & Conquer: Generals*, for example, had several "Follow Waypoint" actions that the designer could use to direct units. The system had a hierarchical menu in the GUI as follows:

```
Team Movement > Waypoint Path >      Follow Waypoint Path
        Attack Follow Waypoint Path
        Flee along Waypoint Path
        Wander along Waypoint Path
        Follow Waypoint Path Exactly (Cinematic)
```

Designers could look at the menu and see that five types of movement along a path are supported. If designers wanted to have a team do an "Attack Wander" movement, they could see that that was not supported. In a text-based scripting system, additional documentation is required.

The parameters are also documented in a GUI based implementation, and values can be provided through a popup menu. The Unreal 3 engine used in *Unreal Tournament 2007* uses a script action called an Actor Factory. This can be used to create a game character. One of the options is to assign an AI controller to the character. This controller can be selected from a pop-up list, so it is not necessary to memorize or look up the names of the available AI controller modules. The user can just pick it from the list.

Reduces Errors

Using a GUI *reduces errors* in the scripting. Many typographical errors are eliminated by allowing the designer to choose values from pop-up menus. The parameters to an action are displayed visually, so it is not possible to leave one out, add an extra parameter, or swap the order. When the GUI is integrated into the game editor, it is possible to add shortcuts, such as selecting a character in the level and automatically referencing that character in the active script.

Implementation Time

With all these benefits, it seems like there would be no reason to use a text-based scripting system instead of a GUI-based scripting system. The drawback of GUI-based scripting systems is that the *implementation time* is long, and a considerable amount of engineering time is required to maintain it on an ongoing basis. Text-based scripting systems can be implemented more quickly.

Courtesy of Blizzard Entertainment, Inc.   Electronic Arts

Game designers can use a graphic user interface when creating game scenarios in both *StarCraft* (left) and *The Sims* (right).

StarCraft contains a GUI editor for creating rule sets called triggers that control behaviors for a mission. *The Sims* uses a graphical editor called Edith that creates the definition of the behaviors for the agents in the Sims world. Adding a graphical user interface to a game engine is a major undertaking, and it should not be taken lightly. However, it has a great potential to significantly accelerate game development, and it supports the creation of a better quality game in the same amount of time.

The field of AI began with stories of monsters, and machines made of gears and pulleys. It has advanced to expert systems in the fields of chemistry and medicine, and a computer that can play championship level chess. Game agents have progressed from simple ghosts on a two-dimensional maze in *Pac-Man* to human and alien characters that move through a complex three-dimensional world in *Half-Life 2*. Video game technology has evolved from assembly language programming on extremely limited consoles, such as the Atari VCS, to GUI based tools to develop games intended to run on systems with multiple processors and thousands of times more memory than the VCS.

Which Brings Us to . . . Here

We have a rich but partial set of technologies from the field of computer science AI. This provides a number of useful techniques, but there is no drop-in "artificial mind" that can be used in video games. As a result, we must combine these techniques with a series of clever ad-hoc methods to "fake" intelligent behaviors in order to create what appear to be intelligent game characters.

Increases in processing power and memory available to video games permits the use of sophisticated programming and scripting languages, and allows for the creation of complex AI systems. However, the creation of these systems is a time-consuming and difficult process, requiring many design decisions. The goal of this process is to create *intelligent agents* in order to make the game fun, interesting, and enjoyable to play.

Intelligent Agents

A principal goal of video game AI development is the creation of intelligent agents. In war games they serve as enemies or allies. In other cases they may be neutral, perhaps selling items to the player. Sometimes they are a part of the background in the game, keeping the world from appearing empty. We expect intelligent agents to:

■ React to the environment. If a guard is patrolling and an enemy unit comes near in a game such as *Command & Conquer: Tiberian Sun*, the agent should stop patrolling and attack the enemy unit. The reaction to the environment is then an important part of the behavior of intelligent agents.

- Solve certain problems in the game environment. One of the more common problems is *pathfinding*. If an agent needs to get to a particular destination in order to enter a vehicle or a building or pick up a crate or bonus object, we expect the agent to be able to figure out a path to get to that particular destination. An intelligent agent does a reasonable job of handling obstacles and terrain so that it successfully gets to the destination.

- *Choose appropriate responses and have a varied set of responses.* If an agent does the same thing over and over again, though very well, this does not indicate intelligence. It often appears mechanical to the player.

- *Exhibit more than one behavior.* In some cases, we expect an agent to be able to converse, sometimes with a player, sometimes with other agents. In modern games, we also expect some display of emotion from the agent.

- *Anticipate the future, although not perfectly.* For example, if a player is running across a field from left to right and an enemy agent attempting to attack is moving toward the player, we would expect the enemy agent to lead the player agent. If a player moves in a particular direction, the enemy agent would respond by also moving in that same direction—anticipating that the player will continue to do so.

- *Exhibit an appropriate level of skill.* Another key aspect of intelligent agents in a game is that they must provide the appropriate level of intelligence. The goal in a video game is to allow the player to win, but at the same time give enough of a challenge that the game is interesting. A stupid AI character that the player can beat easily is not fun, but neither is a inhumanly smart character that always beats the player.

Video game AI systems are written to achieve these goals. Often the behaviors are specific to a game, and are created individually by an AI or game programmer. This makes multiple behaviors and responses possible. A key task in AI development is creating a way to control which behavior is chosen, and making sure that the sequence of behaviors make sense.

We will look at a number of concepts and implementation techniques used to create modern video game AI systems in the next section.

AI Programming Concepts

Game AI is software written in a high level programming language. This can be done using standard programming concepts, such as algorithms and heuristics. In addition, most modern games use object-oriented languages, such as C++. There are several object-oriented techniques that are useful when developing game AI. This section will examine a number of these concepts that will be used later in the book.

Algorithm

An *algorithm* is a well-defined set of steps that will produce a desired result. An algorithm will perform the task that it is intended for and do so at a bounded cost, both in terms of time and memory utilization. There are a variety of standard searching and sorting algorithms—such as *bubble sort, quicksort, binary search*—

Electronic Arts

In *Emperor: Battle for Dune*, the A* algorithm is used to perform pathfinding when units are ordered to move.

with which the AI programmer should be familiar. In addition to the standard algorithms, there are some that are particularly useful for AI programming.

Algorithms can be specified in a programming language such as C++ and thus they can be used in game programs. Frequently, an AI programmer will need to do operations such as searching efficiently, which requires sorting. The AI programmer will frequently use standard computer science algorithms for searching and sorting—as well as data structures for ordering the data—since fairly common activities in AI behaviors include searching for enemies and determining line of sight.

Heuristic

A *heuristic* is a rule of thumb that may solve a problem but is not a guaranteed solution. For example, if a player needs to move a unit to a particular location, a heuristic could be "move in the direction of the destination." This is a fairly reasonable choice

Electronic Arts

Large groups of orcs use heuristics to move into position for melee combat in *The Lord of the Rings: The Battle for Middle Earth*.

and, in some cases, it will actually solve the problem if there are no obstacles between the unit and the target; this will actually succeed in getting the unit to the goal. In some cases, a heuristic is sufficient to deal with the desired behaviors.

In the case of *The Lord of the Rings: The Battle for Middle-Earth*, one of the AI activities is melee combat involving two groups of units that are fighting together. The Mordor orc units are divided up into groups of 12, whereas Gondor fighters are divided up into units of five. Two of these groups will approach to fight, and once they are within range, will begin fighting. Then the individual units use the heuristic of moving towards the enemy units; once they are standing next to them, they begin attacking them with their weapons.

Melee combat does not begin until the two groups of units have moved close enough together that at least one of the individual agents is in contact with an opposing agent. At this point, the simple heuristic of moving towards the enemy unit is adequate to handle the combat.

However, in many cases, the simple heuristic is not adequate to solve the problem. For example, if there is a room with a door and the goal is in the opposite wall from the door outside the room, the heuristic "move directly toward the goal" will take the AI agent to the wall—bumping into it without ever reaching the goal. In this case, we find that the heuristic is not sufficient to perform the task. In some cases, it works well to couple a heuristic with an algorithm.

At the time *StarCraft* was released, computers were relatively limited in their CPU performance. It might take a second or two for a

Courtesy of Blizzard Entertainment, Inc.

StarCraft units use a heuristic to aid in movement.

pathfinding algorithm to execute and return the path for a unit. While this was processing, the game could use the heuristic of "move directly toward the destination" because it was easy to calculate, so the unit could start moving in the direction of the goal while the path was calculating. Most of the time, moving in the direction of the goal was a good start to the path anyway, and the unit would just continue. In a few cases, such as a room with a single exit, moving directly toward the goal would not produce the desired result. The agent would start moving toward the goal, but as soon as a path was available, the agent would turn and follow the path leading out the door and around the side of the room in order to get to the goal destination.

Data-Driven Design and Rapid Iteration

One of the key items that is useful in game development is *data-driven design*. In order to produce good AI, it is necessary to polish, tune, and balance behaviors. The algorithms themselves often produce mechanical results, and most often, these initial results are decent but not great. In order to create *great* AI, the behaviors have to be hand-tuned and polished.

Data-driven design is a programming technique where, outside of the program, data exist that can be modified to change and tune the behavior of the game in general and the AI in particular. The data can range from a simple text file to a full-fledged database. Data-driven design allows designers to modify the game behaviors by simply modifying the data values. This allows them to try out ideas quickly. The more ideas the designer can evaluate, the better the game.

One way to create a data-driven design is to make the parameters that control a behavior available in a text file. For example, the aggressiveness of a unit can be adjusted by setting a value so that the unit requires other enemy units to be 100 feet away before attacking them; that value can be stored in a text file so that it can be adjusted by a designer or engineer without having to rebuild the program. This allows for *rapid iterations*, since the designer can make changes without the help of an engineer, and neither the engineer nor the designer needs to wait for a compile and re-link operation before testing the changes.

We will be using a simple data-driven format to provide values for the AI and demo game in the examples that come with this book. The format will be a name of the field in question followed by an equal sign, and either a "string" or a number. The numbers can be a floating point numbers (e.g., 27.5) or integers (e.g., 100).

The example definition for an agent is as follows:

```
name="AIA gent"
x=20.5
y=15
{
        name = "Body"
        health=100
}


{
        name = "Movement"
        speed=5.7
}
{       name = "AI"
        Goal="FindCoins"
}
{       name = "Appearance"
        icon = "Man"
}
```

::::: Data Format - XML

The key advantage of the previous data-driven format is that it is simple and relatively easy to implement. It is adequate for the sample application presented on the companion DVD and, from that standpoint, it is suitable to those needs. However, if you were actually developing a full game, you would want to use a richer data format, such as XML, because there are a couple of drawbacks to the example data language as presented.

Infected (PSP) uses Kynapse AI middleware.

First, the example data format is limited to strings and numbers. There are some additional data types that are useful, such as enumerations and a named grouping. The other drawback is that there is no verification associated with this language. If an object has a speed and a developer entered velocity instead of speed, the processor accepts it and puts in velocity, but then when the code searches for the parameter speed, it does not find it. One advantage of XML is that it is a standard language, and there are standard editors for it. It is also possible to specify a syntax for a particular set of XML. This is referred to as a *schema* that defines which values are valid, required, and optional. If it is an enumerated type or number of strings, it specifies the format so that the editor itself can verify that the data are correct. If there is more than one person involved in the project, the capability of verifying the data in the editor is a great advantage that will speed up development. A final advantage of XML is that it supports a variety of different data types so that a number of items, including enumerations, can be easily included in the XML using the standard format. Due to these issues, it is a good idea to use XML for the data format of a large scale game development project. The Kynapse AI middleware uses XML as the data language. Kynapse is used in several games: Eden Games' *Alone in the Dark*, Planet Moon's *Infected*, and Real Time Worlds' *Crackdown*.

Object-Oriented Design

Object-oriented design is a powerful technique used in modern video games. The Unreal engine, used for a number of games including *Unreal 2: The Awakening*, makes extensive use of object-oriented design. The engine code implements objects using C++. The scripting language, UnrealScript, supports object-oriented design as well, providing a Java style inheritance model.

Epic Games

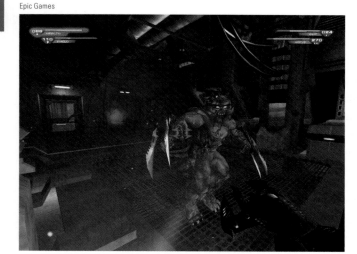

Epic developed *Unreal 2: The Awakening* using a variety of object-oriented techniques.

An *object* at the simplest level is a combination of data and code. Early higher level languages such as C and Fortran did not link code and data together. The code was responsible for making sure the right data were accessed and passed to other code functions. For example, there may be data that define a rectangle and code that draws a rectangle using those data. Other code is responsible for passing the data to the function that draws the data.

Object-oriented programming links the data and code together. A rectangle's data, and the function that draws the rectangle, can be defined as two parts of the rectangle object. This links the two together, so it is obvious which function should be used—and, in fact, an object-oriented system can correctly choose the best function to use.

Let us examine two object-oriented techniques that are useful in AI design and programming: inheritance and aggregation.

Inheritance

Inheritance allows an object to be designed that has a particular behavior and capabilities. A second object can then be created that inherits all of the behaviors and data of the first object. From there, modifications can be made to the second object to create a new, unique object. However, we do not have to duplicate the behaviors for the second object. An example would be in Unreal.

Diagram by Per Olin

Infantry Captain	Castle Guard	Moat Monster
Captain	Guard	Dragon
Character	Character	Monster
Pawn	Pawn	Pawn

Three game agents use inheritance to share the behaviors present in the Pawn class.

For example, there is an object class called Pawn, which contains the data and code that allows agents to move, attack, and carry weapons. Several different game characters can be created using the Pawn as the base class. All the code that does pathfinding, carries weapons, and conducts visual recognition exists in the Pawn class. The code in the Pawn object is automatically available to the other game character classes; in this case Captain, Guard, and Dragon. However, none of the code has to be copied or included directly into those classes. The Captain, Guard, and Dragon can have all of the functionality of the pawn by merely referencing the Pawn class.

An additional opportunity for sharing code exists between the Captain and Guard. There are a number of behaviors that are appropriate for both infantry captains and castle guards. These can be implemented in the Character class. These can be shared between the Captain and Guard, reducing duplication of code. The Monster class would be code that would be useful in other monsters in the game— perhaps attacking with claws or biting.

Finally, any very specific behaviors are added to the Captain, Guard, and Dragon classes. It should take relatively little code to implement the behaviors that are unique to the Captain, as it automatically has the behaviors from the Pawn and Character classes. This is a very powerful technique that helps avoid duplicating code in the game.

The code for pathfinding and for visual recognition can be created once and placed in the Pawn class. Captain objects can automatically use the code, and other objects that have behavior similar to the captain could also use the code as well. Reducing the amount of code duplication is a very good technique for designing AI systems in general for all software projects. Any work that can be done to reduce the amount of code duplication is valuable.

There are three benefits to inheritance. One is that it reduces the amount of memory that is required by the program. A second and more critical benefit is that maintenance of the code is easier. A single instance of the code makes it easier to find the relevant code, and reduces the amount of time required to enhance the feature, or to fix errors.

Finally, when the code is in one spot and shared through inheritance among all the units, correcting an error or enhancing the feature for one unit will automatically propagate all those improvements to all the other objects that have inherited that behavior.

The primary limitation to inheritance is that an object can only inherit from one object. Game AI is sufficiently complex that there are often situations where it would be useful to create an object out of two or more other objects. This can be done by using *aggregation*.

Aggregation

Aggregation is another useful object-oriented design technique. Aggregation is similar to making something out of Legos. You snap pieces together and thus have the resulting whole built out of a number of parts. One way to do aggregation is to build agents out of a list of modules. In *Command & Conquer: Generals*, the agents were built out of a variable list of modules. One module handled the drawing of the agent in the 3D world, and included a model and texture. Another module handled the physics behavior and collision of the object. Those objects that could burn had a "flammable" module that handled the burning behavior. Weapon modules allowed agents to use a variety of weapons.

An armor module would contain the armor information, including how it reacts to particular weapons. An AI module would determine the behaviors associated with the object and also have additional modules added optionally. For special behaviors, such as stealth, there were specific optional modules. The stealth module would control the stealth behavior and detection of the unit.

We can illustrate an example of this approach using a base object that has four slots for modules: an armor slot, a primary weapon slot, a secondary weapon slot, and a movement slot.

The agents are customized by attaching different modules in each slot.

There are two benefits for using this kind of a system:

- It separates the code for each of these behaviors into different modules. The stealth module handles the stealth operations and is separate from the body module, which handles the armor. It is easy to locate the code related to stealth, which is in the stealth module. It does not become mixed in with the code for the other operations.
- It is quick to create new agents. You can combine existing modules together when agents have similar behaviors. For example, a new infantry unit could use the AI for the standard infantry, perhaps with a different body module if the armor was different. The infantry unit could use the standard infantry display module, possibly with a new model created by the art department. Changes can be made, and behaviors can be extended and customized for the particular unit by adding or swapping modules.

The key to aggregation is the use of interfaces to provide the slots for modules. An *interface* is a definition of a set of functions. The interface allows modules to be attached, and easily swapped later.

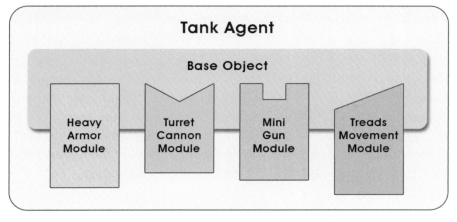

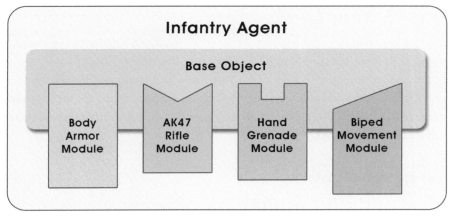

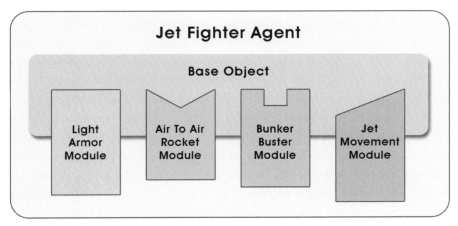

The three agents are created using aggregation. The same base object is used, but different modules are attached for armor, weapons, and movement to create different agents.

It is not a question of one or the other. In most cases both are appropriate. Some systems use aggregation as the primary way to create game objects. In this case inheritance is not used with the base object, but with the modules. The various modules use inheritance to share common code. For example, a base armor class can be created, and then variations such as heavy armor, or a reactive armor, could be created using the base armor class and inheritance. Other systems such as Unreal 3 create agents using inheritance, as noted in the Pawn class example. Unreal 3 uses aggregation as well for weapons, components, and controller modules.

Control Methods

AI routines are written in code that executes sequentially. In a game, many characters may appear to be acting simultaneously. However, the code is being executed sequentially, processing one agent at a time. The order in which the code for each agent is executed, and when it is executed, is important since it determines the structure of the routines that perform the AI operations. The control methods tend to be either time-based or event-based.

Time-Based Control

Time-based control methods are called every few milliseconds. The advantage of a time-based control method is that it is very easy to implement. Most games have rendering code that creates one screen of graphics data (or frame) at a time. After each frame is created, all systems with time-based control are called and given the opportunity to do their processing. The control of a particular system is handled by having a function executed and any processing that needs to be done occurs at that point. This is useful for systems such as a physics module that updates the position of an object based on its velocity. Given the amount of elapsed time since it was last called, the physics module can update the position to the next location for the object or agent. In other cases, time-based control can involve a lot of waiting. For example, an AI control module may need to have the agent move to a location and then start an attack. The movement may take a few seconds, during which the rendering code will produce several hundred frames of data. In a time-based system, the AI will be called several hundred times while waiting for the agent to reach the destination. When the agent finally reaches the destination, the AI will begin the attack.

Event-Based Control

Event-based control calls a function when an event happens. For example, an AI control module could have a collision method that is called when an agent collides with another object or agent. In this case, that method is only called at the moment that an object is detected to have collided with another object. If the object is not moving, the collision method may never be called. In a time-based system, the method is called every few milliseconds regardless of what behavior is going on at a given time. The advantage of event-based control is that the logic is simpler and more efficient. The disadvantage is that a system must be created to detect the events and call the appropriate method when the event occurs. This is generally useful with events that happen frequently, such as collision and entering a trigger region. In addition, handling collision as a system allows the system to be optimized rather than having each object check for collisions individually.

In most games, both types of control are used. There are some calls for the occurrence of particular events. Often most of the processing is handled in a time-based control scheme. In the case of Unreal 3, the time-based method is called Tick. AI entities can then be called by the Tick function, and user interface can be updated by the Tick function. The engine itself is updated every frame by calling the Tick function.

Command & Conquer: Generals, Lord of the Rings: Battle for Middle Earth, and *Command & Conquer 3* use the SAGE RTS engine developed at Electronic Arts. In the SAGE engine, a similar function, known as Update, exists. Operating in a similar fashion to the Unreal 3 Tick function, the Update function is called once each frame to allow the various game systems. This allows each system and object to perform its tasks.

Programming References

Object-oriented programming is a large topic and will only be lightly covered in this book. Any programmer who wants to practice AI programming should study object-oriented design and C++ programming. Here are a few recommended references:

The C++ Programming Language (Stroustrup, 1997)
Effective C++ (Meyers, 1998)
Java2: A Beginner's Guide (Schildt, 2001)
Design Patterns (Gamma, Helm, Johnson, Vlissides, 1995)

History & Concepts: how did we get here (and where is *here*, anyway?)

chapter 1

People have been fascinated with AI for ages. The advent of the programmable electronic digital computer has led to some significant achievements in recent decades. The development of the microprocessor allowed the creation of inexpensive personal computers and video game consoles, which spawned a variety of games. As the hardware became more capable, it became possible to write complex game AI behaviors using a variety of programming techniques, including some from AI research. We will look at creating a system that allows for the creation and controls the sequencing of an agent's behaviors in the next chapter.

:::CHAPTER REVIEW:::

1. A bubble sort is performed by making a number of passes through a list of numbers. Each number is compared with the number that follows. If the first number is larger than the second number, the two numbers are swapped. In the case of the list 5,7,2, and 5,7 would be examined, and since 5 is not larger than 7, so the numbers are not swapped. Next, 7 and 2 would be compared. 7 is greater than 2, so the numbers are swapped, resulting in 5,2,7. A second pass is made, first comparing 5 to 2. 5 is greater than 2, so they are swapped. Next, 5 is compared to 7. 5, which is not greater than 7, so the numbers are not swapped. The resulting list, 2,5,7, is sorted in ascending order. Write an algorithm to perform a bubble sort on a list of numbers. Use a programming language such as BASIC or C++ if you are familiar with one. Otherwise, describe each step in detail.

2. The binary system is used in modern computers to represent numbers. Many modern computers use 32 binary digits, or bits, to access memory. Base 16, or hexadecimal, numbers are often used to represent binary numbers as each hex digit corresponds to 4 bits. The binary numbers 0 to 15 are 0000, 0001, 0010, 0011, 0100, 0101,0110,0111, 1000, 1001, 1010, 1011, 1100, 1101, 1111. In hex they are 0, 1, 2, 3, 4, 5, 6, 7, 8, 9, A, B, C, D, E, F. The 32-bit binary number 00011 01001110100101000100110111 is represented by the hexadecimal number 1574A237. The eight hexadecimial digits are much easier to deal with than the 32 zeros and ones of the binary number. What is the largest number that can be represented with 32 bits? What is its value in hexadecimal, and in decimal? How is this number relevant to the amount of memory in personal computers and game consoles?

3. An arbitrary agent has the following list of attributes: maximum speed, color, name, initial location, health, armor, weapon type, and ammunition count. Define an XML data format that can represent these values, and write an example XML file that contains an arbitrary set of values for an agent. Bonus: Create an XML schema that describes the data format.

4. Advanced: Implement the bubble sort algorithm in C++. Then, using in-line assembly, implement the same algorithm in assembly language. Compare the degree of difficulty and amount of time required to create the algorighm in assembly language vs. C++.

2

AI Agents

creating behavior using a finite state machine

Key Chapter Questions

- How do *agents* work?
- What is a *finite state machine*?
- How are *transitions* managed?
- How are finite state machines implemented using *C++*?
- How is *data-driven modular design* used to build an AI agent?

The purpose of this chapter is to learn and understand how to use *state machines* to create and manage artificial intelligence (AI) behaviors. This will include understanding the concept of state machines and their design, along with how to manage transitions. We will look at an implementation of a state machine system in C++, and build a simple state machine to perform several behaviors. We will then use the technique of *data-driven modular design* to implement an *AI agent*, and a sample application to demonstrate the actual operation of the state machine and agent in an application.

Creating and Controlling
AI Behaviors

AI behaviors are often varied and complex. Different games will require a range
of AI behaviors. Some will be very specific to an individual game. The GLA vehicles
in *Command & Conquer: Generals* could hide in a "Tunnel Network" and pop out
unexpectedly. This behavior was unique to *C&C: Generals*. Other behaviors appear
in a variety of games. Most, if not all, strategy and first-person shooter (FPS) games
have an AI behavior that aims a weapon and fires it at an enemy.

Behavior: A Sequence of Actions

A commonly used AI *model* or *paradigm* (set of concepts and assumptions) is to
consider an AI behavior as a *sequence of actions*—one occurring after another. This
paradigm is used in a wide variety of games, and it is useful for creating a variety
of behaviors. Each behavior is created by adding actions to the sequence, similar to
stringing beads on a wire. We can define an AI behavior using this model by listing
the actions in order. A possible AI behavior would be patrolling an area and guarding against an enemy. The behavior would consist of the following actions: Move,
Scan, Move, Scan, Acquire Target, Approach Target, Fire, Fire, Fire, Reload, Fire,
Fire, Return for Repairs.

Diagram by Per Olin

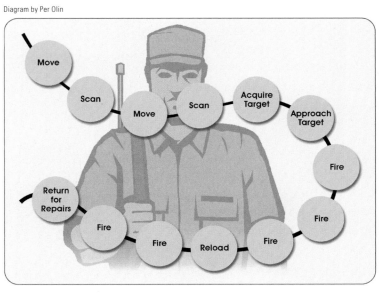

The patrol and guard behavior is defined as a sequence of actions, like beads
on a string.

Dynamic Sequences

An important aspect of AI behaviors is that the actions in the sequence vary depending on the circumstances in the game. The sequence specified for the patrol and guard behavior is correct, given the following conditions:

- The agent's weapon can fire three times before reloading.
- The enemy is destroyed after five shots.
- The enemy damaged the agent.

If a weaker enemy approached, the previous behavior would be incorrect. With an enemy that could be destroyed with two shots, and was unable to significantly damage the agent, a different sequence would be required. The new sequence would be **Move, Scan, Move, Scan, Acquire Target, Approach Target, Fire, Fire, Reload, Return to Patrol.**

An AI system that creates behaviors as a sequence of actions must be able to generate different, appropriate sequences based on the circumstances in the game. We will examine a system, the *finite state machine*, that allows us to create various actions and string them together to form the desired AI behaviors.

> We use finite state machines for the lowest level of the tactical AI—the AI of an individual unit. The behavior within a state is scripted with several heuristic-based rules. This works well because the AI at that level should be lightweight yet robust, since there are so many units on the map.
>
> —Denis Papp
> (Chief Technology Officer, TimeGate Studios)

Finite State Machine

Finite state machines (FSMs)—commonly used in video game AI programming—are good tools for creating and controlling behaviors defined as a sequence of actions. An FSM consists of a number of states and transitions between those states.

A system that is commonly used in video games is a finite state implementation that transfers control from one state to another, using explicit transitions. At any given time, one state is active. The active state performs its action, and all other states are inert. The FSM continues executing the active state until a transition occurs. In the accompanying state machine diagram,

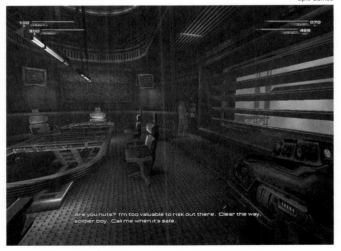

Epic Games

Are you nuts? I'm too valuable to risk out there. Clear the way, soldier boy. Call me when it's safe.

The Unreal Engine, used in a variety of games (such as *Unreal II: The Awakening*, shown), includes a finite state machine in the scripting language, UnrealScript.

Diagram by Per Olin

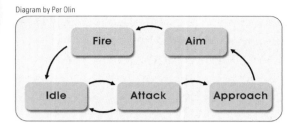

The transition diagram shows the states and the possible transitons between states.

the boxes represent the states, and the arrows represent possible transitions between the states. There are five states: **Idle**, **Attack**, **Approach**, **Aim**, and **Fire**.

The transitions describe and limit the possible sequences of states. Let us assume that the FSM starts in the **Idle** state. It is possible for the state machine to stay in the **Idle** state or switch to the **Attack** state. From **Attack**, the possible states are **Approach** or **Idle**. From **Approach**, the only possible next state is **Aim**. So a normal attack sequence would be **Idle, Attack, Approach, Aim, Fire, Idle**. A possible variant behavior would be **Idle, Attack, Idle, Attack, Approach, Aim, Fire, Idle**. Given this FSM, it would not be possible to see **Idle, Attack, Fire, Idle**.

John Comes on Strategic vs. Tactical Artificial Intelligence:::::

John Comes
(Lead Designer,
Gas Powered Games)

John Comes was born in Reading, Pennsylvania, but spent most of his childhood near Cleveland, Ohio. He graduated from the University of Akron in 1998 with a Bachelor of Science in Mechanical Engineering. In June of 2001, John moved to Las Vegas to work at Westwood Studios on *Earth & Beyond* as a content designer. Since then, he has worked on *Command & Conquer 3, Commander & Conquer: Generals: Zero Hour*, and *The Lord of the Rings: The Battle for Middle-Earth* at Electronic Arts Los Angeles. In 2004, John joined Gas Powered Games, where he recently shipped Supreme Commander. He has been credited as Designer, Senior Content Designer, and Lead Content Engineer— and has most recently moved into the role of Lead Designer at Gas Powered Games.

I usually separate my AI into two parts: strategic and tactical. The strategic part is the part that decides how the AI will act as a whole. The tactical part decides how the AI will go about doing all the things the strategic part wants. Strategic AI is a series of conditions that have to be met to send a unit or group of units to do a task. That task is handled by the tactical AI. I've tried several different strategic AI theories. The one that didn't work well in practice is this:

I had a set of three values from 1 to 100—the willingness to be offensive, the willingness to be defensive, and the willingness to focus on economy. The AI would constantly pole different indicators of its situation and move those three values up and down. Then the AI would send out tasks based upon the severity of each of the three values. In the end, I found myself trying to balance the three-value system to keep these values from always being 1 or 100 more—rather than actually writing a compelling AI system.

> S ince the processors were so basic when I was a programmer in the 1970s and 1980s,
> we used the concept of finite state machines in particular to govern player behavior in
> sports games—and to make it simpler for players to adapt to different game conditions by
> altering their states. Today's AI programmers operate at a level of sophistication and power
> that dwarfs what we had in those days—and use approaches we never dreamed of being
> able to implement.
>
> *—Don L. Daglow*
> *(President & CEO, Stormfront Studios)*

Representative AI States

The states of an FSM can perform many different operations. Part of the AI program-mer's task is to decide what states will be used, and what each state will do. Once this structure is determined, the programmer must then write the code for each state to perform the desired operations and set up the transitions so the states are activated in the correct order. Some states that have been used in video games are the following:

- *MoveTo*: Moves an agent to a destination.
- *Attack*: Attacks an enemy with a weapon.
- *Approach*: Moves an agent to a location suitable for firing a weapon.
- *Aim*: Points a weapon at a target.
- *Fire*: Fires the weapon at a target.
- *Reload*: Reloads the weapon.
- *CollectResources*: Automatically collects and delivers resources (lumber, Tiberium, gold).
- *Idle*: Wait for commands.
- *Guard*: Holds a position and attacks any enemies that approach.
- *Patrol*: Follows a patrol route and attacks any enemies that approach.
- *ReturnToCover*: Moves to a location behind an obstacle that is safe from enemy fire.

These states, and the actions that they perform, are used in games to create the behaviors for the AI agents. Different games will use different sets of these actions, and the exact details of the actions will vary from game to game.

These tanks are performing an attack behavior using the SAGE AI FSM in *Command & Conquer: Generals.*

Command & Conquer: Generals uses the SAGE engine, which includes an FSM for AI behavior implementation. It also uses over 50 AI states to implement agent behaviors. One example is the **Idle** state, which is an AI agent's default state. The **MoveTo** state is used when an agent is moving to a different position. Another state is the **Fire** state, in which an agent fires a weapon at another agent or structure. Another state is the **Collect Resources** state, in which the agent is gathering resources. The **Reload** state is used by an agent, such as a jet that carries two missiles and must return to the airfield to get additional missiles.

By itself, an FSM merely provides the structure for these behaviors, and the information that the agent is in a particular state. The actual behaviors have to be implemented for each state. However, this does provide quite a bit of flexibility and power to create and control agent behaviors.

SAGE State Machine

The implementation of the FSM in SAGE was done in C++ as two object classes: the StateMachine class, and the State class. The StateMachine class consisted of a list of states and a pointer to the active state. Each state was an object of class State. The StateMachine kept track of the current active state and handled any transitions between states.

C++ classes consist of two parts. The first part is data: numbers, strings, and lists of other C++ objects. The second part is one or more methods. The methods (also known as functions or procedures) are a set of instructions that perform operations such as arithmetic, sorting, sending output to the display, and calling other methods. The state objects are implemented as C++ classes, with three methods: OnEnter(), OnExit(), and Update(). The methods for these classes are used as follows: When a transition occurs, the current state is exited; this is done by calling the OnExit() method for the current state; then the new state is entered and becomes the active state by calling the OnEnter() method.

Television shows and motion pictures are a series of images presented to the viewer rapidly, giving the appearance of smooth motion. Movies show 24 images per second, and video displays can show up to 60 images per second. Each image is called a frame. A video game must generate at least 30 frames each second to produce the appearance of smooth movement on the display. At every frame, when processing was done for the AI, the state machine would process any pending transitions—or, if there were no transitions, it would call the Update() method for the active state. These methods functioned in a fashion similar to the EnterState(), ExitState(), and ProcessFrame() methods in the programming example later in this chapter.

MoveTo: A Single-State Behavior

It is possible to implement an AI behavior as a single state in an FSM. An example of this process is illustrated in the **MoveTo** state. Initially, the agent is in the **Idle**

state. At each frame the state machine calls the Update() method of the active state. The Update() method is responsible for performing the actions associated with the state. The **Idle** state is active, so the Idle::Update() method is being called. The Idle::Update() method performs the appropriate actions when an agent is idle. In some cases, it will do nothing; in other cases, it may check for nearby enemies. When the player clicks on the mouse to direct the agent to move to a particular location, a user event is queued and processed. This results in a call to StateMachine::TransitionTo(**MoveTo**). StateMachine refers to the C++ object of class StateMachine. One of the methods for the StateMachine class is TransitionTo(). This

Firaxis Games Inc.

These tanks in *Civilization IV* are in a *MoveTo* state in response to the player's orders.

method is used to direct the StateMachine object to make a particular state the active state. The argument, (**MoveTo**), is the name of the state that will be activated. The next time the StateMachine::Update() is called, the pending transition to the **MoveTo** state is processed.

Diagram by Per Olin

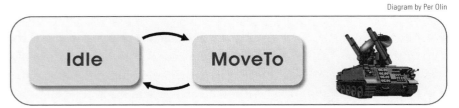

A simple movement behavior can be implemented with a two-state finite state machine.

Idle::OnExit() is called to exit the **Idle** state, and MoveTo::OnEnter() is called as the **MoveTo** state becomes active. The MoveTo::OnEnter() method does any processing necessary to start movement. Likely operations include getting and storing the goal position, and calling or queuing a request to the pathfinding code to find a path to the goal position through a search. In the SAGE engine, a path consisted of a set of intermediate goal positions that could be followed without running into any structures or impassable terrain. In the case of an open field move, the path would be two points—the agent's current position, and the goal position. If there were structures, cliffs, or impassable water in the way, the path would contain more points to go around these obstacles.

The StateMachine object calls the MoveTo::Update() method for the **MoveTo** state once when processing each frame. This allows the **MoveTo** state to perform the appropriate processing to execute the move to behavior. The code in the MoveTo::Update() method looks at the current position, checks the next intermediate goal point, and updates the position moving toward the intermediate goal, based on the agent's speed. If the agent has reached an intermediate goal point, it starts moving toward the next intermediate goal point. When it reaches the end of the path, or the final destination, it generates a transition back to the **Idle** state, since the movement is now be complete. The transition is generated by calling the StateMachine's method StateMachine::TransitionTo(Idle), with Idle as the parameter. This results in the **Idle** state becoming the active state.

Attack: A Multiple-State Behavior

The accompanying state machine diagram is similar to the one used in the SAGE engine created initially for *Command & Conquer: Generals*. The attack behavior is used when an agent has identified a target. This can happen when an enemy agent moves into visual range. A player issues an attack command to a player controlled agent, or scripting supplied by the designer directs an AI controlled agent to attack a particular target.

The attack behavior in the SAGE engine consists of four states: **Approach**, **Aim**, **Fire,** and **Reload**. Dividing the behavior into four states allows us to consider the behavior at two levels. The higher level is the interaction of the states themselves, and the lower level is the detailed behavior of each state.

At the higher level, we can consider questions regarding the sequencing of the states. "Should an AI agent fire without aiming?" In this case,

Diagram by Per Olin

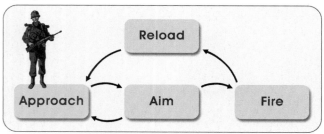

The arrows show the possible transitions between the states of the attack behavior.

the answer is "no." We can look at the state machine diagram and see that the only way to get to the **Fire** state is from the **Aim** state. Thus, the FSM ensures that the AI agent will aim first, then fire. Using the four states allows us to consider and specify the sequencing of states without having to focus on the details of each state.

At the lower level, the code that each state executes, the task is limited to the behavior required for the specific state. The code in the **Approach** state has to be able to handle movement and determine a destination in range of the target. However, it does not need to include any code related to aiming the weapon, firing effects, or animations related to reloading. The smaller scope is more practical to implement in code, and easier to debug.

Approach

The first state in the SAGE engine is **Approach**. This is a movement state that identifies a goal position that is within range of the target. In addition, some weapons require a clear line of sight. The sense of realism is reduced if the agents fire rockets through buildings—and becomes even worse if the rockets explode when hitting the building and destroy the agent that is firing. Agents such as artillery that have a high arc can generally fire over obstacles in the way, and they do not require a clear line of

Epic Games

Dominic in *Gears of War* is moving to a point where he has a clear line of sight to his enemy, and preferably near defensive cover.

sight. Once the agent has moved in range of the target and has a clear line of sight if necessary, this state transitions to an **Aim** state.

Aim

The **Aim** state consists of pointing the weapon at the target. For agents that fire forward (agents with fixed barrels such as artillery, or humans that fire more accurately forward than over the shoulder), it first involves rotating the agent to face the target. Then the weapon (turret or rifle, for example) is rotated to point at the object. The **Aim** state completes when the angle to the target is within the parameters of the weapon

Epic Games

Marcus (left) in *Gears of War* is in the process of aiming at the enemy.

the agent is currently firing. In some cases, the target agent may be moving away from the attacking agent and will move out of range or behind a building. In this case, the **Aim** state will transition back to the **Approach** state in order to move back into range.

Fire

The **Fire** state consists of firing a weapon. In the case of a medieval RTS, "firing" a weapon (such as swinging a sword or shooting an arrow) can be quite complicated, and the **Fire** state is thus somewhat involved and can take a relatively long time. In the case of *C&C: Generals*, which uses modern weapons, most weapons fire quickly, and the **Fire** state is

Epic Games

The Locust Horde character in *Gears of War* has completed aiming his weapon and is now firing.

relatively brief and simple. Beam weapons or flame throwers often have an extended firing time, and the **Fire** state must also track a moving target with the weapon.

Reload

The final state in the attack behavior is **Reload**, which, in the case of a tank, can be a simple delay timer. The reloading happens inside the tank and is not visible to the player. Therefore, it is sufficient to impose a delay to account for the time required to reload the tank's cannon. In other cases, the reloading behavior may be visible to the player; for example, replacing a clip in a rifle or placing a rocket in a bazooka. In these

Electronic Arts

The Orca helicopter in *Command & Conquer: Generals* is returning to the heliport to reload its missiles.

cases, it is appropriate to play an animation of the reloading behavior during the **Reload** state. A more complex reloading behavior involves agents, such as jets and helicopters in *Command & Conquer: Generals*, that have to return to the air base to reload missiles. In this case, the **Reload** state has to include moving the agent back to the base in order to reload.

The four-state attack machine gives us a structure to build the code required to implement the behavior. We can write the code for each state without having to consider the actions performed by the other states, which simplifies the design and implementation. We can consider the sequencing of the states at a higher level, without having to focus on the details of each state. Once implemented, the attack state machine can generate a complex series of actions using the four states. When attacking an enemy, an agent could produce the following behavior:

```
approach the enemy, aim weapon, fire, fire, fire,
fire, reload weapon, fire, fire, fire, fire, reload
weapon, follow the enemy who moved, aim weapon,
fire, fire
```

At this point, the enemy is destroyed and the attack behavior is completed.

Matching States to Game Design

An attack behavior in a tactical shooter such as *SWAT 4* and *Tom Clancy's Ghost Recon Advanced Warfighter* would be rather complicated since there are generally fewer agents, but the agents are seen at closer range and have more detailed behaviors. The **Approach** state may involve considering cover, choosing a location in range of the

target (but out of direct line of sight so it is not in range of the enemy agent), and perhaps deciding to crouch if the cover object is short. The **Aim** state becomes more complex, since the agent needs to either strafe sideways or stand up to get the weapon into line of sight and aimed at the enemy. The **Fire** state can be fairly straight forward: firing the weapon. After firing, a **ReturnToCover** state may be used, or the **Approach** state could be reused to find the original position behind cover or perhaps one closer to the target if the target is moving.

Attack behaviors in *Tom Clancy's Ghost Recon Advanced Warfighter* are complex, with squad members providing each other cover when entering doors.

Designing an FSM

An FSM is a good device for creating and managing well-defined AI behaviors. It cleanly separates the AI behaviors into different states, so it is easy to tell what code is executing when the agent is in the **MoveTo, Idle,** or **CollectResources** state, rather than having one method trying to do multiple behaviors.

FSMs provide structure, states, and transitions in order to create behaviors. However, they do not specify how to divide a behavior into states. This is one of the key tasks for the AI programmer. Dividing behaviors into states provides two benefits to the programmer. First, it allows the programmer to think of the behavior as a series of discrete tasks. Using states for this is similar to using a paragraph as a mechanism for collecting sentences into discrete thoughts. The second benefit is the ability to create complex behaviors out of chains of states. The four states in the attack FSM described earlier produced a behavior consisting of a sequence of 16 actions.

It is possible to divide a behavior into too many states, with the number of states and transitions becoming unwieldy. For example, instead of using one state for the MoveTo behavior, it is possible to divide it into five states: **Request Path**, **Wait For Path**, **Move Agent**, **Check Intermediate Goal**, and **Check Final Goal**. This has the benefit that each state performs only a single task; therefore, it is simple and easy to understand. While it is certainly possible to create a correct AI state machine at this level of detail, there are two drawbacks to such detail. First, it takes the programmer time to create a state object, so it takes more time to set up the structure with four states than with a single state. Second, this level of detail would generate multiple transitions in every frame. The number of transitions makes the behavior of the system hard to understand and debug. One useful debugging technique for FSMs is to output a log message each time a transition occurs. This technique becomes unwieldy if there are a large number of transitions.

A design that has proven effective is one in which transitions occur once every few seconds or less frequently. The states should be designed so that the agent is in a state for a number of frames before transitioning to another state, rather than transitioning between two or more states in a single tick. More complex AI behaviors, such as attacking, fit well into a multiple state implementation.

The granularity of states in an FSM is like the three bears' porridge (in *Goldilocks and the Three Bears*): You do not want a state to be too big, since the state will become cumbersome and difficult to understand, but you do not want the state to be too small, since the number of states and transitions becomes confusing. Each state should be of moderate complexity, where a state will perform an operation that generally will take several seconds or more to complete. You will want to split up a complex behavior such as attack into several states of moderate complexity.

Transitions

Once the states are determined, you must choose the *transitions* that will be used and the conditions that will trigger them. The transitions are potential changes from one state to another, but only one can happen at a time. For example, in the **MoveTo** state, no transitions will be generated until the agent reaches the goal position.

There are two ways for transitions to be generated for FSMs: internal and external. Internal transitions are generated by the states inside the FSM and often occur when a state completes an operation. The **Fire** state will generate a transition to the **Reload** state when the **Fire** state has fired all the ammunition in a clip. External transitions come from outside the FSM, often from designer-controlled scripts. A designer may decide that it is appropriate for the AI agent to be more alert and direct the AI to transition from an **Idle** state to a **Patrol** state. The timing of transitions can be immediate or deferred. An immediate transition occurs when it is requested. With immediate transitions it is possible to get two or more transitions one after another. Deferred transitions are stored and occur when the next frame is processed.

Internal

It is always the case that transitions can be generated *internally*. The active state may generate a transition to another state, depending on conditions tested by the active state. For example, a player may direct a tank to return to base. The tank uses a **MoveTo** state to move to the destination. When the **MoveTo** state reaches its goal at the base, the **MoveTo** state generates a transition to the **Idle** state.

It is possible to build an FSM that is self-contained and only generates transitions internally. This type of FSM is not affected by player input or scripts outside of the FSM. A self-contained FSM is suitable for a sys-

The Lord of the Rings: The Battle for Middle-Earth uses a self-contained finite state machine that tracks the emotional states of agents.

tem that tracks the emotional state of an agent. *The Lord of the Rings: The Battle for Middle-Earth* uses this kind of emotion system. The emotion FSM has three states: **Afraid**, **Calm**, and **Enthusiastic**. The **Calm** state periodically checks for frightening events, such as the death of several allies, or the arrival of a very powerful enemy. At this point, the **Calm** state generates a transition to the **Afraid** state. When the frightening enemy leaves or is killed, the **Afraid** state transitions back to the **Calm** state. When a powerful ally arrives, or the enemy is greatly outnumbered, the **Calm** state transitions to **Enthusiastic**. The states play appropriate animations and sounds to display the emotional state to the player: cowering in the **Afraid** state and cheering and taunting in the **Enthusiastic** state.

A self-contained FSM is not suitable for agent AI, since the agent needs to respond to player input and commands from the strategic AI system and scripted commands written by the designer or programmer.

External

Transitions can also be generated *externally* or outside the FSM. For example, in an RTS a player may click to command an agent to move to a location. The command is processed, and a request to transition to the **MoveTo** state is sent to the agent's FSM. In another case, the player may need to destroy an enemy radar installation. The player selects tanks and clicks on the enemy target. Inside the game, a button click generates a transition to the **Approach** state in the tanks' AI FSM. The tanks then move to the radar installation and begin firing.

Illustration by Per Olin

The player clicking on the guard button in the user interface generates an external transition in the artificial intelligence finite state machine to the *Guard* state.

Deferred

Once a transition is generated, the transition can be performed immediately, or *deferred* and performed at a later time. The deferred transition is preferable in most cases. Video games usually have a processing loop that is executed once for each frame. An example loop would update each system in order. When processing a frame, the input system is updated to check buttons pressed by the player; the physics system is updated to move the game objects; the AI system is updated to perform the active AI behaviors; the animation system is updated, adjusting each animated character; and, finally, the graphics system is updated to generate the frame image for the player. The frames are usually numbered sequentially for reference.

This processing is repeated while the game is running. The deferred (normal) transition happens during the next frame's processing loop, when the AI system is updated. Therefore, a transition generated when processing Frame 7 would be executed during the processing of Frame 8. This has several advantages.

First, state transitions will always occur at a specific time: at the beginning of the update of the AI update. This way, you only have FSM transitions executing during the AI system update rather than sometimes having transitions occur during the input system update and other times during the AI system update. With a system as complex as a modern electronic game, it is beneficial to make the execution as consistent as possible. It can make a difference whether the processing occurs before the physics system has updated an object's position, or afterwards.

The second advantage is that deferred transitions enforce a maximum of one transition per frame. An FSM that allows external transitions can receive several transitions during a processing loop from multiple external and internal sources. When multiple deferred transitions are generated during a frame, only the last transition requested is performed. This prevents state thrashing (executing multiple states during one frame) and animation "twitching" (visual artifacts caused by activating multiple animations on a single mesh during one frame).

Finally, the executions of states are distinct and sequential. In the case of a deferred transition from **Aim** to **Fire** in Frame 7, the deferred transition occurs as follows: The **Aim** state is executed during the AI system update in Frame 7. The transition is requested during Frame 7. During Frame 8 the transition is performed during the AI system update time, and the **Fire** state is executed. At Frame 7 the **Aim** state is active, and at Frame 8 the **Fire** state is active.

In contrast, an immediate internal transition results in both states being active during Frame 7. AI control code often issues instructions to other systems such as the physics system to move the agent, or the animation system to play an animation. With two states issuing instructions at the same time, it is possible to have multiple contradictory instructions, which can result in twitching that is apparent to the player.

The deferred transition is the preferred transition for an FSM. It prevents state thrashing and animation twitching. It results in an orderly sequential execution of states. This execution is intuitive and easy to understand and debug.

The only potential drawback to a deferred transition is that it introduces a small delay between the time one state ends and the next one begins. If a game updates the FSM 30 times a second or more, as *Command & Conquer: Generals* does, the delay is very small. However, some games do not update the FSM every frame. In order to improve game performance, the AI system containing the FSMs is updated less frequently, perhaps only five times per second. In this case, a deferred transition may result in a delay of $\frac{1}{5}$ of a second, which can be apparent to the player as a stutter in a unit's movement. In this case, an immediate transition can be used, removing the delay and correcting the stutter in the movement.

Immediate

The *immediate* transition causes the state machine to immediately exit the current state and enter the new state. This removes the delay associated with deferred transitions. Care must be taken to avoid the twitching and thrashing problems mentioned previously. In general, the deferred transition should be used as the default and the immediate transition only when timing issues arise.

Tom Clancy's Splinter Cell: Double Agent was developed using a finite state machine system that performs immediate transitions.

In some systems, the only transition available is an immediate transition. It is possible to implement a system in this fashion, but *spin* becomes more of a problem. Spin occurs when the state machine cycles through several states repeatedly.

External transitions should be deferred. They occur less frequently than internal transitions, and they are not time-critical, so the advantages of deferred transitions make them the best choice for external transitions. Internal transitions can be deferred or immediate, but deferred transitions are the preferred choice for most situations. Immediate transitions should be used only when there are critical performance or timing issues.

Spin

There is a potential problem with immediate transitions that can occur if there is an error in the logic and the states spin. For example, if the **Fire** state inappropriately checks range—and that check gets out of sync with the approach state's range check—the FSM will spin "**Approach** —> **Aim** —> **Fire** —> **Approach** —> **Aim** —> **Fire**" and the game will lock up. This spin is most often due to a programming error, but it can occasionally happen in unusual circumstances during normal gameplay, such as when two agents happen to briefly occupy the same location. It is a good idea to add a limit to the maximum number of immediate transitions that can occur in one frame. Ten is a reasonable limit. This will prevent the game from locking up, and often the condition causing the spin is transient, and the situation will correct itself.

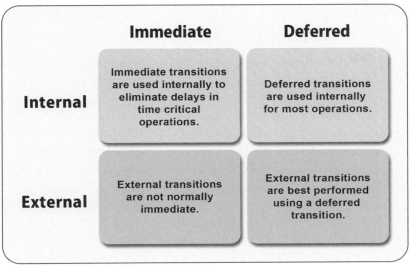

Diagram by Per Olin

Comparison of internal, external, immediate and deferred transitions.

The accompanying diagram illustrates three types of transitions. The external deferred transition begins the processing with the **Aim** state. In Frame 121, the **Aim** state performs a deferred internal transition to the **Fire** state. This causes the **Fire** state to begin executing at the start of the next frame. Finally, at Frame 123 the **Fire** state performs an immediate internal transition to the **Dodge** state. The **Dodge** state starts processing immediately, beginning its processing during Frame 123, rather than waiting to begin during Frame 124.

Diagram by Per Olin

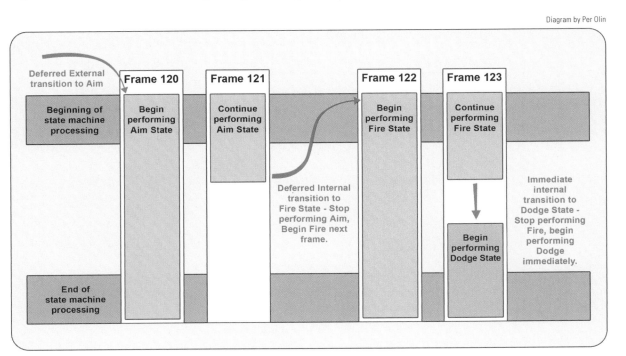

Three types of transitions performed by the **Aim**, **Fire**, and **Dodge** states.

An AI System Controlled by a Finite State Machine

The AI code for a number of games has been implemented using one or more FSMs. The SAGE engine, for example, uses one or two FSMs to control agent AI behaviors. SAGE uses scripting to select specific AI states, such as **Guard** or **Patrol**.

We will examine an implementation of an agent implemented in C++ that uses an FSM to control the agent's behaviors. The agents will be implemented as an AI *module*. In this example, a module is a C++ object that performs a particular task. The module uses a C++ interface, which is a list of pure virtual functions. The use of an interface allows the creation of multiple modules that perform the task. This allows the creation of different styles of AI that can be interchanged easily.

Other agent systems are implemented as modules as well. For example, the movement interface is specified to allow the agent to move from place to place. Once the interface is defined, we can create multiple movement modules that perform the task of movement. A walking movement module would move the agent along the ground. A flying movement module would move the agent through the air, then land it at the destination. A spider movement module could allow the agent to crawl up walls and across ceilings, in addition to moving on the ground.

The technique of aggregation allows us to build an agent using one or more modules. The choice of modules defines the properties of the agent. A rock that serves as an obstacle could be built with two modules: a display module so it could be seen, and a collision module so that other agents would collide with the rock instead of just passing through the rock.

Diagram by Per Olin

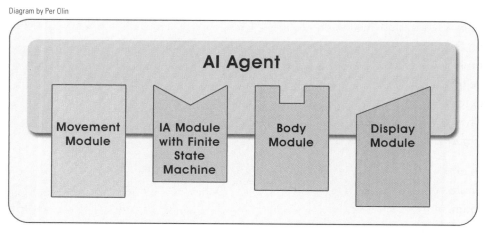

The AI agent is assembled from four modules: a movement module, an AI module, a body module, and a display module. Different modules can be used to create several different kinds of AI agents.

The example agent will have a display module, so it can be seen, a movement module, so it can move, an AI module, to control the movement, and a body module to track health and damage received. A simple two-dimensional space will give the agent an environment and allow other agents to exist as well.

:::::: Modular Design

Building an agent from a set of modules is a technique called *modular design*. Modern video game engines such as SAGE and Unreal 3 create agents from a set of modules. SAGE provides modules for collision, AI, display, physics, weapons, and movement. Unreal 3 builds agents from a list of modules called components, which define the agent's collision, display, particle systems,

Epic Games

The Unreal Engine (*Unreal Tournament 2007* pictured) uses modular design.

and lights. In addition, Unreal 3 provides a control module interface and provides modules for AI control and human control of agents.

Sample Application

The working implementation of this agent and the game environment are included on the *Game Artificial Intelligence* companion DVD. The source code for the project is available for programmers with access to Visual Studio.NET, and can be modified for other environments as an exercise for the programmer. Also, an executable version, Simpleagent.exe, is available for the non-programmer to run. The InitialData.txt file can be edited with any text editor, allowing all readers to experiment with the application.

In order to test and demonstrate the concepts in the agent, we are going to create a limited two-dimensional environment where the agent can operate. The game environment is implemented in Visual Studio.NET C++ using the Microsoft foundation classes and standard template library.

The game environment provides:

- the ability to create agents
- maintenance of a list of agents active in the world
- an interface that allows agents to find other agents in the environment
- graphics support to draw the agents in the game window so that the player will be able to see the agents

Agent Design

The agent class uses data-driven modular design to assemble the parts of the agent. The agent uses interfaces and the aggregation technique to attach modules to the agent. Each of the four modules—body, movement, appearance and AI—use this technique to allow agents to be created using different combinations of modules without having to change any of the C++ code. This allows rapid creation of different types of agents on the part of designers and artists. The details of the implementation can be found in the documentation file on the companion DVD and in the source code.

Movement Module

The data for the agent and the environment are provided in InitialData.txt. The following data specifies the movement module information.

```
{
        Section = "Movement"
        MovementType = "Normal"
        Speed = 5.7
}
```

The MovementType="Normal" selects the C++ object NormalMovement as the movement module for the agent. In addition to specifying the module, the data file can provide parameters to the movement module as well. The line "speed = 5.7" directs the NormalMovementModule to move the agent at a maximum speed of 5.7 pixels per frame.

© Valve Corporation. Used with permission.

The ImmobileMovementModule would be appropriate for an AI agent such as the *Half-Life 2* sentry gun that is unable to move.

We can change "Normal" to "Immobile":

```
MovementType = "Immobile"
```

The agent will use the ImmobileMovementModule and become unable to move. The use of this module ensures that the unit doesn't accidentally receive a movement command and move. In addition, this module uses less memory than the normal movement module.

Data-Driven Design

There is an alternative method that accomplishes the same task as data drive design: data and modules that can be defined in C++ code. For a programmer, it is often faster to work in C++ code. C++ compilers provide built-in ways to specify data and modules. Data-driven design requires additional work on the part of the programmer. In early video game development teams were very small, and most, if not all, of the developers were programmers. In this environment, data-driven design was more of a burden than a benefit. Modern video games are developed by teams of people, and most of the team members are not programmers. In this environment there are several benefits to data-driven design. There is a cost benefit, because designers can make changes without a compiler license. A full set of programming tools including a compiler can cost several hundred dollars. There is a time benefit to the designer, as she doesn't have to wait to get assistance from a programmer. Finally, there is a time benefit to the programmer, as interruptions are reduced. The net result is that data-driven design makes game development faster and more productive in the modern environment.

Appearance Module

The Appearance module displays a visual representation of the agent in the example environment. The SimpleAppearanceModule is an Appearance module for the agent that uses a Windows two-dimensional icon bitmap to represent the agent. A data section for the SimpleAppearanceModule follows:

```
{
        Section = "Appearance"
        AppearanceType = "Simple"
        icon = "Man"
}
```

The AppearanceType of "Simple" creates a SimpleAppearanceModule. The SimpleAppearanceModule represents the agent with the icon specified in the data section. The module appends .ico to the icon name, so *icon = "Man"* would draw the agent with the icon file Man.ico.

Body Module

The Body module tracks the health of the agent and notes when the agent is killed. A data section for the Mortal module follows:

```
{
        Section = "Body"
        BodyType = "Mortal"
        health=100
}
```

This allocates a MortalBodyModule C++ object with 100 health points. The agent dies when it receives 100 or more points of damage. A second body module, the ImmortalBody, is available. By specifying BodyType = "Immortal" in the data section, the agent receives an ImmortalBodyModule. The ImmortalBodyModule behavior is that the agent never dies, regardless of the amount of damage received.

:::::: SAGE Engine

Electronic Arts

Agents in *Command & Conquer Generals: Zero Hour* are assembled from multiple modules specified in a data file.

The SAGE engine, used in *Command & Conquer Generals: Zero Hour*, uses a data-driven modular design. This design is similar to the one used by the example agent. A system was created to manage the modules, allowing each object to have an unlimited number of modules. The system managed the allocation of the modules and called the appropriate methods in the modules. The AI module is a time-controlled module, so its Update method was called once per frame by the module system. This allowed the AI module to perform the necessary processing for each frame.

Some events were handled by the module system. Rather than being called each frame, these modules were only called when a particular event occurred. The most common event module was the collision module. This module would be called when an object collided with another object.

AI Module

The AI module, in the example agent, performs the AI tasks. In the example, these tasks include patrol movement, searching for a target, and moving to the target.

The AIModule reads a goal from the data file and sets the state machine to the appropriate state to accomplish that goal. At each frame, the AIModule's Tick() method calls the state machine's Tick() method, and the active state of the state machine performs the AI behavior. The desired AI behaviors are as follows:

- *Idle*: The agent will remain motionless.
- *Patrol*: The agent will move in a rectangular pattern, indefinitely.
- *Find coins*: The agent will move in a rectangular pattern, periodically searching for a coin. When it finds a coin, it will move to the coin and pick it up. After picking up the coin, the agent will resume moving in the rectangular pattern and searching.

These behaviors can be specified and implemented in an FSM. The AI module uses a C++ object, AgentStateMachine, which implements an FSM. The AgentStateMachine has one or more states for each behavior that is required. The **Idle** and **Patrol** behaviors are each implanted with a single state, while the **Find Coins** behavior requires two states. The AgentStateMachine performs the AI behaviors supported by the AI module.

AgentStateMachine Class

The AgentStateMachine class implements an FSM that will control the movement of the agent and perform the required AI behaviors. The AgentStateMachine class supports a variable number of states, as different combinations of behaviors will require different numbers of states. In the example, there are four states: **Idle**, **Patrol**, **Patrol For Coin**, and **Pick Up Coin**. **Idle** is a simple state that does nothing. **Patrol** moves the agent in a simple rectangular patrol path. **Patrol For Coin** patrols and searches for a gold coin in the game environment, and **Pick Up Coin** moves to the coin and picks it up.

The AgentStateMachine implements external and internal transitions. An external transition is used to select the desired behavior. For the patrol behavior, an external transition is generated to the **Patrol** state. Internal transitions are used when the FSM is performing a behavior. When a coin is found, an internal transition is generated to the **Pick Up Coin** state, in order to pick up the coin. After the agent has picked up the coin, an internal transition is generated back to the **Patrol For Coin** state so the agent can continue patrolling and looking for additional coins.

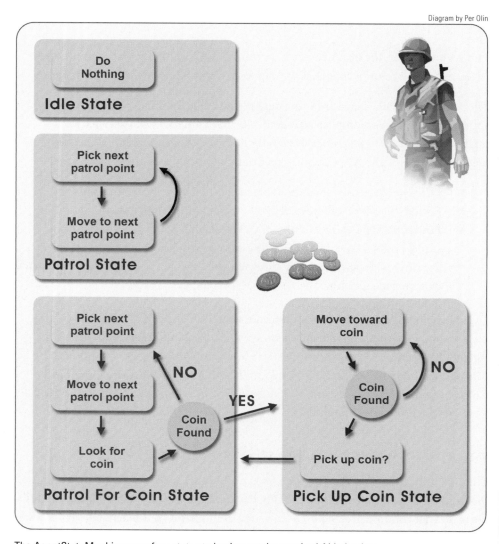

Diagram by Per Olin

The AgentStateMachine uses four states to implement the required AI behaviors.

This example demonstrates the use of an FSM to control the agent's behaviors. An external transition is used to specify the agent's behavior—idle, patrol, or pick up coins. Simple behaviors—idle and patrol—are implemented with a single state. A more complex behavior—search and pick up coins—is implemented using two states. Internal transitions are used in the two-state behavior to switch between states when necessary. The AI systems in many video games are written using FSMs. In actual games, such as *The Lord of the Rings: The Battle for Middle-Earth,* the FSM had over 100 states. Complex behaviors were implemented using ten or more states.

::::: Debugging FSMs

FSMs quickly reach such a degree of complexity in games that programmers spend a significant amount of time debugging them. It is useful to create some tools to support debugging, since they can reduce the amount of time required to identify and correct problems. The first tool is included in the example StateMachine class. Each time a transition occurs, and a state is exited or entered, the FSM writes a message to the console.

```
agent StickMan, Exit state NO_STATE
agent StickMan, Enter state PatrolCoins
```

This creates a log of state transitions so that we can review the sequence and verify whether the expected transitions occurred in the correct order.

Electronic Arts

In an actual game, such as *Command & Conquer: Generals*, there may be 40 or more agents active at one time. Searching the log of all transitions is akin to searching for a needle in a haystack. In order to make this capability more useful, we added the ability to log the transitions only for a single agent. This greatly improved the usability of the log. A debug window that allowed programmers to stop the game and step through game frames was helpful as well. An additional feature that was useful in conjunction

A group of agents in a battle generate a large number of state transitions in *Command & Conquer: Generals* This is difficult to track and debug.

with pausing the game was a debug switch that would cause the name of the current AI state to be displayed as a tool tip when you moved the game cursor over an agent. The combination of these three tools—logging, pause, and step—and the interactive display of state made debugging of complex state machines possible, if not easy.

Speculative Features

A trap that AI programmers can fall into involves speculative features and programming. A speculative feature is a potentially useful and valuable feature that occurs to programmers when they are implementing a system, but has not yet been specified in the game design. A speculative feature is one that occurs to programmers looking at the situation. It may be because the programmer has run into a problem while working on a feature. In other cases the programmer is anticipating a problem that

Illustration by Per Olin

may occur when the feature is used. Often the programmer will anticipate problems based on past experience. This is in contrast to a feature that is in the game design and is planned to be supported.

Another source of speculative features is the desire to create a system that handles all possible situations correctly. For example, a game may have water and land, and include boats, tanks, and hovercrafts. The boats move on water, the tanks and soldiers on land, and the hovercrafts on both. The movement system would need to support movement on land, on water, and, in the case of the hovercraft, on land and water. These are the required features. Submarines and scuba divers are speculative features at this point. While the game has water, ships, and soldiers, there are no submarines or scuba divers. Code to support submarine and scuba diver movement is at this point speculative.

A speculative feature may appear at first glance to be a good idea. The programmer is exercising initiative, and dealing with problems before they arise, rather than waiting. However, more often than not, speculative features delay the project and reduce the overall quality of the game.

Attraction

The attraction of speculative features often comes from a programmer's past experience. Video game code is often developed in iterative cycles. A programmer creates a first version, which is then available for use and testing. The programmer works with the designer and testers to polish the feature to the desired level of quality.

Often, once a set of features is working, the designers may discover that a gameplay mechanic is not working. For example, in the initial design of the game, units in an RTS may only be required to fire when stationary. This means that units that are retreating cannot fire. In order to actually play the game, several systems must be working: graphics, weapons, animation, movement, and AI. These systems are tested, and are working as designed. However, gameplay testing may indicate that players find the failure of their retreating units to shoot back is irritating and unrealistic. When implementing firing while retreating, the programmers discover that the firing animations and the movement animations are not compatible, and parts of the system must be re-written to support this combination.

Note that the process that we have just followed is a classic, normal development cycle that will occur in AI development for games:

1. The initial implementation is made.
2. It behaves correctly for the initial game design.
3. Changes are made to the game design.
4. It is discovered that systems that were finished now need additional work to support the design changes.

Can you see how it would be better if the systems correctly anticipated our future needs? In the case of the fire-while-retreat feature, it would be useful if the animation system supported simultaneous fire and move animations. Unfortunately, doing this requires either extreme over-engineering or correctly predicting the future. Over-engineering is not a productive use of time and resources, and any design methodology that requires accurate prediction of the future is doomed to failure.

Hidden Cost

The key question is: Should the animation system been written to support simultaneous fire and movement animations? It seems that it would be a good idea to have a more broadly capable animation system. However, the answer is "no." It would be a mistake to put this code into the animation system initially unless the game design had specifically indicated that the agents were going to be required to fire while retreating.

There are several reasons for this:

1. Speculative features delay the project. The additional code required to implement the speculative feature is going to take additional time. This is a serious issue because the best implementation of games is done in an iterative fashion. Features are implemented, the game is played, modifications and refinements are added, and the game is played again. The amount of time to finish a particular revision is critical because it determines a number of cycles that can be done to refine the design.
2. The speculative feature may not be necessary. At the point the animation system is initially implemented, it is not known whether the game will support firing while moving. It may be that the initial behavior is acceptable, and this feature will never be used. In this case the speculative feature is a waste of time. In addition to wasting time, unused code makes the game harder to debug and support.

3. If needed, the speculative feature will be easier to implement after the details are known, at which point the feature is no longer speculative. It is much easier to correctly implement the fire-while-retreating behavior after the designers have determined the details of the new behavior, rather than attempting to implement a system that will support an unknown future design decision.

4. As the exact details are not yet known, it is very difficult to adequately test a speculative feature. Untested code also makes a game difficult to maintain and debug.

5. The number of errors in a project is usually proportional to the number of lines of code. Adding additional code for speculative features often reduces the quality of the game.

Although it may be tempting to implement speculative features, they delay development, negatively impact the game's quality, and thus should be avoided. It is better to wait until the need is obvious, since this will eliminate wasting time by implementing unused features.

An FSM is a powerful and flexible method for creating and controlling AI behaviors. The use of an FSM allows the programmer to divide the behavior into states that each perform a relatively simple task. The transitions allow the FSM to create complex behaviors by executing long sequences of these states. The behavior of a state is determined by the programmer, and can be as simple or complex as necessary. The states can make use of other AI techniques such as the path search algorithms presented later in this book. The results of the path search can be used to produce AI agents with realistic movement.

Modern video games using FSMs may require in excess of 100 states. This number of states is difficult to design, implement, and debug. The use of hierarchy makes this process faster, and the resulting FSM easier to understand. We will examine the use of hierarchy in the next chapter.

:::CHAPTER REVIEW:::

1. A hypothetical real-time strategy game requires some strategic AI behaviors for the player's AI opponent. Each player, human and AI, starts with an agent that can build structures and factories. A vehicle factory can build tanks and armored personnel carriers. The land factory requires power and iron to build vehicles. An iron refinery automatically gathers iron ore and creates iron. The iron refinery requires power to refine iron. A power plant provides power, and has no pre-requisites. The strategic AI is specified by the lead designer. The AI can perform the following types of actions: A) Build structure X; B) Use factory X to produce N vehicles of type Y; C) Direct a group of vehicles to guard the base; D) Direct a group of vehicles to attack enemy structure Z. What actions are required on the part of the AI in order to build a tank, while meeting all the game's prerequisites?

2. The lead designer requests the following behavior: The AI is to build four armored personnel carriers to guard the base. Then the AI is to build six tanks and attack the opposing player's air-field structure. List the required actions in order for the AI to perform this behavior.

3. Create an FSM that will generate this list of actions. Use labeled circles for the states, and arrows for transitions. If a state has more than one transition out of the state, label each transition with the condition(s) that will trigger that transition.

4. During gameplay, unexpected events often occur; in one case the player destroys the AI's power plant and most of the armored personnel carriers, stalling vehicle production and leaving the base defenseless. In this case, the lead designer requests the following behavior: Rebuild the power plant first, then build another set of armored personnel carriers. Once this is complete, resume the previous plan. List the required actions to perform this behavior.

5. In another case the player constructed a missile base in addition to an air field. In this case the lead designer wants the AI to attack the missile base. Would the state machine in exercise 2 be capable of creating this sequence of actions? If necessary, extend the state machine to be capable of creating the sequence of actions required for exercises 1,3, and 4.

6. Consider the use of internal and external transitions to make the changes required for example 4. How could each type of transition be used? What are the advantages and disadvantages of either type? Where would you recommend that either be used, and why?

Complexity & Broad Scope

multiple states and hierarchical state machines

Key Chapter Questions

■ What are the advantages of a *hierarchical finite state machine*?

■ Which state machine control mechanism makes use of *procedural transition generation* and what are its advantages?

■ What are two state machine control mechanisms that examine *multiple states* and what are their advantages?

■ A *goal-oriented* system is more work than a hierarchical finite state machine. When is the additional work worthwhile?

■ Which is more efficient—*active state generated transitions* or *child states compete*? What is one way to improve the efficiency of the more costly control mechanism?

A modern electronic game will often have in excess of 100 behaviors that the various agents in the game can perform. These behaviors range from patrol and attack to search to flee. Choosing the most appropriate behavior at a given time is a key to good game artificial intelligence (AI). Many AI programmers use a hierarchical finite state machine (HFSM) to structure the states in order to make the code easier to create, understand, and maintain. The appropriate behavior is chosen by searching the hierarchy, or by allowing the active state to control the state machine. We will examine several methods for searching the hierarchy in this chapter.

Hierarchical Finite State Machine

In a modern electronic game, a finite state machine (FSM)—described in Chapter 2—is often used to control the AI behaviors. However, the number of states may easily exceed 100 in order to provide all the necessary behaviors for the different agents in the game. When dealing with this number of states, it becomes very difficult for the programmers and designers to keep track of what is going on. Consider the several issues that need to be managed in an FSM, including:

- which states are available
- which states are active at a given time
- what transitions are between states
- how the transitions are represented

One good way to make it simpler for the code—and more comprehensible for the designers and programmers—when dealing with a large number of states is to use a *hierarchical finite state machine (HFSM)*.

Eidos Interactive Ltd.

Freedom Fighters uses a hierarchy of states to control complex AI behaviors.

Diagram by Per Olin

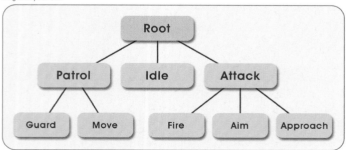

The primary states in this hierarchical finite state machine have from 0 to 3 sub-states.

In an HFSM, the root machine has a list of states. Each of those states may have one or more sub-states, and each sub-state may also have sub-states. At any one time, a state is active at a given level, and if it has sub-states, one of the sub-states is active. At the top level, the total number of states is reduced, so we can look at a unit and say it can be in one of three states, rather than one of 100. The unit is in the **Idle**, **Attack**, or **Patrol** state. At the top level, we only have to concern ourselves with selecting one of the three top-level states. This greatly simplifies the conditions that have to be specified, and it increases the ability of the designers and programmers to understand what is going on and debug it. After the top level is defined, sub-states are defined to elaborate on the details of the high-level states. In addition to being easier to understand, the reduced number of states at the top level is more efficient, potentially resulting in faster game performance.

Example State: Attack

The **Attack** state has the following sub-states:

Approach (when it is out of range of the enemy)
Fire (when it is within range and the weapon is ready to fire)
Aim (when the agent is not facing the target)

This structure makes an AI behavior easier to implement, understand, and debug. For example, if there is a problem with a unit not firing, we can examine the state machine. If we determine that the unit is stuck in the **Aim** state, we know to look at the **Attack** state and sub-states. We do not have to look at the **Patrol** sub-states. In the case of a simple FSM, there is no division of states, so it is more difficult to understand, and we are cannot easily focus on the relevant portion when there is a problem.

Procedural Transition Generation

Once we make use of an HFSM, we need to consider how to specify the transitions between states. Classical computer FSMs (or finite state automata) use a table of inputs and current states to specify the next state. The inputs to an AI state machine are the entire game state. This does not map well into a table of inputs, so state machines in game AI generally use *procedural transition generation*, where the AI code calls a function in the state machine to cause a transition to a particular state. This mechanism is implemented in the state machine example presented on the companion DVD. The function TransitionToState() causes the state machine to transition from the current state to another state, executing the appropriate ExitState() method for the current state, and EnterState() for the new state.

BioWare Corp.

The Unreal 3 engine, used in BioWare's *Mass Effect*, generates procedural transitions between states.

TransitionToState() is a public function. This means that as far as the C++ language is concerned, the function can be called at any time from anywhere in the game. While this is certainly flexible, it makes it difficult to design and maintain the state machines when we have no idea where or when the transitions will be generated.

Models

In order to make the design and maintenance of state machines easier, we use a *model* that limits when and how transitions are generated. This is a self-imposed restriction that makes the state machine easier to understand. For example, it is possible for a state transition function to be called while saving a game to a file. This is problematic, since it is not clear which condition is saved and which state will be active when loading the file. Using a model that specifies when transitions occur can prevent problems like this from arising.

Models and Hacks

As we have noted, using procedural transition generation means that a transition can be generated at any time. Using a model to limit this is helpful, but the model does not always exactly match the needs of the AI system. In this case, it is possible to generate transitions that do not follow the model. This is one of many techniques that are called *hacks*. A hack is not the first choice, since it defeats the use of the model in the first place. However, at the end of the day, the driving goal is the gameplay and not the purity of the coding model. Hacks are occasionally unavoidable, and they should be documented to give others information as to the situation that required the hack, and the hack's implementation, so they can understand what was done and why.

Externally Generated Transitions

In most cases, it is possible for the player, or a game designer, to give an agent a command. A player uses the user interface and may click on an target to direct the agent to attack the target. A game designer may use scripting (discussed in Chapter 6) to direct an agent to patrol a given area, or use an *area trigger* to direct an agent to attack the player. An area trigger is a two- or three-dimensional area with an action attached to the area. When the player, or other specified agent, enters the area, the action is executed. In this case, the action directs the agent to attack the player. This often generates a transition to a particular state that performs or initiates the performance of the task. For example, when a player directs a tank to attack, the tank enters an **Attack** state. Similarly, if an enemy enters an AI controlled agent's line of sight, the AI agent may enter an **Attack** state.

Externally generated transitions are out of the control of the state machine. They may be generated by systems external to the AI, such as the user interface, or by other parts of the AI, such as designer supplied scripting. A good way to fit external transitions into a model is to make them deferred. Rather than changing the state immediately, the information is stored until the normal AI state machine processing occurs. At this point the external transitions are executed. In this fashion, all transitions occur during the normal AI state machine processing phase.

Internally Generated Transitions

Once the state machine has entered a state (such as **Attack**) that performs a task, the state machine will continue to execute the task. This will involve generating transitions; for example, from **Move**, to **Aim**, and then to **Fire**. Internally generated transitions account for the majority of the transitions in AI state machines.

A state machine can be built using different models to control the transitions, or no model at all. We will look at several different models for implementing transitions. The use of a model that fits the needs of the AI will result in a design that is easier to implement, debug, and understand. The use of a model that does not fit the AI, no matter how elegant, will require hacks to produce the desired behaviors, eliminating the benefits of using a model in the first place.

Active State Generated Transitions

One model for generating transitions involves the active state. The Unreal 3 engine Engine used in *Unreal Tournament 2007* and *Gears of War* supports this model, and

it is the same model used by the state machine in the Chapter 2 programming example included on the companion DVD. In a hierarchical model, there may be multiple active states—one per level. In the **Attack** state, the machine would begin with an active **Attack** state, which would then generate a transition to the **Aim** state. Both **Attack** and **Aim** would then be active states. Since the parent state (**Attack**) is active, it can generate transitions if necessary. However, the sub-states generate the transitions for the most part.

Epic Games

The Unreal 3 engine, used in *Gears of War,* supports the active state model for generating transitions.

In the case of the **Harvest** state, we have a relatively simple control flow. When the **Harvest** state is entered, it activates the **Move To Source** state, which moves the harvester to the nearest supply source. After the move completes, the **Move To Source** state generates a transition to the **Load** state, which contacts the supply source and loads supplies. When loading is complete, the **Load** state generates a transition to the **Move To Depot** state, which allows the unit to move and unload

Diagram by Per Olin

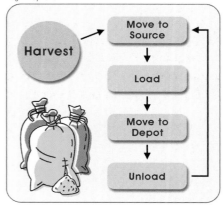

The **Harvest** state and sub-states are controlled using transitions generated by the active state.

Diagram by Per Olin

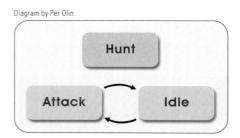

supplies. The parent **Harvest** state then has to allow the sub-states to run and does not generate any state transitions among the sub-states after the initial entry.

In some cases, the parent state is more active in generating transitions. One example is a **Hunt** state. The goal of this state is to attack and destroy the nearest enemy unit, and repeat the process. In this case, the **Hunt** state will find the closest enemy when it is entered and generate a transition to the **Attack** sub-state the next level down.

Like the **Harvest** state, the **Hunt** state will execute the active sub-state, performing the attack. However, the **Hunt** state will do two additional checks. First, it will monitor the active sub-state. If the active sub-state becomes **Idle** (normally because the target has been destroyed, but the target could have become invisible or in some other fashion become impossible to attack), the **Hunt** state searches again for the closest enemy and generates a transition to the **Attack** sub-state. The black transition in the diagram from **Idle** to **Attack** will be generated by the **Hunt** rather than the **Idle** state. The second check **Hunt** performs is to see if another enemy unit has moved closer than the original target. If so, it will change the target unit for the **Attack** state.

Advantages and Drawbacks

The advantages of active state generated transitions are *simplicity* and *speed*. Since only the active states can generate transitions, all other states and sub-states can be ignored. The primary drawback is that these transitions only do one thing at a time.

This model fits straightforward AI behaviors such as those found in a real-time strategy game (RTS) reasonably well. These behaviors range from guarding a location or patrolling an area to attacking an enemy until the enemy or attacker is destroyed. Once an agent starts one of these behaviors, it is appropriate to keep doing so until directed otherwise. This focus on the active state is useful and appropriate in this environment.

The active state model uses an explicit transition-oriented control mechanism. The state machine only has to keep track of the current state, and that state remains active unless the active state generates a transition. This is a very efficient approach, since only the active state does any processing. It is also clear what state the agent is in, and when transitions can occur.

There are also drawbacks to active state generated transitions, which do give the currently active state complete control of the state machine. If the state machine is currently in the **Guard** state, it will only transition out of this state if the code in the **Guard** state invokes a transition. This model fits RTS AI quite well and is used as the backbone in several RTS games since RTS agents are supposed to do as they are ordered most of the time and generally ignore distractions. In other cases, "distractions" are important. For example, in a first-person shooter (FPS), an intelligent reaction when detecting that someone is shooting a rocket at you is to dodge. This response is pretty much independent of what the agent may be doing at the time. If an agent is moving to pick up an item, attacking an enemy, guarding, or just idling, it makes sense to dodge. In the active state model, switching to a **Dodge** state from whatever state the agent currently in means all states must check for dodging and generate the transition, or we have to add code outside of the state machine that checks for this and forces the state machine into the **Dodge** state.

In some cases even an RTS may require more than a simple active state generated transition model. A tank is given an order to move to a particular location on a map, and midway through the movement it passes an enemy tank that fires on it. Using a simple HFSM with the sub-states generating the transitions, the tank is in a **Move** state. The default behavior of the FSM in this case would be for the tank to keep moving and possibly be destroyed without retaliating. If a game design decision indicates that units should not keep moving but retaliate by stopping and firing back, the FSM must be changed. A simple change would be for the **Move** state to check for damage, and, if there is damage, switch to the **Attack** state. However, this causes the move to be aborted since the attack state transitions to **Idle** after destroying the target, and the unit will stop after attacking. The **Attack** state then needs to be extended so that it "remembers" whether it was moving when it was entered, and so that it goes back to moving. However, it could be that the unit was moving to enter a vehicle. As you can see, these sorts of design decisions can greatly complicate the otherwise simple HFSM. Fortunately for an RTS, it is generally preferred that the units follow the orders given rather than stop and perform an "intelligent" but not requested action; so the simple HFSM model still works rather well for an RTS. However, other games such as squad-based tactical shooters call for more human behavior from the agents, and this would require extensions to the simple active state transition model.

Denis Papp on Artificial Intelligence for Real-Time Strategy Games : : : : :

Denis Papp
(Chief Technology
Officer, TimeGate
Studios)

Denis Papp joined TimeGate Studios in 1999 and served as the lead programmer on the award-winning *Kohan* series of RTS games, the *Axis & Allies* RTS game, and *F.E.A.R.: Extraction Point*. Prior to this, he developed *Loki*, the first version of what is now the strongest poker AI in the world (*Poki*), with the Games Research Group at the University of Alberta. Denis began his professional career at BioWare Corp., taking over during his first year as the lead programmer on *Shattered Steel*.

For the artificial intelligence opponents in a RTS game, there are so many resources available and goals that can be accomplished in parallel. Here are some basic ideas that work particularly well:

- Treat it as a resource allocation problem.

- Reduce decisions down to fuzzy scoring heuristics as opposed to a linear script.

- Quantize the game space to manageable chunks.

- Simplify the problem by breaking the AI into a well-defined hierarchy; solve the strategic and tactical levels separately.

Consider Multiple States

Another way to control the transitions in the state machine is by *examining multiple states*. In this model, the state machine considers all states and picks the best one to become active, rather than having the states generate transitions and only considering the active state.

Bungie Studios

AI agents in *Halo 2* consider multiple states in the state machine in order to control behaviors.

When considering multiple states, the state machine examines all of the states in order to determine the best state. This state then becomes the active state. Rather than the **Attack** state generating a transition to **Patrol** when the enemy is killed or flees, the **Root** state determines whether the agent should **Attack, Patrol**, or enter some other state entirely. This method has two major differences from the active state generated transitions. First, all substates are considered. This is more expensive than just processing the active sub-state, but it supports a more dynamic and flexible state machine. Second, sub-states do not have to know about each other. In the **Harvest** example, the **Load** state had to know to transition to the **Move To Depot** state. In the state search model, the states do not have to be aware of the other states, since the transi-

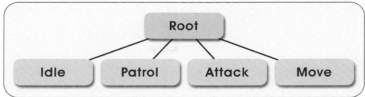

Diagram by Per Olin

This hierarchical finite state machine considers multiple states to determine which state is active.

tions are generated in the state machine. Thus, the logic of the state machine is more complex in this case, since it has to decide which state is best at a given time; however, the logic in the states is simpler, since they are not generating transitions to the other states.

Child States Compete

One method for handling the state search is to have the *child states compete* to become the active state. Each child state has a relevance function, which returns a number indicating the relevance of the state to the current situation. Generally, zero indicates that the state is not relevant and that higher values are more relevant.

The root in this case will examine the states and choose the most relevant one. For example, if the unit has a goal destination, the **Move** state is relevant. If there are enemies nearby, the **Attack** state is relevant. In order to provide the parent with the state's relevance, each state has a function that evaluates and returns the relevance of that state. For the example, let us say that the relevance ranges from 0 to 100. A state with a relevance value of 0 is not relevant. A relevance of 100 is most relevant.

The **Move** state has a relevance function of:

```
int Move::Relevance(Object &thisObject)
{
    if (thisObject.hasGoalDestination()) {
        return 75;
    }
    return 0;
}
```

Thus, if the game object has a goal destination, the **Move** state is of high relevance.

The **Attack** state has the following relevance function:

```
int Attack:: Relevance(StateMachine& machine, agent& owner)
{
    Const Object * nearestEnemy = FindClosestVisibleEnemy();
    If (nearestEnemy == NULL)
        return 0; // Attack is not relevant if no enemies are
        visible.
    int relevance = 50; // slightly relevant if we can see it.
    If (thisObject.GetWeapon().InRange(*nearestEnemy) {
        Relevance = 70;
    }
    return relevance;
}
```

In this case, we have the classic RTS move and attack behaviors. When the unit is issued a move order and has a goal destination, its relevance is 75, and it enters the **Move** state. If an enemy is sighted, the **Attack** state relevance is 50 (lower than 75) and the unit continues moving. Even if the enemy is in range, the **Attack** relevance is 70 (lower than 75), so the unit continues to move.

The advantage of the child states compete is that the state machine and the other child states do not have to know details of the child states. The code for the state machine is simple and does not change when states are added, removed, or modified.

There are drawbacks to the child states compete control model. The first drawback is *computational expense*. If there are 50 possible states, the simple implementation requires that all 50 states' relevance functions be evaluated. In the case of the **Move** state, the relevance function has trivial cost, but the **Attack** state has a rather expensive relevance function, since searching for other units is rarely a cheap operation and weapon range testing can be non-trivial. A second drawback is the possibility of *state twitching*. If a unit with a relatively short-range weapon is attacked by slow-firing artillery, it may have the artillery in view, but not in range. It then returns a relevance of 50, and the move at 75 is higher, so it moves. But the artillery with longer range hits the unit, and the unit is damaged. The **Attack** relevance is now 80 (higher than 75), so it turns to attack. While the artillery is reloading—and before the unit gets in weapon range—recently damaged artillery expires, turns around, and starts moving again. However, it is again damaged, so it switches back to the **Attack** state, moves back to attack, moves away, and then moves back. This is called *twitching* (since the unit twitches back and forth) or *dithering* (because the unit cannot decide for sure if it wants to attack or move). With a large number of possible states—and a variety of units with different speed, weapon ranges, and vision ranges—it is easy to accidentally come up with combinations that produce twitching in some cases.

::::: Improving Child Competes

There are a number of techniques that can be used to improve performance and dithering. The first, and most important, is *creating a hierarchy*. In this case, the best hierarchy is one that is relatively narrow and as deep as necessary.

Diagram by Per Olin

The narrow hierarchy improves both computational expense and dithering. In the accompanying diagram, the **Patrol**, **Attack**, and **Fire** states are active in the first, second, and third levels, respectively. As there are only four states at the top level, the root only has to get relevance values from **Patrol**, **Idle**, **Escort**, and **Recon**. At the second level, only **Guard**, **Attack**, and **Move** are evaluated for relevance. At the third level, **Fire**, **Aim**, and **Approach** are evaluated. Thus, only 10 states have to be evaluated, rather than all the states. In the previous example, the child states of **Escort**, **Recon**, **Guard**, and **Move** do not have to be evaluated. This improves the performance of the AI. Evaluating 12 states also reduces the opportunity for dithering. Thus, while hierarchy for an FSM is a good idea for readability, hierarchy in a state search model is necessary for performance and improving the behavior of the system, as well as readability.

The **Fire** state is the active sub-state in this hierarchical finite state machine.

Bungie Studios

Another method for improving performance is *masking states*, or using *temporary states*. In the case of masking states, all states are present in the hierarchy. In many cases, a state will never be used for a particular unit. For example, there may be a **Flee** state for

Halo 2 uses hierarchy and state masking to improve artificial intelligence performance.

lightly armored units that are fast. The heavily armored, slow moving units would never enter a **Flee** state. Thus, the evaluation of relevance of the **Flee** state for these units is, well, irrelevant. In this state, having a *bitmask* for all the states is a useful technique. A bitmask is an array of binary values, called a *bit*, each of which is zero or one. If there were 70 states, the bitmask would contain 70 bits, one for each state. If the value for a state's corresponding bit was one, the relevance function would be evaluated, and the value returned. If the bit value was zero for a state, the state would never be made active, saving the cost of executing the relevance function. In the case of the heavy units, the **Flee** state bit would be zero, and the state would never be evaluated for relevance.

Similarly, there may be states that are relevant only for a short time for specific units. For example, if the squad leader is killed, there may be a **Retreat** state that is only triggered immediately after the squad leader's death. It is inefficient for all units to always evaluate this state, since most of the time it will return zero. Therefore, it can be masked off, and in an event (squad leader death) can temporarily enable it for certain units in the bit mask.

Retaliation

Retaliation behavior is an example of an AI behavior that is easier to implement in the child competes control model, as opposed to the active state transition model. In the case of the state generated transition FSM, adding a retaliation behavior increased the complexity of the states considerably. With a child competes control model, the retaliation behavior can be added by just modifying the **Attack** state. We only need to add the following lines to the **Attack** state's relevance function:

```
int Attack:: Relevance(StateMachine& machine, agent& owner)
{
    Const Object * nearestEnemy = FindClosestVisibleEnemy();
    If (nearestEnemy == NULL)
        return 0; // Attack is not relevant if no enemies are
        visible.
    int relevance = 50; // slightly relevant if we can see it.
    If (thisObject.GetWeapon().InRange(*nearestEnemy) {
        Relevance = 70;
    }
    If (thisObject.RecentlyDamaged()) {
        // If we have been damaged recently,
        // we are more inclined to attack.
        Relevance += 30;
    }
    relevance = clamp(relevance, 0, 100); // in case we get out
    of range.
    return relevance;
}
```

The behavior of stopping, attacking the enemy, and continuing the move is accomplished without having to modify the **Move** state. In addition, no changes are needed in the **Root** state. If another state is added, such as **Enter Vehicle**, the unit can stop and attack enemies without the **Enter Vehicle** state having to be aware of the **Attack** state. This model can produce quite complex behaviors while limiting the amount of information that states have to know about each other, unlike a simple FSM.

Parent State Control

Another method for handling the state search is to have the *parent state* have custom code to control the search. In the accompanying diagram, the **Root** state would contain code to determine which sub-state should be active. This mechanism can be very powerful, but it has several drawbacks. First, it requires that information about a state be separated. The **Move** state contains the code to perform a unit movement.

However, the parent state must contain the code that decides whether or not to enter the **Move** state. This makes it easier for the code to get out of sync, and it requires that it be updated in two places when it changes. The second drawback is that it is inflexible when adding or removing states. When a state is

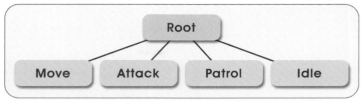

The parent state (**Root** in this case) generates the transitions in the parent state control model.

added, the custom code must be updated to choose the new state when appropriate. Similarly, when a state is removed, the code related to that state must be removed from the parent state.

In light of its drawbacks, the parent state control as the primary control mechanism should be avoided for the state search. Also, it should be used late in development (after the state machine is essentially complete), and only to implement specific behaviors required for the gameplay that could not be achieved using the normal control mechanisms.

::::: Blended State Machines

In actual use, state machines are often a *blend* of control models. They have a primary mode that handles most operations, but in some cases it is necessary to use another control mode to generate the required behaviors. In the case of the SAGE engine, the primary control method was the active state transition model. However, in some

Halo 2 uses a child competes model in its artificial intelligence state machine.

rare cases code was used that performed the parent state control, and generated a transition outside of the normal control flow.

Although *Halo 2* uses a child competes model in its AI state machine, the details of the competition vary. The basic model is similar to the one presented in the example. The most relevant state is performed, and if another state becomes more relevant, it interrupts the current state and becomes active. Other models include a sequential mode (where the states are executed sequentially if they are of non-zero relevance) and a probabilistic mode that randomly chooses among states with non-zero relevance.

:::::: SAGE2 and Halo 2 Control Mechanisms

Bungie Studios

Halo 2 uses a state machine that examines multiple states to generate complex AI behaviors.

The control mechanisms associated with the SAGE2 (RTS) and Halo 2 (FPS) engines have different characteristics and demonstrate how form follows function. The SAGE2 engine is intended for large numbers of agents, and the individual agent behaviors are varied, but not extremely complex. For example, units do not ever take cover or spontaneously flee in the SAGE2 engine. The *active state transition* model works well in the SAGE2 engine. Only the active state and the active sub-states are processed in a given frame, so there can be a top-level "garrison building" state added, and it will not incur any processing overhead while in the **MoveTo** or **Attack** states. However, the **Garrison** state can only be entered by some other state explicitly transitioning to it, or by an external command generating the transition. This is appropriate for an RTS, where units are (for the most part) expected to follow the player's orders and not come up with ideas on their own.

One control mechanism used in *Halo 2* examines multiple states using the child states compete model. *Halo 2* actually uses several state machine control mechanisms, as well as custom code when necessary. In the case of *Halo 2*, the child states compete by returning a relevancy value that is a Boolean value: yes or no. As more than one sub-state could answer yes, there needs to be method for breaking ties. In this case, a prioritized list is used. (Again, note that *Halo 2* uses a number of methods for breaking ties; this is just one of them.) So the sub-states are queried in priority order, and the first one that returns yes becomes the active state.

The control mechanisms for *Halo 2* are more powerful than those in SAGE, but potentially more expensive. A higher priority state can become active at any time, and the lower priority state that is active does not have to know anything about the higher priority state. However, all higher priority states have to be evaluated for relevancy at each frame, so as the number of states increases, the processing requirements increase. In this we see an example of form following function. The SAGE 2 control model is simpler, generally more efficient, and suitable for a large number of moderately complex agents that occur in an RTS, whereas the *Halo 2* model described is more powerful, potentially more expensive to process, and suitable for a small number of more complex agents expected in an FPS.

Abstractions and Models

Abstractions and models are ways to describe and think about the way something works. A state machine is one model that specifically describes how the AI controls and chooses its behaviors. It is very flexible, and states can be used for different purposes. The transition model gives us some idea of the sequence of states. However, a state machine by itself does not illustrate much about the intention of the AI; it tells us that the AI can potentially be in one of the defined states, and is in the active state at the current time. The meaning comes from the definition of the state and the transitions defined by the programmer. For example, a **MoveTo** state can represent a goal and an action. The goal is to move the agent to the destination. The action is to use the agent's movement system (legs, wheel, or wings, for example) and the game's physics systems to move the agent to the destination. It can be useful to consider the behavior at a higher level than simply a state. One way to look at AI behaviors is to consider goals, actions and tools:

Goal: A goal is a desired state in the game world. A positional goal would be a desired position for the agent. Another goal could be that a particular enemy agent be destroyed. A third goal could be to guard an area or object in the world. Note that goals can be complex and require multiple sub-goals in order to achieve the primary goal. For example, attacking an enemy may require that the agent first move to a position where the weapon is in range and within line of sight of the enemy, then aim, and finally fire the weapon, repeating the sequence until the enemy is destroyed.

Action: An action is a method or behavior for achieving a goal. Some actions, such as moving to a position, take a relatively long time. Others, such as aiming or firing a weapon, are relatively quick. Actions require a tool to perform the action. If the tool is unavailable (for example, if the agent does not have a weapon), then the action "fire weapon" cannot be performed.

Tool: A tool is something required to perform an action. Sometimes the tool is optional (such as a weapon or vehicle) and it may not be available. Other times, the tool is part of the agent (legs for movement, for example) and is always available.

State Machines

State machines can represent goals, perform actions, and manage tools. In some cases, such as a **MoveTo** state, a goal and an action can be represented by a state. A **Hunt** state represents a goal (destroy all enemy units), and it contains a state machine that represents another goal (attack a particular enemy agent). The state machine manages tools by virtue of the fact that only a single state is active.

State Search Goals

We have already seen how the states in a state search model use a goal to help determine their relevance. In a hierarchical state machine, a high-level state may correspond to a particular goal.

For example, a **Harvest** state may represent the goal of gathering as many resources as possible. The sub-states represent a sequence of actions that will achieve the goal. However, this information is implicit in the state machine. Not all high-level states represent a goal, and not all sub-states necessarily correspond to an action.

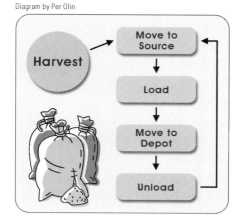

Diagram by Per Olin

The **Harvest** state is implemented using state generated transitions.

HFSM Implementations

The companion CD contains additional information and two working implementations of HFSM's, one using active state generated transitions and the other using the child states compete control mechanism. Documentation, executable files, and full source code are provided.

Advantages and Drawbacks of the State Machine Model

One of the advantages of a state machine is that, due to the fact that only one state is active at a time, access to actions and tools is limited to a single action and tools. This automatically prevents the agent from trying to move to two places at once or fire a weapon at two different targets simultaneously.

The drawback is that the state machine has difficulty handling interrupted goals and more than one goal at a time. If an agent is moving to a new location and is attacked, there are two easy behaviors available using a state machine: complete the current action (which makes the AI look unresponsive), and stop and attack the enemy agent (which switches the agent out of the **MoveTo** state so that it is no longer moving to the position). The handling of two goals would allow the agent to continue moving to the desired position while shooting back at the attacking agent. This is difficult to do with a single state machine. There are several techniques that allow these problems to be addressed to some degree: state suspend and continue, state stack, and multiple state machines.

State Suspend and Continue

One method of addressing these problems is through *state suspend and continue*—allowing a state to be suspended, executing another state machine until it finishes, and then returning execution to the current state. An excellent candidate for this is the dodge behavior. When the AI determines that the dodge behavior is appropriate, it can pause the current state processing and run a state machine containing a **Dodge** state. When the **Dodge** state completes and returns to **Idle**, the AI can return to the previous state machine processing. This corrects the problem of the AI "forgetting" what it was doing. The Unreal 3 and SAGE engines support this capability in two different fashions. Unreal 3 provides a *state stack*, which allows more than one state to be suspended at a time. SAGE provides a single *alternate state,* which only allows a single state to be suspended.

State Stack

A *state stack* can be used to implement a multi-level suspend and continue capability. Gears of War uses the Unreal 3 state processing in UnrealScript. This provides a PushState and PopState mechanism that implements the suspend and continue behavior. When a state is pushed, the current state is paused, and the new state is executed until PopState is called. At this point the original state continues execution. Since this is implemented as a stack, this mechanism allows multiple states to be pushed on the stack at a given time.

Epic Games

Gears of War allows more than one state to be suspended and continued.

Alternate State

Command & Conquer: Generals uses a single additional state machine, which allows a single state to be interrupted in order to run another. In the Unreal 3 model, you could have the following:

```
MoveTo active
The need for Dodge detected.
MoveTo suspended   Dodge active
The need for a Duck detected.
MoveTo suspended   Dodge suspended   Duck active
Duck action completed.
MoveTo suspended   Dodge active
Dodge action completed.
MoveTo active
```

The SAGE model supports a single interrupting state. In this case the behavior would be:

```
MoveTo active
The need for Dodge detected.
MoveTo suspended  Dodge active
The need for a Duck detected.  Dodge aborted.
MoveTo suspended  Duck active
Duck action completed.
MoveTo active
```

In practice, having the AI remember the top-level state, in this case **MoveTo**, is generally adequate.

Multiple State Machines

One relatively simple way to support two goals is to use *multiple state machines*. This works well, and it was used in the AI for *Counter-Strike: Condition Zero*. One drawback of this method is that it is necessary to make sure that the two state machines do not conflict. For example, if both state machines try to move the agent simultaneously, the conflict may cause the agent to twitch back and forth. One straightforward method to address this, used in *C&C: Generals*, was to limit the state machines to separate parts of the agent (in this case, a tank). One state machine controlled the turret and cannon, and the other state machine controlled the chassis and treads. The turret AI could not move the tank, and the chassis AI could not rotate the turret or fire the cannon. This required a bit of coordination between the state machines. If the chassis received an attack command, it would move the tank into range of the victim agent, then request that the turret AI fire at the victim. One convenient result of this was that while the chassis was moving into range, the turret could track and fire at enemy targets on the way to the ultimate goal. This made the tank appear to be more realistic. The infantry were implemented with a single state machine, and were unable to fire while moving.

The AI control is handled by multiple state machines in a number of games. *Counter-Strike: Condition Zero* and *Command & Conquer: Generals* use two or more state machines per agent.

Using hierarchical state machines, multiple state machines, and the suspend and continue technique permits complex state machines to be developed to perform game AI behaviors for modern video games. The state machines and states can manage the agent's available tools and represent goals and actions. However, much of this information is implicit in the implementation of the state machines. As the behaviors become more complex, it may be useful to make goals, actions, and tools more explicit, and give formal support to handling multiple goals.

Goal-Oriented AI Model

A goal-oriented model starts with a set of goals. In a fashion similar to examining multiple states, the AI chooses a goal to activate from the set of available goals. Each goal has one or more actions that are possible in the game that can meet the conditions of the goal. Without this, there is no way of achieving the goal, and the goal is not particularly useful.

This goal-oriented model consists of three parts: goals, actions, and tools. A goal is a result that can be achieved by the AI. If the AI can move, then one of the goals can be to move to a location. If the AI can fire a weapon, then one of the goals can be to destroy an enemy.

Actions are behaviors that can achieve a goal. A goal needs to have one or more actions that can achieve the goal. In the case of a tank, a goal to move to a location may have one action: drive to the goal. For a soldier, there may be multiple actions. The soldier could walk, swim, or ride in a jeep.

Tools are resources or objects required to perform an action. Sometimes a tool is a part of an AI agent. For example, a soldier usually comes with legs that can be used to walk. A benefit of considering "built in" parts as tools is that we can account for damage. If legs are considered a tool, when soldier takes damage to his legs we can treat this as if he no longer has the legs "tool." The AI will recognize that the soldier can no longer walk to a location, although it may be possible for the soldier to ride to the location in a jeep if a jeep is available.

Goal Operation

Goals can be selected by the player or by a virtual player. The goals are given a priority and the system attempts to activate the goals starting with the highest priority.

Goals can be activated based on two criteria. First, the goal has to have at least one, and possibly more than one, action that will meet the goal. For example, if your goal is to get an agent to a particular point on the map, it must be able to walk, ride in a vehicle, or have some sort of flight capability such as a jet-pack or a flying vehicle that can get the unit to a different spot. Second, the tools to perform the action must be available. For walking, the legs must be undamaged. If a jet-pack is necessary, the jet-pack must be available. If the action and tool are not available, the goal is temporarily impossible and cannot be activated. If action and tool are available, the goal is activated and the actions are performed.

The system will continue to perform the actions of the active goals. The active goals will be re-evaluated periodically. Tools may be lost due to damage, making some goals temporarily impossible. Tools may be acquired, or become available by the completion of an active goal. At this point, new goals can be activated. The goals are prioritized so that the agent will always have at least one goal until the game is won or lost.

Goal Hierarchy

The complexity of the AI behaviors is such that a simple list of goals is generally not sufficient to implement the AI. The same requirements that make the use of hierarchical state machines necessary are met by the use of *hierarchical goals*. Simple goals, such as a change in position, may be met by a single action. High-level goals, such as hunt, require multiple sub-goals to be reached in order to achieve the high-level goal. In some cases, it is possible that the sub-goals may themselves be high-level goals with their own set of sub-goals.

One source of hierarchical goals is a strategic AI. The AI may evaluate a situation and decide that a squad of units needs to flank attack another unit. This Flank goal then generates a sub-goal for each member in the squad, specifying the position for the squad member necessary to achieve the flanking effect.

Note that this is a somewhat more complex and detailed description of the behavior than we used for the state machines. The goal "Joe Move To Position," action "Walk To Position 1," and toolset "Legs" could be handled by a single **MoveTo** state in a state machine implementation. In some cases, the simple state is adequate and corresponds well to the AI agent. For example, an infantry unit in an RTS game usually has one way of moving (legs), and they are always available. Thus, the additional work of separating the **MoveTo** state into a goal, an action, and a tool results in additional complexity, but no added value.

However, consider a more complex game mechanic. An AI has multiple means of movement: legs, jet pack, or motorcycle. In addition, damage is applied to specific body parts. Thus, it would be possible for the agent to be shot in the legs and be damaged, but not be killed. In this case, the added detail is very helpful in controlling the AI. By specifying three tools, the AI could make use of a jet pack if the legs were damaged.

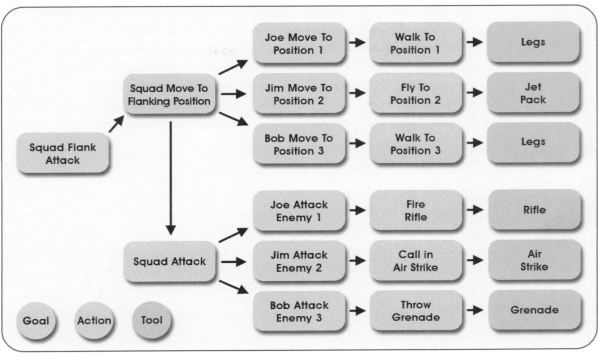

The Flank Attack goal is achieved with two actions that generate an additional six sub-goals.

Goal Selection

One of the key activities in a goal-oriented AI model is determining which goals to activate. The inclusion of tools in the design provides some explicit information regarding whether it is possible to activate a particular goal at a given time. Assume that the AI is evaluating whether to activate the Squad Flank Attack goal.

The initial question is whether it is possible to activate the goal. The first requirement is that we have a squad. If Joe, Bob, and Jim have been killed, this goal cannot be achieved. The second requirement is that the squad members have some way to move: legs, or a jet pack, or some other means. The third requirement is that each member has some kind of weapon that can be used to attack. If any of these requirements cannot be met, then we do not have the resources to achieve the goal and cannot activate it.

Another question is whether the tools are available. For example, the squad may have a move goal active, and the members and their legs are busy. There are two ways to handle this. First, note that the resources are busy and that the goal cannot be activated. Second, prioritize the goals. If the Flank goal has a higher priority than the Move goal, the Flank goal can deactivate the Move goal and activate the Flank goal.

One of the benefits of the goal-oriented system is that, unlike a finite state machine, multiple goals can be active at one time. The required tools information allows goals that use different tools to be active at once. For example, a move goal and a fire goal can be active at the same time, since the Move action requires the feet, and the fire goal requires the weapon. Both can be active at one time. Of course, the movement and animation system have to support firing a weapon while moving as well, but the AI system is perfectly capable of handling this behavior.

Action Selection

The Flank Attack goal diagram on the previous page is simplified to only show the actions actually used. One of the strengths of this model is that it can represent multiple actions with respect to a goal. In the case of the Flank Attack, there are two actions required to achieve the goal. The first action (Squad Move) had to be completed, and then the second action (Squad Attack) was completed to achieve the goal. There are also several possible actions, any one of which will accomplish the goal.

In this case, performing any of the four actions will achieve the goal. We first need to choose an action. The tool can be used to eliminate actions. For example, if we do not have a jet pack in our inventory, we can eliminate the Fly action as a means for achieving the goal. The next thing to do is give the actions a priority. This can be done numerically, or simply by ordering the actions in a list. We then choose the highest priority action for which we have the required tool or tools. Note that a goal may require multiple actions. One action, all actions, or one or more actions may be required to achieve a goal.

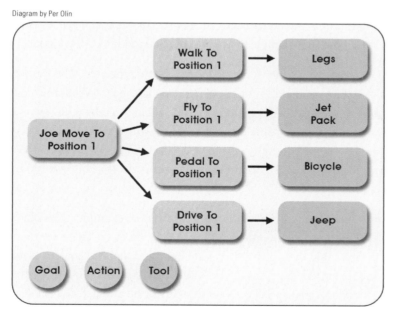

Diagram by Per Olin

Four possible actions can be used to achieve the Move To goal. Each action requires a different tool, so one action will be chosen based on the available tools.

When we have multiple actions, there are three ways that the sub-goals can meet a goal. Each is useful in different situations.

One Is Sufficient

In some cases, meeting a single sub-goal may be sufficient. The preceding Move To goal is achieved by any one of the four actions. In another case, we may have a squad of four AI characters. It is necessary to open a door, so the squad has an Open Door goal. Four sub-goals are for each of the members to move to the door and open it. Any one of these sub-goals meets the goal.

All Are Required

In other cases, all sub-goals must be met to achieve the goal. The squad may need to enter a helicopter to be transported to another location. The Enter Helicopter goal is not met until each squad member has entered the helicopter.

One or More

Finally, there are some goals that can be met if one of the sub-goals is met, but as many of the sub-goals should be performed as possible. An example of this is a goal to provide cover fire. In this case, at least one squad must provide cover fire to achieve this goal. However, having as many squad members as available provide cover fire is better.

This mode is useful in combination with the *one is sufficient* mode. The squad can activate the Open Door and Provide Cover Fire goals. The Open Door goal is given a higher priority, so one squad member is sent to open the door. This squad member is busy, and therefore not available to achieve the Provide Cover goal. However, the rest of the squad can perform the Provide Cover goal.

Multiple Actions: Sequential or Simultaneous

When *multiple actions* are required, or permitted in the case of *one or more*, there are generally two cases available: *sequential* or *simultaneous*. In the first case, the actions must be performed in sequence. The first action is performed, and when it is completed, the second action is performed. The Flank Attack goal uses this mode for the Squad Move to Flanking Position action followed by the Squad Attack action. The squad does not attack until the squad has moved into position. However, the actions that make up the Squad Move to Flanking Position are performed simultaneously. Each of the squad members begins moving immediately. The goal is achieved when the last of the actions is completed. The implementation of the goal-oriented model should allow specification of sequential or parallel execution of actions and, in the sequential case, the order of execution of the actions. The order specification can be simple, such as ordering the actions in a list.

Diagram by Per Olin

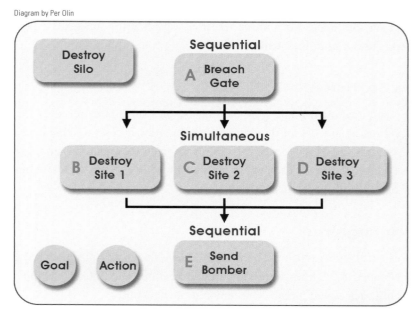

The Destroy Silo goal requires a combination of sequential and simultaneous tasks.

A more complex goal may require mixing the two modes. For example, goal Alpha is to destroy a hardened nuclear silo. A bunker-buster bomb is available, but the target is guarded by three anti-aircraft sites with surface to air missiles. The anti-aircraft sites are inside a compound with a high wall. In order to achieve goal Alpha, the following tasks must be completed:

Task A: Breach the walls
Task B: Destroy anti-aircraft site 1
Task C: Destroy anti-aircraft site 2
Task D: Destroy anti-aircraft site 3
Task E: Send bomber in with bunker-buster bomb

Task A must be performed first, as the gates must be breached before the anti-aircraft sites can be attacked. Task E must be performed last, or the bomber will be destroyed by the surface-to-air missiles. Tasks B, C, and D should be performed simultaneously in order to destroy the anti-aircraft sites as quickly as possible.

However, complex combinations can be broken up into groups and handled either simultaneously or in parallel. Actions B, C, and D can be grouped into a goal Beta: Destroy Anti Aircraft sites. The actions in goal Beta would be executed simultaneously. Then goal Alpha becomes Tasks A, F, and D executed sequentially, where Task F is achieving goal Beta.

Diagram by Per Olin

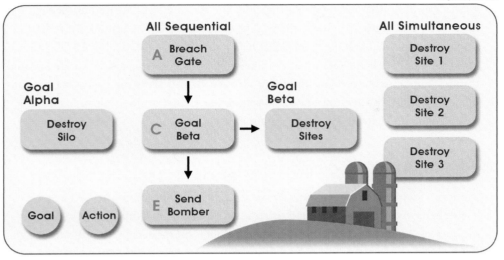

The Destroy Silo goal can be performed without combining sequential and simultaneous execution by separating the actions into two goals.

Keep It Simple

It is preferable to use basic control structures and keep the control structure simple, either simultaneous or sequential. Adding an additional complex control structure that allows mixing simultaneous and sequential tasks requires more programming work, maintenance, and debugging. It only provides another way to do the same tasks. In some cases a redundant method for performing tasks can be a time saver. More often, it is a source of confusion and bugs in the software.

Obtaining a Tool

An interesting case is when we have a goal, but no tool available for any of the actions. For example, what if we have no weapon, or our weapon is out of ammunition? We have an attack goal, but it cannot be performed because none of the actions to achieve this goal have the required tool (in this case, a working weapon). One way of handling this case is to understand that we cannot activate the attack goal, since we have no weapon. Another way to deal with this is to generate a new, additional goal. The new goal is to obtain the tool required for the action. In the case of the weapon, the new goal would be to pick up a weapon or ammunition for a weapon we already have. Once this goal is complete, it would be possible to activate the attack goal. This is somewhat complex to manage, but it allows for very interesting behaviors.

The goal-oriented AI model is useful in designing and implementing AI behaviors. This model can be used explicitly or implicitly. An explicit implementation would have C++ goal objects for each of the possible goals, and a system that held a list of the goals and selected the active goal or goals. In an implicit implementation the goal is known to the designer, who specifies the series of actions, perhaps using finite state machines, to achieve the goal. An explicit system is time-consuming to implement and requires that every goal be specified in C++ code, but has the advantage that complex behaviors, such as linked goals when getting a tool, can be created. Implicit implementations are simpler to implement and allow the designer to create new goals easily, but require that the designer keep track of the goals in his head, and provide no support for linking goals.

Handling Complexity

Modern video games require numerous complex behaviors from their AI agents. These behaviors can be controlled using state machines, but this requires a large number of states. It is helpful to organize the states hierarchically in order to design, implement, and debug the state machines. A simple, efficient hierarchy can be achieved by creating states that contain another instance of a state machine. Each level of the hierarchy is the same, consisting of a state machine with additional states. A more complex hierarchy can be created using goals, actions, and tools. Each level consists of goals, and each goal requires actions and tools.

Procedural transitions generated by the states are efficient and easy to implement. However, this control model only considers the active state. All other states are ignored. Each active state is therefore responsible for considering all possible reasons that another state should become active. An alternative is to consider the other states in addition to the one that is currently active. This requires more processing, but each state can be responsible for determining when that state should be activated. New states can be added easily using this control model.

A well designed state machine can do a good job of handling complex behaviors under normal circumstances. For example, the state machine can ensure that an agent only fires when his weapon has ammunition. Similarly, the state machine can send the agent to get more ammunition when the agent runs out. This can handle the majority of an AI agent's behaviors. However, game designers often add a few special events in a game that require unusual behavior. For example, a game may have rifles, so the agent can shoot at the player, but also allow a melee attack where the agent runs up to the player and strikes the player with a bayonet attached to the rifle. In general, the expected behavior for an AI agent would be to fire at the player from a distance. However, the game designer has a particular point in the game where the he wants the player to experience the shock of an enemy rushing up and attacking with the bayonet. The designer only wants this behavior at this particular spot in the game, as it would not be shocking if the enemy always ran up and attacked with the bayonet. This requires that the game designer be able to temporarily modify the behavior at a specific time. We will examine a way for designers to modify the agent's behavior in Chapter 4.

:::CHAPTER REVIEW:::

1. Create two state diagrams for an **Attack** state consisting of at least three sub-states—one using active state generated transitions, and one using child competes model. Describe the function of each sub-state. Are the same states used in both state machines?

2. Describe the transitions generated in the first state machine, and the relevance functions for the child states compete.

3. Create a goal-oriented diagram for the **Attack** behavior. What information does the goal-oriented diagram specify that is not present in the state machine diagrams?

Part II:
Controlling
Behaviors

CHAPTER

Customizing AI Systems

allowing others to modify and implement the AI

Key Chapter Questions

- Early video games were written in programming languages, often assembly language and C. What changes have taken place to make scripting languages useful tools in video games?

- What is an example of a game system that requires minimal setup by a game designer, and when is this kind of system useful?

- What is an example of a game system that requires that substantial information be supplied by a game designer, and what are its advantages?

- Building a custom script system is time-consuming. What are two ways to make game scripting available more quickly?

- What are the advantages and drawbacks of text-based scripting? Given unlimited resources, what are some ways to address the drawbacks?

It is important that we allow members of the development team, particularly designers, to control artificial intelligence (AI) behaviors, because the specification of the AI behaviors generally comes from designers in the first place. The job of the AI programmer is to implement behaviors and control for those behaviors, such as creating a finite state machine (FSM) or putting behaviors in as rule primitives. However, the AI programmer is generally not responsible for determining what the behaviors are or when they should occur. This is the task of the designer. Determining the amount of control, and how that control is provided, is an important task when designing AI systems. The designer must be provided enough control to customize the AI, but at the same time should not have to specify unnecessary details in order to get the desired behaviors. Scripting systems are commonly used to customize AI behaviors by game development teams, and allow the game playing community to modify the games as well.

Black Box & White Box Systems

Programmers and designers collaborate in the development and tuning of AI in modern video games. The programmer develops the lower-level systems, and the designer is responsible for the high-level behaviors and timing of the behaviors. The division between high-level and low-level systems is somewhat fluid. In some cases, the low-level systems built by the programmer are relatively complete, or "plug and play." The designer just has to use the system at the appropriate time. This is called a Black Box, since the designer does not have to see what is going on inside. In other cases, the low-level systems are like a toolbox, or "some assembly required." This is called a *White Box*, since the designer needs to know how the pieces are used together. An important design decision when building AI systems is whether to make a particular AI system or subsystem a Black Box or White Box system.

In a Black Box system, there are relatively few inputs; the AI system makes decisions and controls a variety of actions or behaviors inside without requiring specific instruction or external control.

Created by Jason Bramble

Created by Jason Bramble

A Black Box system is easy to use, while a White Box system is more complex.

An example of a Black Box system would be the engine on an automobile. The engine itself has one input, which is the accelerator. However, by basing its behavior on this one input, the engine control system (or Black Box for the engine) controls the amount of air allowed into the engine through the carburetor. On a millisecond-by-millisecond basis, the Black Box controls the amount of gasoline that is injected into the cylinders, the timing of the spark, and how much electricity is either sent to guide the engine through the electrical motor or generated from the electrical generator motor in order to charge the batteries. All of these behaviors and decisions are handled by the Black Box based on the single input of the throttle position.

An example of an AI-based Black Box system is the base building AI for *StarCraft*. In order to direct the AI to build a base, there is one operation that the designer calls, which is the campaign AI script. The designer sets a trigger with the action "Execute AI Script 'Terran Campaign Difficult' at 'UpperLeftCorner,'" and the AI builds a Terran base at the specified location. The designer does not have to specify anything else.

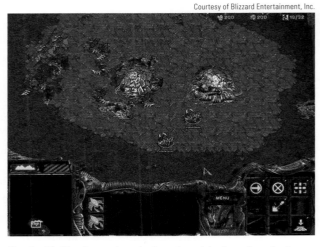

StarCraft's AI only requires the location of the base in order to construct it.

Another example of a Black Box system was an early implementation of the AI for *Populous*. The AI was controlled by five floating point numbers that gave the weight for creating structures, building units, attacking, defending, and harvesting resources. In the case of *Populous*, the Black Box approach did not provide enough control; consequently, more control of the AI was added before the game shipped.

A good example of a White Box system in a car is the steering system. In this system, the steering wheel controls the positioning of the tires. When the steering wheel is rotated to the left, the tires rotate to the left. When it is rotated to the right, the tires rotate to the right. When it is not moved, the tires do not move. Thus, the steering wheel precisely follows input from the driver. The driver has to completely specify the input, and there are no behaviors generated that are not directly controlled by the driver.

The transmission in a car can be either Black Box or White Box, depending on whether it is automatic or manual. An automatic transmission is another example of a Black Box system. The driver specifies whether the car should go forward or reverse. After this, the transmission makes all the decisions regarding which gear to use and when to change gears up or down. This is done automatically with no additional input from the driver.

An example of a White Box system would be a six-speed manual transmission on a sports car. In addition to indicating whether the driver wants to go forward or backward by using a forward or reverse gear, the driver also chooses the gear to be used. The driver can choose a higher gear (which will produce more fuel-efficient behavior but lower power output) or a lower gear (which will allow faster acceleration but produce

less fuel efficiency and more wear on the engine). The driver has to be aware of the characteristics of the engine and know that if the gear is too high (causing the RPM to drop low), the engine could be damaged. Similarly, if the gear is too low, the engine can run too fast and also cause damage. In addition, there is a clutch, which is another input to the transmission that has to be coordinated with the shift. When doing all this together, it also becomes necessary to take the accelerator into account. In the case of a Black Box automatic transmission, the driver does not have to worry about the accelerator with respect to the transmission because the transmission takes care of it.

As a result of the multiple, related inputs to the White Box manual transmission, the driver can do some things with a manual transmission that are not possible to do with an automatic transmission. For example, the driver can pop the clutch in order to get a very rapid acceleration from a standing start. The automatic transmission is not capable of providing this behavior because it does not have the clutch and the variety of inputs necessary in order to perform the operation.

Electronic Arts

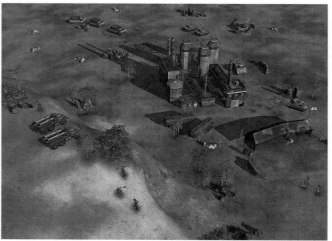

The AI base building function in *Command & Conquer: Generals* requires that the designer place each structure, allowing the designer to control the sequence and position of each structure.

The base building by the AI in *Command & Conquer: Generals* is a White Box system, requiring that the designer specify a great deal of information, including the position for each structure that will be built in the base. Specifications are implemented in the World Builder map editor, where the structures are selected from a menu and placed onto the terrain, rotated, and aligned. The designer specifies a rule set that indicates for each structure in what order that structure should be built. Additionally, the designer specifies a list of teams of units that will be built in order to defend the base and attack the opposing player. Each team has specific rules that indicate when those teams should be built, and what behavior should be exhibited by those teams once they are built. Finally, the designer has to create rules that specify how many units should gather resources, and when additional resource collection structures are to be built.

The use of the two systems is quite different. In order get the AI to build the base in *StarCraft* (Black Box), the designer specifies one line of script command in the Campaign Editor. In *Command & Conquer: Generals* (White Box), the designer specifies 30 building locations, 10 or 15 team definitions, and up to 100 rules that describe when the structures should be built, when the teams should be built, and when resource collection should be completed and increased.

Keep in mind that systems can be Black Box to some of the game development team and White Box to others. In the case of an automatic transmission in an automobile, most consider it a Black Box. However, to a hydraulic engineer who designs automatic transmissions, it is a White Box. Similarly, the *StarCraft* base building AI is a Black Box to the designer using the Campaign Editor and creating a scenario. To the AI scripting engineer, the system is a White Box system.

White Box systems are not inherently better or worse than Black Box systems. Each has different strengths and weaknesses, and each tends to be strong in the area where the other is weak.

A key to good AI design is to understand the strengths and weaknesses of both Black Box and White Box approaches, and to apply the most appropriate method based on the needs of the situation, which often depend on the specific problem and the staff on hand to solve it. For example, if you were building a car and had a skilled race car driver available, you might choose to build a manual transmission, which is easier to build and produces superior results in the hands of a professional. However, if you had no trained drivers, and a brilliant mechanical engineer, you might choose to build an automatic transmission that will be easier to drive and takes advantage of your engineering strength.

Diagram by Per Olin

White Box

- Requires less training & skill to use
- Average user gets better results
- Takes more expertise to build
- Difficult to modify

Black Box

- Requires more training & skill to use
- Expert user gets better results
- Takes less expertise to build
- Expert user can tune the system

White Box and Black Box systems are each useful in different situations in video game design. It is helpful to choose the system whose strengths fit the needs of a particular situation.

Similarly, with a wealth of game programmers, the Black Box approach may be preferable in order to take advantage of the project staffing. Alternatively, a team with great designers accustomed to working with rule-based and/or scripting systems may be able to make better use of a White Box system.

Don L. Daglow
(Chief Executive
Officer, Stormfront
Studios)

Don L. Daglow has served as President & CEO of Stormfront Studios since found-ing the company in 1988. Stormfront's major titles include the action-adventure *Eragon* (Xbox 360, PS2, Xbox, PC; published by Vivendi Universal Games, based on the 20th Century Fox film) and *The Lord of the Rings: The Two Towers* (PS2, Xbox, published by EA, based on the film by Peter Jackson). Electronic Games has called Don "one of the best-known and respected producers in the history of the field," and in 2003 he received the CGE Award for "groundbreaking achievements that shaped the video game industry." Prior to founding Stormfront, Don served as director of Intellivision game development for Mattel, as a producer at Electronic Arts, and as head of the Entertainment and Education division at Broderbund. He designed and programmed the first-ever computer baseball game in 1971 (now recorded in the Baseball Hall of Fame in Cooperstown, NY), the first mainframe computer role-playing game (*Dungeon* for PDP-10 mainframes, 1975), the first sim game (Intellivision *Utopia*, 1981), and the first game to use multiple camera angles (Intellivision *World Series Major League Baseball,* 1983). Don co-designed Computer Game Hall of Fame title *Earl Weaver Baseball* (1987) and the first mas-sively multiplayer online graphic adventure, the original *Neverwinter Nights* for AOL (1991–1997). In 2003 he was elected to the board of directors of the Academy of Interactive Arts and Sciences. He also is a past winner of the National Endowment for the Humanities New Voices playwriting competition. Don holds a BA in Writing from Pomona College and an EdM from Claremont Graduate University.

In today's games, roles are becoming increasingly more complex and special-ized. In some cases the AI implementation may be driven by a designer, a programmer, or a close-knit designer-programmer team, depending on the game and the available team members. In other kinds of game AI challenges the problem may chiefly be one of programming, focused on development of optimal algorithms.

For example, if we're defining the behavior of a second-tier enemy boss in a console action-adventure, a designer can start work on the AI using special-ized tools. Here at Stormfront Studios, the engineering team has evolved a sophisticated "sandbox" game level where enemy and player characters can be inserted onto a playfield. Artists can easily modify the playfield for flat or slop-ing terrain in order to introduce basic architectural geometry like walls, etc. By hitting a hot key the designer can expose a large number of variables for the enemy in an on-screen chart. He or she can then change those values to influence the enemy's behavior, and immediately replay a confrontation to assess those changes. How fast should the enemy be able to turn? If stunned, how long does it stay that way? What are its forward, lateral, and backpedaling speeds? After a player character initiates an attack, how long does the AI delay before it "recognizes" the danger? Is it more likely to flee or block/parry in melee combat? How likely is it to counterattack? After what delay?

In this way, the designers can get the basic characteristics and behaviors of any character down. For bosses or more sophisticated enemies, they can then specify in writing what kinds of custom behaviors are necessary, things you could never get just by assigning values. That spec goes to the AI programmer, who uses his specialized knowledge and implements the spirit of what the designer created. Typically, the two interact and share ideas about how to make the enemy the most fun to combat and the most interesting to defeat.

Black Box Design

There are a few scenarios that favor Black Box design; in particular, those that encompass well-defined problems and repetitive behavior.

Well-Defined Problems

The best indicator pointing toward Black Box design is that the problem is *well-defined* and unchanging. In this case, the Black Box advantages shine. Since the problem is well-defined, we know what to expect when we push the button. It does not require a lot of communication and iteration, so the programmer can implement the solution with a minimum of interruption. The Black Box does not need to have a large number of inputs, which means that the programmer does not have to write interface code to provide ways of parsing into script or a graphical control language to get the input into the Black Box.

Repetitive Behavior

The Black Box solution is better suited toward *repetitive behavior* in which a single behavior is repeated. For example, a low-level behavior such as an AI agent crouching behind cover, moving out from behind cover, raising a weapon, firing a weapon at the player, and moving back behind cover is well suited for a Black Box implementation. The behavior is reasonably well-defined, since one would generally expect enemy agents to move out from behind cover and shoot at the player. In addition, this behavior may be used repeatedly throughout several different levels. Implementing the behavior as a Black Box minimizes the amount of work required of the designer.

::::: *Counter Strike* Bot

© Valve Corporation. Used with permission.

The *Half-Life* mod *Counter-Strike* AI bot was developed as a Black Box, which was a good choice because the game had been released at least a year before the bot was implemented. The style of gameplay had been well established, and the engineer who created the bot had played *Counter-Strike* and thus had an excellent idea of how the behavior of the bot should perform. Therefore, it took a few months to create the bot and get it in place.

White Box Design

There are a few scenarios that favor White Box design; in particular, those that involve collaborative projects and iterative development.

Collaborative Projects

White Box design scales especially well in *collaborative projects* where multiple people with different skill sets are working on a project, such as a software engineer and a designer, whereas a Black Box system is most efficient when a single person is doing the work. The White Box implementation is often very suitable for a designer working on a high-level specification, since the programmer only has to get the low-level behaviors and interface working. Thus, it is possible if you have additional staff to get a faster turnaround on a White Box rather than a Black Box implementation.

Iterative Development

White Box design also works well with situations requiring *iterative development*. One case is when designers are evaluating gameplay scenarios. A White Box design allows the designers to quickly make modifications and test them without requiring a software engineer to make changes. This results in faster turnaround for the designers and in more iterations, allowing designers to try more variations and pick the best ones. In addition, the software engineer can work on other tasks while the designers are focusing on the gameplay, without requiring the software engineer to be involved directly in the process.

An example of a White Box effort was the strategic AI implemented for *Command & Conquer: Generals*. One AI programmer worked on the low-level engineering part, the interface to the White Box, and the lead designer created the rules set, base layout, and team lists to drive the AI. The total work was accomplished in about three man-months; however, the work was overlapped and it was completed in a total of approximately six calendar weeks, which is a relatively short amount of time. However, with the compressed schedules that are granted in the current game industry, six weeks was all the time available, so it was fortunate that the work was completed in such a short amount of time. This demonstrates the potential for White Boxes to allow the application of additional resources, which can reduce the calendar time to complete a particular feature.

The strategic AI in *Command & Conquer: Generals* was controlled by an extensive rules set created by the lead designer.

Consider Staffing

Sometimes it is obvious whether to create a White Box or a Black Box design. For example, low-level AI behaviors in a real-time strategy (RTS) game such as *Lord of the Rings: Battle for Middle-Earth* are numerous, repetitive, and efficient. A Black Box implementation in C++ is appropriate. Responding to triggered events in a first-person shooter (FPS) such as *Medal of Honor: Pacific Assault* should be White Box, using scripting or data in the editor to control events that will change frequently, since managing them in C++ code is not appropriate. In other cases, it could be done either way, like the transmission in a car. You could use an automatic or a manual transmission, depending on exactly what is more important in what you are trying to accomplish. Some features in the game could be implemented in either fashion, and the best choice may depend on the staff available to implement the feature. As discussed earlier, the Black Box approach is good for repetitive, low-level activities. It is usually engineering intensive. One staffing question would be whether you are heavy or light in AI engineering on your team. If you have a lot of engineering talent in the AI area, and the game AI is fairly well-defined, you may want to lean toward a Black Box implementation and give the AI engineers more of the AI work. If you have the resources to handle it, the AI Black Box approach can be more efficient in a total number of months to get a particular job done. However, if you have more design staff than engineering staff, the White Box approach can be more efficient. The engineer can implement the specific well-known lower-level tasks, such as pathfinding, point-to-point movement, and weapon firing. In addition, an interface to create higher-level behaviors is provided to the designers. The engineer can do this part of the work and move on to other tasks while the designers work on the higher-level AI behaviors using the system provided by the engineer.

Mark Skaggs on the Coder-Designer Relationship:::::

Mark Skaggs
(Chief Executive
Officer, Blue Nitro
Studios)

Mark Skaggs is one of the game industry's most successful and innovative talents. He is best known for his work in the RTS genre, leading award-winning products such as *Command and Conquer: Red Alert 2*, *Command and Conquer: Generals*, *The Lord of the Rings: The Battle for Middle-Earth*, and more. With a game career spanning over 13 years, Mark has been responsible for production, game design, technical direction, and art direction on hit products that have sold over 10 million units since 2000.

Designers should think carefully about the behaviors, actions, and emotions of the various "actors" of their game world. Looking at the game from the perspective of what they want the player to see, hear, and experience while playing the game is critical to building the list of functionality they need from the coding staff. When they have that clear in their minds, they can then develop a list of behaviors, attributes, and actions they need the programmers to create for the game world.

Once the programmers have the list of "needs" from the design staff, their job is to come up with ways to deliver those features into the game world in the most simple and direct fashion that allows designers flexibility to rapidly iterate through the tweak and polish phase.

Given that there are no perfect solutions, for each of the "needs" from design, the programmers and designers will most likely have a series of discussions to refine some of the design elements according to the harsh realities of coding up real-time AI systems. These discussions are a give and take where sometimes the solution involves a change from the coding side and other times a simple design change can save weeks or months of coding.

When the chemistry is right between the coders and the designers, I've seen real magic happen as their discussions yield inspiration for even better design through great code solutions.

One word of caution for AI programmers: Please remember that your best win is for designers to be able to make a great and fun game on top of the code you write. Don't fall into the trap of trying to make the best, most clever implementation of the "true thinking AI brain" that you just know "the world is waiting to see." I've seen coders do this and it usually leads to bloated code that is very difficult to maintain and nearly impossible for designers to use to make a fun game. Instead, just focus on giving the designers what they need in an intelligent, easy to use form. They'll love you for it and the game will be even better because of it.

During the debugging phase, designers and coders should work hand in hand.

Development Techniques

One of the advantages of Black Box systems is that the associated interfaces are minimal. Exposing the various controls of a White Box system requires some kind of interface, which can increase development time (something that is always in short supply). On the other hand, an awkward or incomplete interface to the system can make it difficult to use, squandering one of the benefits of White Box design. The best of all worlds is an interface that is quick to develop and easy to use. A variety of techniques are available to the AI programmer to provide an interface to the system. A parameter file allows the parameters such as agent speed, timing, or armor to be adjusted. A state mask can be used to enable and disable states in the AI in order to customize an agent's behaviors. Rule sets can be used to specify the conditions that trigger particular AI behaviors.

Data-Driven Systems

One key to efficient development is a *data-driven* design. Earlier chapter exercises used the InitialData.txt file that can be modified independent of the program to control the behaviors of the game and AI. This allows a designer to make modifications to the AI outside of the scope of the program itself. Thus, the programmer and the designer can work independently and in parallel on different aspects of the program.

This is in contrast to the older model, which would require the designer and the programmer to work together at the same time on the code with the designer specifying changes, the programmer making the changes and updating the program in real time, and the programmer testing the program with the designer present and iterating on that cycle. Using data-driven design, behaviors may be adjusted, tuned, added, or removed without requiring the services of the programmer. Simultaneously, the programmer can be working on tasks, such as adding new behaviors and debugging existing behaviors, without having to be present while the designer is working. This produces a much more efficient result.

Gas Powered Games

Supreme Commander uses a data-driven design in order to allow the game's designers to modify an agent's behaviors and attributes, then quickly test the new behavior.

> ## Simple & Usable Tools
>
> Data-driven, visually oriented tools that allow rapid paced short revision cycles are the best. The designers and the tool builders should work together to design the tools to ensure ease of use, and simplicity can be maintained after the initial specification. I also think the best designed tools have limitations built into them that are central to the design and agreed to by the designers ahead of time. By limitations I mean having the smallest set of features and functionality needed to complete the design task well. I've seen situations where the design tools were so complex and all powerful that the designers didn't figure out how to use them well. I've also seen the situation where amazing things were accomplished simply because the designers learned everything about the tool and then turned on their creativity about how to use the tool to create new and unexpected scenarios, missions, etc.
>
> —Mark Skaggs (Chief Executive Officer, Blue Nitro Studios)

Parameter File

There are a number of ways the designer can use a data-driven system in order to control AI behaviors. The first is a *parameter file*, such as the one that was used in Chapter 2 to specify the behaviors for the simple agent. The parameters allow the designer to tune various aspects of the behaviors. One of the parameters might be *sight range*, which specifies how far an AI unit considers other units to be visible. An enemy has to be within sight distance to respond to the presence of another unit. Another value might be *weapon range*, which has a similar impact upon behavior, since the AI unit must move to within weapon range. The designer can give the agent a larger weapon range, causing the AI unit to remain back and take long range shots. Alternatively, the designer can give the agent a shorter range and force the AI unit to rush the player. These modifications give the AI behavior and gameplay a different behavior and feel. The challenge for the designer and AI programmer is to determine in advance which parameters shall be modifiable via the parameter file. In general, it is a good idea to put most, if not all, tunable values into the parameter file. This gives the designer maximum flexibility in tuning AI behaviors.

State Mask

Another method of allowing the designer to control behaviors is available when using an FSM. The method used in *Halo 2* is to specify a *state mask*, which specifies whether certain states are enabled or disabled, allowing the designer to enable or disable states for a particular agent. AI agents may then have different behaviors while sharing the same state machine. One example is the **Retreat** state for agents in *Halo 2*. Specific units (the Grunts, for example) will retreat in certain situations, such as if they are surprised or are attacked by a devastating weapon such as the energy sword. However, other units such as the Elite never flee because they are the tough senior agents in the game. One way that the designer can control this behavior is to specify a state mask that enables the **Flee** state for the Grunts. The Elites have the **Flee** state disabled. Thus, the designer can configure the behaviors of different units without actually having to change the code or the structure of the FSM.

Rule-Based Systems

Another way of handling behaviors is to use a *rule-based system*, where the rules are created by the designer. In this method, the programmer creates a system that can read, evaluate, and execute rules. For example, the following could be a rule: *If the player has more than 10 tanks, build an anti-tank team.* The engineer would be responsible for implementing the code to test whether a player has a number of units of a given type and build a team of AI agents. The designer can create the rules that control the behavior of the AI system under a variety of conditions. (Rule-based systems will be examined in more detail in the next chapter.)

Frank Gilson on Sharing the Load:::::

At Wizards of the Coast, Frank T. Gilson manages project development in the Digital Games department. Frank was a producer at Atari's Santa Monica, CA office, managing aspects of third-party development, contracting with talent (such as composers and writers), and overseeing external development. Prior to working at Atari, Frank was an associate producer at Blizzard for *Warcraft III: Reign of Chaos* and the *Frozen Throne* expansion. He also worked in quality assurance as a technical engineer (*Diablo 2*), lead analyst (*StarCraft: Brood War*), and analyst (*StarCraft* and *Mac Diablo*). Prior to joining the game industry, Frank was a graduate student at UC Irvine in Mathematical Behavioral Sciences, studying formal models for economics, voter choice, and psychology.

Frank T. Gilson
(Senior Developer,
Wizards of the Coast)

Design and programming leads need to meet during initial project planning phases to lay out the requirements for artificial intelligence for the game project, just as they would for tools, pipelines, or anything else. Initial development phases need to account for AI prototyping. No one person should be allowed to become a bottleneck with respect to AI design or implementation.

It's always a good idea to have the tools available to allow some of the engineering workload to fall on artists, designers, and other production personnel rather than requiring an engineer for every change. This permits staff to do valuable development work, tweaking, and exploring at a greater rate. Tools that permit designers to attach and tune AI to "actors" (units, objects, creatures, etc.) help facilitate this.

> ## Programmers & Designers: Division of Labor
>
> For TimeGate, the division has always been that designers define the game rules that the AI must abide by. Programmers design and implement the AI, but they use a data-driven approach (i.e., adjusting parameters and limited scripting). Designers tweak the AI and can define different personalities. We like to expose the same tools to the user community as well.
>
> —*Denis Papp (Chief Technology Officer, TimeGate Studios)*

Scripting Systems

A powerful way to allow designers access to the configuration of the AI behaviors is to use a *scripting system*. The following scripting languages have several useful features:

- The scripts are in data or level files, and they can be modified without changing the game engine. This allows a faster and more productive change and test cycle.
- Individual levels can have custom scripts, so the AI behavior can be customized for individual missions.
- Scripting languages used in games are customized for the particular game, making it easy to develop gameplay using the scripting language.
- Scripting systems can be programmed for robustness and ease of use.
- Text scripting systems allow the user community to make modifications to the game using a text editor.

Scripting languages can be used in a variety of ways within a game environment, and there are several possible methods for doing game scripting. One option is to use a text scripting language, which can be either custom or open-source. Another option is to use a graphical user interface (GUI) in conjunction with a text scripting language. Finally, a graphical scripting language can be implemented.

> We give designers the ability to customize and tune the AI. Character variables are all exposed to the designers in a way that lets them tune behavior and performance. We also have proprietary tools for level layouts for 3rd person and 1st person games, and a straightforward scripting language that both designers and programmers can use to define behaviors for objects as well as characters.
>
> —*Don L. Daglow*
> *(Chief Executive Officer,*
> *Stormfront Studios)*

There are two primary ways to support text scripting in a game engine. The first is to write a custom implementation of a scripting language that is built specifically for the game engine. Examples of this include Quake C, written for the Quake Engine by id Software, and UnrealScript, written for the Unreal Engine by Epic Games.

The following is a sample of the Quake C scripting language:

Courtesy of id Software, Inc.

```
void() meleeDamage=
{
   local vector      vDelta;
   local float       damage;

   if (!self.enemy)
{
        return;            // enemy gone.
   }

   vDelta = self.enemy.origin - self.origin;

   if (vlen(vDelta) > MAX_MELEE_DISTANCE)
   {
        return; // not close enough to do melee damage
   }

   damage = random()* MAX_MELEE_DAMAGE;
   AttemptDamage (self.enemy, self, damage);
};
```

Quake C is a subset of the C programming language used in the Quake Engine (*Quake 4* shown) for gameplay programming.

Another approach is to use an existing implementation of a scripting language. A common and efficient way to accomplish this is by integrating an open source scripting language into the game engine.

Custom Scripting Languages

There are several advantages to creating a custom scripting language:

- The scripting code can be made as minimal as necessary to reduce memory and processor requirements.
- The custom implementation can interface directly with the game data structures because the script code has access to the game engine code.
- The scripting system can be customized to do specific operations necessary or useful in the game.

Electronic Arts

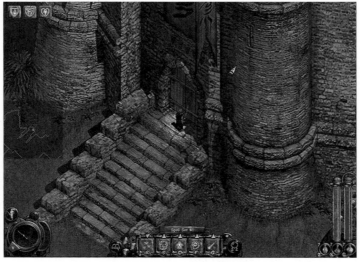

The developers of *Nox* created a custom scripting language for internal use while developing the game.

The primary and overwhelming disadvantage of building a custom scripting implementation is that it creates delays and ongoing distractions in the game development process. It takes time and engineering resources to develop a scripting language implementation. Most game development projects are short on both of these. Integrating an open source scripting language such as Lua takes many days of work, but building a minimal scripting language takes several months. This engineering time is better spent on gameplay and tools rather than on creating yet another scripting language.

Another problem with a custom scripting language is that it is *custom*. Many books have been written about open source languages such as Lua and Python. It is unlikely that a custom scripting language will be documented as well.

Debugging a custom scripting language is often challenging. Since it is written from scratch, there is no built-in debugging support. Either additional programming resources must be added to support debugging or the debugging must be done by the programming team, which has access to the low-level engine debugging tools.

In general, creating a custom scripting language for a game is not the best way to use resources, and it is not recommended. Incorporating an existing scripting language is a better use of time and development resources.

Open Source Scripting Languages

Two commonly used open source scripting languages in games are Lua and Python. Lua has been used in games such as *Grim Fandango, Baldur's Gate, MDK2, Psychonauts,* and *Blitzkrieg.* Python is used in games such as *Toontown Online, Eve Online, Blade of Darkness,* and *Earth & Beyond.*

One way to take advantage of an existing scripting language is to use an open source implementation. Lua and Python—available on the Web at *http://lua.org* and *http:// python.org,* respectively—are two open source solutions that have been successfully used in games. You can get the full source for these systems, and there is no charge to license them in applications. If you are doing a commercial game, you need to make sure that the licensing agreement is acceptable. You should always examine the requirements, which do change over time.

The first advantage of an open source solution is the cost. Both Python and Lua are free software. Another advantage is that you can get the scripting system up and running very quickly compared to a custom implementation. All you have to do is interface the scripting system with your game, which takes much less time than implementing a custom scripting solution from scratch. Python and Lua come with a full implementation of the scripting system, including a parser. There is also a standard library of functions that comes with each scripting language.

World of Warcraft uses the Lua scripting language.

The final advantage is that you get a full implementation of a standard language. This means that all of the features of the scripting language are complete and available. Since they are standard languages, you can purchase manuals to help your developers learn the language, and it may even be possible to hire programmers and designers that have used the language before.

The disadvantage of the open source solution is that it is a general purpose implementation. The memory requirements may be higher than a custom implementation, since they include their own memory manager and garbage collection system. Game specific features can easily be added to the scripting system, but they do not come with the basic systems. Console systems prior to the Xbox 360 and PlayStation 3 had limited memory, and supporting this could be a problem. However, current PCs and next-gen consoles ship with 512MB of memory, and the 200k for a scripting system is not a significant overhead, particularly if you consider the features and speed of development that you gain from using an open source system.

Licensed Scripting Languages

Another way to take advantage of an existing scripting language is to license one. For example, Epic's Unreal Engine comes with UnrealScript, and Garage Games' Torque Engine comes with Torque Script.

Epic Games

Unreal Tournament 2007 uses the UnrealScript language, which is provided with the Unreal 3 Engine.

The advantages of a licensed solution include all the advantages of a custom scripting language and an open source scripting language. The scripting system is integrated into the game engine and supports game specific features. Debugging support is already available. You can begin developing gameplay code immediately. UnrealScript is based on Java and thus has a standard language interface and syntax, while Torque Script uses a subset of C++. Both support object-oriented programming and are very flexible and powerful. In addition, they have the advantages of the custom code because they are both game-specific and have extensions that are available. UnrealScript has a state machine built into the language and a powerful extension that is latent execution, which allows behaviors that span time to be written. This greatly simplifies the implementation of certain operations.

Given the advantages of a licensed language, why would you possibly not use one? The primary reason is that the rest of the system is not available on your target platform or is otherwise unsuitable for your game. Both of these solutions are integrated into a game engine, Unreal and Torque, respectively. If the engine is not available for your target platform, then you will not be able to take advantage of that particular licensed scripting language. Also, the engine may not be the best suited for a particular game. This is sometimes the case when creating sequels and the custom code from the previous game is available for re-use.

We have discussed how text scripting languages can be implemented through *open source, licensed,* or *custom* solutions. The best choice is to use a licensed scripting system, as long as the license fee is reasonable and its associated engine is suitable for your game. The open source solution is a good choice for new engines or for those that do not have an associated scripting system. Custom solutions, on the other hand, can be too much work for most uses.

Interfacing a Text Scripting Language to a Game

Models for interfacing a text scripting language to a game can either be *procedural* or *object-oriented*. Procedural interfaces are straightforward to implement and use. Object-oriented interfaces take more time to implement, and are more complex in use. It is possible to do more varied operations using an object-oriented model.

Procedural Model

The *procedural model* incorporates events and functions. When an even occurs (such as an AI agent seeing the player character), a script function is called. This function is specified by the designer, and it determines the agent's response to that event. Game functions are made available in the scripting environment to allow the designer to respond to the event. The system could be set up so that a function OnSeePlayer is called when the AI agent sees the player. A sample function to handle this event is:

```
function OnSeePlayer(agent, player)
    if (Health(agent) < DefaultHealth(agent)*0.1) then
        Retreat(agent);
    else
        Attack(agent, player);
    end
end
```

This version causes the agent to retreat if it sees the player and the agent's health is less than 10% of its normal health; otherwise, the agent will attack. In this model, a script function is called when certain events occur and the designer is allowed to respond to them. This requires coordination between the programmer and designer, since the designer has to specify the list of events that can be scripted. The programmer must detect these events and call the script function. In addition, the designer must specify which actions must be available in the scripts, such as the Retreat and Attack actions, and the programmer must implement and make them available to the scripting system. The available events and actions limit the scope of which events can cause a response, as well as the complexity of the response. As a game progresses and the system is used, the designers will likely request an expanded set of events and actions.

Object-Oriented Model

The *object-oriented model* allows a designer or programmer to create and manipulate game objects via the scripting language. Lua provides support for interfacing with C++ objects, allowing the implementation of systems where pre-defined C++ objects can be created and manipulated in Lua scripts. The UnrealScript language allows the definition of new object types, as well as the creation and manipulation of C++ objects. The Python scripting language has object-oriented features in the language, including multiple inheritance. This allows the programming of substantial functionality in the scripting language.

Division of Labor

There are generally two ways that the scripting system can be used. One is a relatively straightforward procedural system that can be used by designers that have some familiarity with programming. In this kind of system, the major programming tasks are performed in C++ by the software engineers, and the scripting is used primarily for control and modification of behaviors. Often, the designers write the bulk of the scripts for this system. An object-oriented scripting system, such as UnrealScript or Python, results in a scripting system that is more powerful in that much or all of a behavior can be implemented in the scripting language. However, this level of programming expertise usually requires a software engineer. In this situation, therefore, the engineers tend to write the bulk of the script code.

The Importance of a Technical Designer

In my experience, it is best to find a technical designer that can fulfill both the design and the implementation role. Other programmers are often needed to give hooks in to the data stored in the game but it's really just one or a few technical design minded individuals who can iterate on AI again and again. Only the people that are embedded into the process and actually have hands on can make the good decisions to progress an AI forward.

—*John Comes (Lead Designer, Gas Powered Games)*

Graphical User Interface Scripting Languages

Sometimes it is necessary to create a GUI to speed up the scripting process. Text scripting is time-consuming, and minor typographical errors can cause a script to fail to compile, or to execute incorrectly. We have already discussed how custom text scripting implementations are usually too cumbersome for most users. However, the extra programming time associated with custom implementations is well worth it when creating GUIs.

Even though scripting languages are easier to use than programming languages such as C++, they are very particular about how they are written. Needless to say, writing programs in them can be difficult. For example, something that a designer might want to do in a game is the following test and action: *If the player has entered an area named "Defend7," then create a team to defend it called "Foxtrot3."*

This is not a particularly complicated concept. In a Lua implementation, however, you do not get to program in a natural language so it would look somewhat like this:

```
If PlayerEnteredArea(ThePlayer, "Defend7") then
    Local teame = BuildTeam("Foxtrot3");
    DefendArea(team, "Defend7");
End
```

There are several difficulties associated with writing this in an open source scripting language such as Lua or Python. First of all, you have to learn the specific script language format. All programming languages have very specific syntax that must be entered correctly. If a person is not familiar with the Lua or Python scripting language, details such as whether a semicolon is required at the end of a line become stumbling blocks. Do you use 'single quotes' or "double quotes" to specify a string?

Another problem is that you are using named references. For example, the area named "Defend7" was probably named in the level editor. At this point, there can be errors because it is necessary to type the name correctly. It makes a difference whether the name is "Defend 7" with a space, "Defend7" without a space, "Defend_7" with an underscore, or even "defend 7" with a lower case "d." A GUI integrated into the level editor can alleviate many of these problems.

Text-Based GUI

One way to implement a GUI is to have a text-based language, but allow the scripter to enter the scripts via a series of dialogue boxes, or forms. Some examples of games that use this include *C&C: Generals* (SAGE engine) and *StarCraft*.

Courtesy of Blizzard Entertainment, Inc.

Electronic Arts

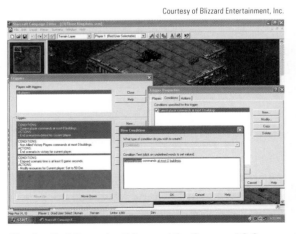

The *StarCraft* Campaign Editor and the *Command & Conquer: Generals* Worldbuilder tool use a series of dialogue boxes to assist in entering script data.

In order to create the "PlayerEnteredArea" script, the scripter would first select from a drop-down list of script tests. The scripter selects "Player Entered Area." This performs two useful functions. First, it prevents any typographical errors. Second, it gives the scripter a hint regarding which tests are available. If the test "NPC Entered Area" is in the list, then the scripter knows to test for an NPC entering an area. If it is not, then it may not be implemented yet.

Once the PlayerEnteredArea test is selected, a dialogue is available for the scripter to fill in the parameters of the test. The scripter can select a player from a drop-down list of the players defined for the current mission, and select an area from a drop-down list of all the areas that have been drawn in the map. This easily shows the scripter that there are two required parameters to the test, and it allows the scripter to select values that are valid for the current mission. Both of these features speed the creation of the script by prompting the scripter to enter all required parameters and prevent typographical errors.

This type of interface can be used in several different environments. First, it can be implemented on top of a text scripting language. The GUI would then generate a line of Lua or Python script that would be run by the scripting engine. Alternatively, the GUI can produce binary data that can be executed directly by the application. The script method has the advantage that you can write scripts directly and produce scripts that are more complex than the capabilities supported by the GUI. A programmer could write a script using a text editor and use script language elements that were not supported in the GUI.

Producing a binary format from the GUI produces small amounts of data in an efficient format. Interpreting the script data directly in the engine is fast and easy when the elements in the GUI are converted into binary data. This can be interpreted very quickly and efficiently inside a scripting engine in the game. The SAGE engine uses this type of implementation where the scripts are defined in the GUI and stored as binary data for execution in the game engine. The parsing and conversion from text to binary format is handled in the editor. Interpreting and executing the scripts in the engine requires little more than a case statement in C++.

Custom Graphical Programming Language (Kismet)

Another method for GUI scripting is to create a graphical language that can be used to build the script operations that are performed in the game. The previous example used a GUI to speed creation of scripts. However, the scripting was text-based in nature. Each script was displayed to the scripter in a text format and was actually converted into script text in some cases. A node-based graphical system allows the scripter to actually create a graphical representation of the script. An example of this is the Kismet scripting system in the Unreal Engine, used by games such as *SWAT-4* and *Tribes*. This graphical interface allows the scripter to place nodes and connect using the mouse.

This type of system is complex, and it takes more work to implement than a text-based GUI. It would be hard to justify the amount of time and effort to implement this for an engine intended for a single game. However, licensing a language with such a graphical editing system can be very useful. Game developers who think visually find working in this environment more friendly and productive than programming in a text-based scripting language.

The Unreal 3 Engine (*Gears of War* shown) uses the Kismet GUI scripting language.

Support for Non-Programmers

We use a proprietary format: text files that are similar to XML. There is support for templates, inheritance, and error checking, which gives the designers an intuitive environment to both tweak numbers and do some limited scripting. Ideally, we would have GUI tools as well.

—*Denis Papp (Chief Technology Officer, TimeGate Studios)*

Grouping Scripts in a Graphical Environment

One issue to consider when developing a GUI is to include a mechanism for grouping the scripts. There may be several hundred scripts in a game, and ordering them in a structured fashion makes it possible to quickly find the script you are looking for.

The Kismet scripting system has the ability to group nodes into a sequence. Each sequence is named and displayed in a tree browser in the lower-right side of the Kismet editor. You can create hierarchical subsequences, and then you can view the hierarchy in the tree view.

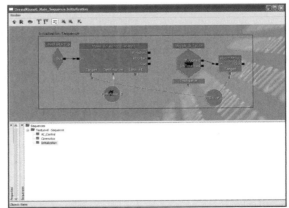

The Kismet system allows script grouping visually. Script groups can be located quickly with the hierarchical text-based tree control on the bottom of the screen.

The SAGE engine used in *C&C Generals: Zero Hour* provides a hierarchal directory structure for the scripts. They can be divided up into arbitrary groups based on the designer's personal preferences. The groups are named and can be hierarchically grouped as well. For example, all the initialization scripts can be placed in the initialization group, and the player trigger scripts can be placed in another group.

Task Specialization

There was a lot of cross-disciplinary development going on in early game development. Most games were developed by very small teams in small shops. Much of this was due to the fact that the early game systems were very simple compared to current game systems; for example, early electronic games only supported 2D graphics.

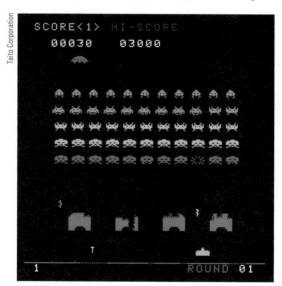

Taito Corporation

Space Invaders had one game screen consisting of nine two-dimensional icons (including five aliens, mothership, player's ship, barriers and bullets).

In many cases these games had a single level of display so that there was one 2D plane that needed to be dealt with. In many cases, the color and resolution were extremely limited, so the amount of art possible was also very limited. Thus, the programmer could often create adequate art, since the best possible art had to be very simple anyway. You could, therefore, have a programmer who was also the artist and designer of the game. What was possible with the primitive microprocessors that controlled the game was very restricted in terms of processing speed and memory size. The design of the game was thus relatively simple. In many cases, a designer might also be a programmer. You basically did not have to be a great and detailed expert in programming, design, or art to develop early video games, since the systems were so limited, although the ability to use simple systems in a fun fashion was actually the hallmark of early designers. In many cases, tasks such as art and design development could be done in code by the same person because the designer was able to develop in code, and the programmer could produce art from the code as well.

From this, the model of controlling behaviors in code emerged, and it worked reasonably well, as long as the designer was also a programmer. However, modern development is generally done with a separation of disciplines, which is primarily due to the complexity of the games and their associated systems. Currently, systems are written in C++, which is a deep and powerful programming language. Even after years of use, even the most knowledgeable users often do not consider themselves experts or authorities on the language.

Game design has also gotten extremely complex, with designers having to understand the overall design and behaviors intended from each level; there is a great deal of thinking, planning, and specification required just to come up with the design of the behaviors, and it requires the designer's full-time attention and thought. To get a behavior to work in code requires attention to detail such as memory management, robustness, the C++ language itself, source control systems, and compiling linking and optimization issues; the designer does not have to worry about any of these elements. There is enough to keep the designer busy figuring out the behaviors themselves without having to worry about all the details

Earth & Beyond included a client-server game implementation and complex gameplay, requiring a development team with numerous C++ experts and game designers.

associated with implementation. Similarly, the programmer has enough to keep busy: getting the behavior to work; implementing in the associated code; dealing with custom hardware present in current platforms; and handling exceptions, robustness, memory management, and so forth. Therefore, we have a division of labor where the designers specify the behaviors and the programmers implement the behaviors, and the question becomes how to get the most efficient game development out of that combination.

Benefits of Scripting Over C++

Scripting has a variety of advantages over programming in C++. First of all, there is no compiler necessary, so in the case of mod-makers or in the case of designers working at a company it is not necessary to supply them with a C++ compiler in order for them to do their work.

Second, the scripting code is often data rather than linked into the application. This allows the code to be customized to a particular level in a map; thus, you can use scripting code to allow for certain behaviors in one level or mission that is not displayed in all the other missions. Alternatively, if code is written in C++, it is straightforward to link it into the application, which results in having general code available for all levels. The customization capability of scripting also provides a safety mechanism because that code is not linked and will not affect the gameplay of any other level.

Third, scripting language can generally be created in such a fashion that errors in scripting do not cause the game to crash. One of the drawbacks of working in C++ is that it is relatively easy to crash the application due to errors in coding. However, a

chapter 4

well-designed scripting system can be coded with appropriate checks so that even if errors are made in the scripting, they do not cause the game to crash.

:::::Glue Functions

Humongous Entertainment's *Backyard Hockey* uses Python as its scripting language. Humongous wrote a utility (YAGA) that reads an interface description of the functions and arguments and automatically generates the C++ glue routines.

C++ functions called from script languages are normally called using a calling convention defined by the script language. This convention is different than the standard style of passing arguments to C++ functions. For example, in Lua all C++ functions called by Lua scripts have the same argument list: a pointer to the Lua state. In addition, most script languages allow a variable number of arguments. Since C++ is a strongly typed language, we cannot easily call a C++ function with a variable number of arguments. We have to use a "glue" function that takes argument information, evaluates the arguments, and calls the "native" function with the specified arguments. Each C++ function we wish to call from a scripting language requires its glue function. In the Lua example code on the DVD, the glue routines are coded by hand to clearly demonstrate the operations being performed. However, in an actual game there may be hundreds of functions that require glue functions, and it may be useful to automate this process. It is possible to use C++ macros or templates to automate the generation of the glue functions. The UnrealScript system used in *Gears of War* automatically generates the glue functions necessary to call C++ functions from script, and script functions from C++ code. *Backyard Hockey* uses a utility program to generate the C++ code for the glue functions needed to interface C++ with the Python scripting language.

Using Scripting in a Game

A scripting system can be used in a variety of ways. A simple use is to provide data values to the game. A more powerful use of scripting is to call script functions in response to events, allowing the script to determine the AI's response to a particular event. Object-oriented scripting can be used to create complex scripts and create and control new AI behaviors.

Provide Data Values

The scripting system can be used to provide data values, similar to the way we used the InitialData.txt file in earlier examples. Instead of returning the time to generate a new coin from the data section, we can create a function in Lua called CoinTime and have the function return the amount of time to wait before creating the next coin. In Lua, it would look like this:

```
function CoinTime()
    return 7.5;
end
```

By itself, this is a bit of overkill for the data that we are storing here. However, if we did do it this way, it would open up certain capabilities that may be useful. For example, we can make a C++ function available to Lua called GameTime() that returns the number of seconds that have elapsed from the start of the game. It would then be possible to add more tests in the Lua code so that during the first 30 seconds of gameplay, the coin appears every 7 seconds, whereas during the 30–90th seconds of gameplay, the coins could be generated every 5 seconds. After the 90th second of gameplay the coins could be generated every 2 seconds. The Lua script code for this function would look like this:

```
function CoinTime()
    local curTime;
    curTime = GameTime();
    if (curTime<30) then
        return 7.5;
    elseif (curTime<90) then
        return 5;
    else
        return 2;
    end
end
```

The C++ function LuaInterface::CallFloatFunction() handles the required Lua operations to call the script function and return the floating point return value.

The advantage of handling the data in Lua rather than in the data file we have used before is that it can be made dynamic and the values can change over time. Thus, if there are gameplay values that need to be adjusted, they can be done in this fashion by using a scripted interface rather than a simple data file.

Events and Functions

At this point, we can implement the events and functions described earlier. The OnSeePlayer() script function could be called from the game at the point that the agent sees the player character, and appropriate call back glue functions to attack or retreat could be made available using the methods already described.

Controlling Animations

Another use of scripting is to control behaviors in the game. One example is the control of an animation system. A similar system was used in *The Lord of the Rings: The Battle for Middle-Earth*. When animations change, it is useful to play a transition animation to prevent the animations from changing positions suddenly, or "popping." For

Electronic Arts

example, if a character is running and stops, one foot may be up in the air. In the idle animation played for the character, both feet are on the ground. One solution is to blend the animations to smooth the transition. However, blending can sometimes result in unnaturally fast movement. Elephants move so slowly and ponderously that even blending animations looks odd. If an elephant is walking and its feet are in the air, it is necessary to play an animation that sets his feet back down so the movement appears natural. Depending on where the elephant is in its walk animation, any one of its four legs may be in the air at a given time. Thus, there are four different transition animations necessary to get the elephant to place its feet back down on the ground,

Lua scripting was used in *The Lord of the Rings: The Battle for Middle-Earth* to coordinate animation transitions for complex characters such as the Ent.

depending on where the elephant is in its animation cycle. The advantage of a Lua script to control the animation is that it can query the animation playback position using a callback into the C++ code. This callback returns the percentage amount that the animation has played, and it can be used to select the correct animation.

```
Function ElephantSelectTransition()
   Local pctComplete;
   pctComplete = AnimationOffset();
   if (pctComplete <0.25) then
         PlayTransition("ElephantWalkTrans25");
   elseif (pctComplete<0.5) then
         PlayTransition("ElephantWalkTrans50");
   elseif (pctComplete<0.75) then
         PlayTransition("ElephantWalkTrans75");
   else
         PlayTransition("ElephantWalkTrans100");
   end
end
```

Script Interface Design

The key to design using a scripting system such as Lua is that you have to anticipate which methods you want to have available in the C++ code that be can called from Lua and also determine which functions will be called in Lua at a particular time. For example, in the data case of the coin, we need to determine in advance what will be querying Lua for the time to generate the coin.

In the case of animation control, we first need to decide that we will use a Lua function to determine the animation transition. In this case, we call:

```
ElephantSelectTransition()
```

Next, we need to determine which callbacks will be needed by the Lua function. In order to blend the elephant animations, we need a function to select the transition:

```
PlayTransition()
```

and a function to query the position of the current animation. The name of the preceding animation may be useful as well. This is an inexact science, and we will always have to include additional callbacks as the need arises. It is very helpful to get as much as possible right initially. This will ease the development of the game and reduce the amount of rework necessary later.

Object-Oriented Scripting

The scripting examples so far use functions, passing data between script and C++ functions. This can be used for a variety of operations in the game, and it may be all that is necessary. In order to do more work in scripting, it may be necessary to create and manipulate objects in the game. Access to game objects, and the ability to create game objects, allows more complex operations to be performed using the script system. It is possible using a simple script function to order an agent to begin an attack. However, the details of the attack behavior are not specified in the script but in C++ code, which does not require object access. It is possible to create the attack states, and thus customize the AI behaviors, with object access. Script programming with game objects is time-consuming and difficult as well as being powerful and flexible. Advanced programming training is necessary in order to create sophisticated object-oriented scripts.

Lua has support that can be used to link it to C++ objects. However, the Lua language does not support object-oriented techniques such as inheritance or interfaces directly. You can make use of objects defined in C++ and exported from the game environment via a mechanism such as Luna, a C++ template class for use with Lua, but you cannot create new types of objects in Lua. Languages such as Python and UnrealScript support object-oriented programming in the language. Using either of these as a scripting language allows the creation of new objects and the inheritance of existing object behaviors by new object classes.

Benefits of Using a Scripting Language

A benefit of scripting is that it allows modification of the game without the use of a C++ compiler and programmer. Non-programmers, such as designers (and potentially artists and producers), can make modifications. This allows for multi-tasking, with a programmer working in one area of the AI, and the designer working on scripts in another area. In addition, it opens the game to the user community. Users can edit scripts and modify the game.

Implementing an object-oriented scripting model has additional benefits. Scripting states in a state machine allows AI behaviors to be modified to a far greater extent than just using parameter files. We can create new states and modify the behaviors of existing states. This allows programmers to create state machines that can be modified by designers who do not have access to the C++ build system, and it also gives a great deal of potential for expansion and change to the mod community.

Another benefit of using a scripting language is that you can do custom scripting for a level or mission. This allows you to create custom behaviors that are appropriate to a specific part of a game. At this point, you would need a mechanism for unloading scripts. Lua loads script files into the global name table, and when you have map-specific scripting, it modifies the global name space. You would not want the first map's scripts to

Electronic Arts

Python scripting was used to create the artificial intelligence in *Earth & Beyond*.

remain loaded when you load scripts for a second map, since it would potentially interfere with the scripts in the second map. A reasonable method in Lua is to delete the lua_State scripting context, create a new one, and then load the game's global scripts and the scripts for the second map.

Lua Game Scripting

A programming example is included on the companion DVD that demonstrates the integration of the Lua scripting language into a game environment. The example allows object-oriented programming of a state machine using Lua, including creation of states and implementation of state behaviors. Lua scripts can be modified with a text editor, and full C and C++ source code is included as well.

Automatic Fun

I've found that the specific coding or design techniques didn't matter as much as the overriding philosophy that we should sacrifice "real thinking" and "scientific approaches to proper AI design" in order to make sure the game experience was fun for the players.

When I say "fun" in this context, I'm not talking about game mechanics, but instead all the little things that give the creatures in the game world a sense of being real. These things can range from having the AI creatures "stumble" or do other "non-perfect" actions all the way to them showing emotions players expect if these AI creatures were truly experiencing the scenario we're watching on screen. One of the techniques that always seems like a good idea but never works out is what I call "programming AI for automatic fun." "Programming AI for automatic fun" basically boils down to programmers working to code up complete simulations of everything in a gameplay scenario with the expectation that the fun will magically emerge with very little work from the designer. The expectation is that the code will allow new emergent gameplay to happen with designers only needing to tweak a number or two before release of the game. It's not that I think simulations can't be the basis of great games (look at what Maxis and Wright have been doing for years), I just know from experience that you need a designer to be deeply involved every step of the way to make sure that "fun" is actually built into and supported by the code.

—Mark Skaggs (Chief Executive Officer, Blue Nitro Studios)

Implementing AI and gameplay functionality using a White Box approach combined with scripting gives both designers and users the ability to modify and extend the game. It enables designers to work on scripts at the same time programmers are developing C++ code. During development, this allows faster turnaround when tuning the AI, resulting in more polished gameplay. After the game is shipped, mod makers can use this capability to create additional game scenarios.

Scripting can be added to a game quickly using an open source language such as Python or Lua. Commercial game engines such as Unreal and Torque come with licensed scripting languages customized for games. Both approaches provide extensive functionality immediately. In the past, custom scripting languages were created, but the availability of open source and licensed scripting languages provide extensive features more quickly than a custom language. It is rare that a custom solution is a wise use of resources. GUIs can be created to speed script development as well.

Another tool for developing White Box systems that facilitate collaboration between AI programmers and designers is a rule-based system. These systems allow designers to control the AI by creating a set of rules that direct the AI's behavior. We will examine these systems in the next chapter.

:::CHAPTER REVIEW:::

1. Consider an AI behavior of a squad of soldiers attacking the player. The game design dictates that the squad will attack in two fashions: straight on as a group, and in a flanking fashion with half the group moving to one side of the player and the other half attacking straight on. Design a Black Box system to provide this behavior, and design a White Box implementation. Given that both programmers and designers are working on this feature, estimate the percentage of work done by programmers vs. designers for both scenarios.

2. Using the systems from Exercise 1, consider what will be necessary if the game design changes, and a third attack behavior is needed with the squad encircling the player. What work will be required in the Black Box case? The White Box case? Based on this information, would you make any changes to the White Box design?

3. Consider adding a procedural vs. an object-oriented scripting interface to a game. Which is more useful to the modding community, and why? Should this impact the game's design?

CHAPTER

5

Expert Systems

capturing high-level knowledge and improving behavioral control

Key Chapter Questions

- What are the three components of an expert system? Which part is created in advance, and which is modified during the use of the expert system?

- What are the two styles of inference engines? Which is more suitable for games, and why?

- Which style of inference engine is more suitable when we only know some of the facts? What is the name of an expert system that uses this method?

- When an expert system is embedded in a game, what is the source of facts? Do we have partial or complete knowledge?

- What are inconsistent facts? Describe two mechanisms to handle them.

Expert systems are one of the more commonly used forms of artificial intelligence (AI) programming in games as well as in medicine and industry. An expert, or rule-based system consists of rules that operate based on a set of facts using an inference engine. This chapter examines the construction and operation of rule-based systems and the process of embedding an expert system into a video game.

Expert Systems Defined

Expert systems (or rule-based systems) are powerful and useful in game development. Their strength is their ability to capture the knowledge of an expert, but this is their weakness as well because they require experts to generate the rule set that captures the desired knowledge.

An algorithm such as A* has the advantage that it does not require any help from an expert. The algorithm can successfully find the shortest path to the goal. Unfortunately, many of the problems associated with game AI do not have an algorithmic solution. In this case, the best and only solution is to capture the game designer's expertise. Rule-based systems encompass one way to capture this knowledge.

Expert System Components

An expert system consists of three components: a knowledge base, inference engine, and working store. The *knowledge base* consists of a set of rules that are created from the knowledge of the expert, often in conjunction with a knowledge engineer familiar with the operation of the expert system. The knowledge base, or rule set, is unique to the particular use of the expert system. For example, a medical expert system contains rules pertaining to the diagnosis of illnesses. A computer configuration expert system contains rules relating to controllers, I/O devices, and the compatibility of different memory cards.

The second component is the *inference engine*, which is a computer program that is common across different uses; for example, both medical and computer systems may use the same inference engine, but a different knowledge base.

> **G**ranted, there are usually 5–10 different "IF"s before I get to the "THEN," but I still use them quite often. The "IF"s are usually based on the situation the AI perceives.
>
> —*John Comes*
> *(Lead Designer,*
> *Gas Powered Games)*

Finally, there is a *working store* that contains the facts for the current application of the system. For example, the computer configuration expert system will have the facts describing the current computer being configured in the working store.

The key component that makes an expert system work is the rule set.

A rule is of the form: IF condition THEN action or result.

An example rule would be: IF stoplight is red THEN stop.

We can refer to the condition as the Left Hand Side or LHS of the rule. The action/result is the Right Hand Side, or RHS.

During the operation of an expert system the inference engine processes the data in the working store and rule set. When the conditions in the LHS of the rule are valid, the inference engine performs the action specified in the RHS of the rule. This may add new facts to (or in some cases remove them from) the working memory.

Knowledge Base

The knowledge base consists of a series of rules that are IF THEN statements. The rules are generally named for easy reference. It is much easier to refer to the YellowLightRule by name than to refer to the complete rule. In an expert system, the knowledge base is created beforehand by entering the rules. During processing, the rules are not added to or removed from the rule base. They may be enabled or disabled during processing by the inference engine.

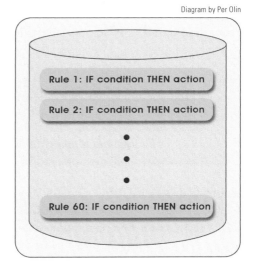

Diagram by Per Olin

The knowledge base is a pre-defined database that consists of a set of rules.

Rule Sets in Real-Time Strategy Games

For years, real-time strategy (RTS) games have used rule sets for artificial intelligence to control the behavior of both units and armies in scripted solo play missions and also in skirmish battles. We've also used rules to help control the pace of gaming and to invoke key action during the middle of missions. You can download the mission/map editor for *Command & Conquer: Generals* and *The Lord of the Rings: The Battle for Middle-Earth* to get some hands-on experience with creating rule set based AI for RTS games.

—*Mark Skaggs (Chief Executive Officer, Blue Nitro Studios)*

Sample Rules

From the MYCIN system for diagnosis of meningitis and bacterial infections:

```
IF
      The site of the culture is blood AND
      The identity of the organism is not known with certainty AND
      The stain of the organism is gram negative AND
      The morphology of the organism is rod AND
      The patient has been seriously burned
THEN
      There is weakly suggestive evidence (.4) that the identity of
            the organism is pseudomonas.
```

From the XCON/R1 system for configuring DEC VAX computer systems:

```
IF
      The current context is assigning devices to Unibus modules AND
      There is an unassigned dual port disk drive AND
      The type of controller it requires is known AND
      There are two such controllers, neither of which has any
            devices assigned to it AND
      The number of devices that these controllers can support is
            known
THEN
      Assign the disk drive to each of the controllers AND
      Note that the two controllers have been associated and each
            supports one drive.
```

Example Rule Set

Here is a small knowledge base for a stoplight that will be used to demonstrate the operation of an expert system. We will start out with just a few rules. The rules are:

- RedRule=IF red light is on THEN stop.
- GreenRule=IF green light is on THEN go.
- YellowFarRule=IF yellow light is on AND vehicle is moving 30 miles an hour AND distance to stoplight is greater than 150 feet THEN stop.
- YellowCloseRule=IF yellow light is on AND vehicle is moving 30 miles an hour AND distance to stoplight is less than 150 feet THEN go.
- RedFlashingRule=IF red light is flashing THEN caution is required.
- CautionRule=IF caution is required AND vehicle is moving THEN stop.
- ProceedRule=IF caution is required AND vehicle is stopped THEN proceed with caution.

We will look at the operation of these rules in more detail later in the chapter.

:::::: *Warcraft III*'s Rule System

The *Warcraft III* trigger editor is a rule-based system in the map editor. The system considers two types of facts, referred to as events and conditions. An *event* is a transitional fact—an agent entering or exiting a trigger, for example. A *condition* is a longer term fact—the game difficulty level, for example.

Courtesy of Blizzard Entertainment, Inc.   Courtesy of Blizzard Entertainment, Inc.

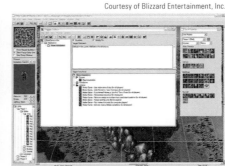

Warcraft III controls behaviors specific to a map by embedding a set of rules, called triggers, in the map. The sample trigger shown in the *WarCraft III* map editor performs initialization on map start-up.

The trigger editor allows the rules to be entered using a graphical format. The rule entered above is

IF Difficulty Level = Normal THEN StageOne = TRUE

StageOne is a Boolean value that can be tested in subsequent rules. The *WarCraft III* trigger system comes with a wide variety of game specific facts that can be tested, such as the amount of resources the player has and the amount of time that has elapsed. Variables can be set in rules. In addition, game actions such as assigning resources or spawning agents can be performed as well.

Working Memory

The *working memory* contains the set of known facts. It starts empty, and the initial set of known facts is entered. An important item to note is that the absence of a fact does not mean that the fact is false; it only means that we do not know that it is true. In our example of a stoplight, we have the following fact: "Distance to stoplight is greater than 150 feet." If this fact is not in our working memory, it does not mean that the distance is less than 150 feet, which is a separate fact: "Distance to stoplight is less than 150 feet." It may mean that we do not know what the distance is. In this case, neither fact would be in the working memory.

Diagram by Per Olin

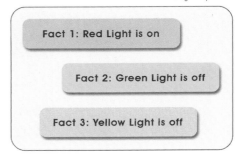

Working memory consists of a list of facts that are added during the operation of the expert system.

A benefit of a rule-based system is that we do not necessarily have to know all the facts. We could know the fact "Red light is on." We do not know what the distance is, or whether any of the other lights are on, but we can still draw the conclusion that we should stop.

Inconsistent Facts

It is possible to have *inconsistent facts* in the working memory. A distance to stoplight fact is a case in point. The two facts "distance to stoplight is less than 150 feet" and "distance to stoplight is greater than 150 feet" are separate facts. It is possible to enter both into the working memory. While it is possible as far as the expert system is concerned, it makes no sense in the real world as both facts cannot be true at the same time. If they are both set, it means either that the operator made an error when entering the data, or there is an error in the knowledge base. One solution to this is relatively simple. We add a rule IF "distance to stoplight is less than 150 feet" AND "distance to stoplight is greater than 150 feet" THEN message "Current facts are invalid" AND HALT. This rule notifies the operator that there is a problem, and processing stops.

Inference Engine

The *inference engine* is the part of an expert system that processes the rules in the knowledge base and the facts in the working memory. The inference engine examines the rule set for rules whose conditions are met by the known facts. If a rule's conditions are met, the rule is executed. This may add additional facts to the working memory, which may trigger additional rules.

Diagram by Per Olin

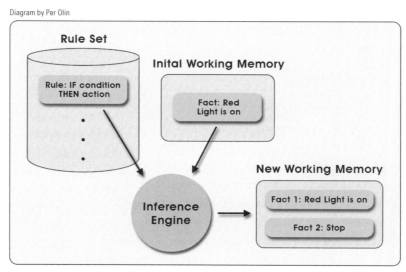

The inference engine processes a rule and a fact and adds the new fact ("stop") to the working memory.

The following is a sample of an inference engine:

```
WHILE not done
    Conflict Resolution: If there are activations then select the
        one with highest priority, else done.

    Act: Sequentially perform the actions on the right hand side on
        the selected activation. Those that change working memory
        have an immediate effect in this cycle. Remove the activation
        that has just fired from the agenda.

    Match: Update the agenda by checking whether the left hand
        sides of any rules are satisfied, if so activate them.
        Remove activations if the left hand sides of their rules are
        no longer satisfied.

    Check for halt: If a halt action is performed or a break
        command given then done.

END-WHILE
Accept a new user command.
```

Let us consider the example stoplight rule set. Assume that the fact "the light is red" is present in the working memory. The inference engine can execute and discover that the condition for rule 1 is met and add the fact "stop" to the working memory. At this point, the user could query the expert system with regard to what facts were known, and the expert system would then list that "the red light is on" and "stop" are the two known facts at this point.

Capturing High-Level Knowledge

An expert system is valuable for being able to store and use *high-level knowledge* in the rule set. For example, we can create a rule relating to determining whether to stop for a yellow light.

IF the light is yellow AND the car is more than 150 feet from the stoplight AND the speed of the car is no more than 30 miles per hour THEN stop.

This carries some information that we need about how to proceed in approaching a yellow stoplight. The rule considers three facts of data and determines whether the car should stop. The rule is relatively easy to evaluate and understand, and if applied to driving will produce good results. However, the rule is dealing with a situation that is complex, with many variables. The answer depends on the interaction of friction between the tire and street, brake pads and brake drums, anti-lock brake system, human perception time and reaction time, and the operation of stoplights in general. However, we can simplify the situation to the given rule and still get good results without having to consider coefficients of friction between different surfaces. There are several ways to create rules: either through analysis, empirical study, or expert intuition.

Analysis

In order to create rules through *analysis*, consider the situation regarding how to proceed when approaching a yellow stoplight. The actual time for a car to stop depends on the physics of a car, along with the perceptual time for a driver to perceive the light and press the brake to stop the vehicle. The amount of time to slow a vehicle down from 30 miles per hour after the brakes are applied depends on the relative coefficient of friction between tires on the car and the average road surface. It may be necessary to factor in the fact that in some cases the coefficient of friction may be lowered due to extenuating circumstances such as rain or debris on the road. Ranges for these values can be determined by study and analysis. The results can be calculated for a variety of conditions, and the value of 150 feet can be compared to the stopping distance. If 150 feet is sufficient distance to stop in most cases, then the rule can be created with that value.

Empirical Study

A variety of cars and drivers can be studied *empirically* to determine how long it takes them to stop for a yellow light. We can do this by observing and recording the distance required to stop in a large number of instances. This will provide a set of distances. From an inspection of the results, we can choose a good value for the stopping distance. Empirical study requires that we are able to observe a number of cases. It has the advantage that no theory or scientific research is necessary; we do not need to understand momentum, friction, or reaction time. We simply measure a number of cases.

Expert Intuition

If we have an *expert* available who has done work and study in the area of cars stopping for traffic lights, we can use the expert's opinion to develop the rule.

The Power of Expert Systems

One aspect that makes the rule-based systems very powerful is that they can encapsulate any or all of these types information into a single rule. A rule can encapsulate the results of extensive analysis, or represent knowledge that is gained through experience and observation. It is possible to use rules developed through any or all of these methods in a knowledge base.

Through observation in the field of medicine, for example, we may come up with the following rule: If the temperature of the patient is two degrees above normal, there is a 60% chance that the patient has an infection. We do not have to prove a causal link between the infection and the fever, and in fact the mechanism may be unknown. Through observation we have determined that this is valid medically and that this can be used in the knowledge base even though we do not have any way to prove on a biochemical basis that this is the fact. Often information that we have in the knowledge base comes from secondary sources such as observation, inference, or intuition on the part of the expert, which is why they are called expert systems. The expert system, therefore, allows us to represent the high-level knowledge that we have in our rule base.

Explanation

In addition to giving information as to which facts are true, the expert system can also give an *explanation* for why a particular fact is true (or not, as the case may be). In this case, if the system lists that "the red light is on" and "stop" are the two known facts, the user can then query the system with regard to the reasoning for those two facts. The reason the fact "red light is on" is known is that it was specified to be true by the operator. The reasoning for "stop" being true then is that RedRule executed and added "stop" to the working memory. The explanation would look like this:

```
"red light is on" -> input fact from operator
RedRule -> fired because "red light is on"
"stop" -> set by execution of RedRule
```

We can examine the chain of reasoning and judge whether we agree with the reasoning. In more complex cases, there may be a number of rules involved in the reasoning. There are several benefits of this behavior. First, it gives the users of the system much more confidence in the system. The person using the system can see the chain of reasoning and, if necessary, verify the applicability of the rules to the current situation. Second, it is very helpful in the development of the expert system. For example, in the early stages of the development of a rule system, it is common to get a "wrong" answer from the system. The explanation shows which rules were involved and how they interacted. This often provides insight into correcting the problem. In the case of game AI, it can provide insight into how to improve AI behaviors.

Challenges

Problems can arise when creating a rule set and using an expert system. High level knowledge can be inconsistent; the real world often includes exceptions and special cases that may invalidate a rule. Rules can be modified, or additional rules can be added to handle these situations.

Conflicting Information

Part of the power of knowledge-based systems is that they can represent high-level knowledge. One of the drawbacks of high-level knowledge, though, is that it can be inconsistent, whereas deep knowledge is inherently consistent.

Deep Knowledge is Self-Consistent

In the next chapter, we'll look a an A* algorithm for pathfinding. The pathfind search in general is a very *deep* form of knowledge where the algorithm works on data that actually specifically represents, though simplified, the areas of a simulation where movement is possible (and where it is not)—representing the position of the agent and this network. We know where the agent is and where the agent could move, and it is as such internally self-consistent. In other words, the agent is always at one spot—not at another spot. So there was no question where we consider the agent to be during the pathfinding operation and simulation—and there are no paths that are both possible and impossible at the same time for the agent to take— so either path is possible or it is not, and it is well-defined.

High-Level Knowledge May Not Be Self-Consistent

High-level rules are unfortunately not constrained to be completely self-consistent. For example, we have two bits of folk wisdom:

Absence makes the heart grow fonder.

Out of sight, out of mind.

Both fit into the rules of human behavior, but, unfortunately, they happen to be opposite from one another. As a result of this, it is possible to have contradictory facts in a rule-based system.

For example, we could have the rule: IF light is green THEN go. This is a reasonable rule for dealing with stoplights. However, as we work on making our rule set more complete, we may add another rule: IF pedestrian is in the walkway THEN stop. Surely we would all agree that this is a reasonable rule as well. However, it is possible for the following facts to both be true: "The light is green" and "A pedestrian is in the walkway." In this case, the rule set indicates that we should go and stop. This is not an uncommon result with rule sets. Fortunately, knowledge-based systems are capable of both representing this situation and resolving the conflicts that occur.

There are ways to represent, handle, and interpret these situations. One of the cases can be that there are valid reasons that support multiple conflicting conclusions, in which case interpretation could basically go either way. Our knowledge base is not sufficient in this case to give us a specific answer. This is one of the areas you have to watch for to make sure that the knowledge base is built to be internally self-consistent and handle cases where there are conflicting rules or facts.

Inconsistent Results

In some cases, there can be conflicting facts resulting from a rule set. For example, you may want to extend the stoplight situation to add another rule which is:

- PedestrianRule=IF pedestrian is in walkway THEN stop.

If we simply add the rule then we have the following rule set.

- RedRule=IF red light is on THEN stop.
- GreenRule=IF green light is on THEN go.
- YellowFarRule=IF yellow light is on AND vehicle is moving 30 miles an hour AND distance to stoplight is greater than 150 feet THEN stop.
- YellowCloseRule=IF yellow light is on AND vehicle is moving 30 miles an hour AND distance to stoplight is less than 150 feet THEN go.
- RedFlashingRule=IF red light is flashing THEN caution is required.
- CautionRule=IF caution is required AND vehicle is moving THEN stop.
- ProceedRule=IF caution is required AND vehicle is stopped THEN proceed with caution.
- PedestrianRule=IF pedestrian in walkway THEN stop.

If we input the following facts, "green light is on" and "pedestrian in walkway," the inference engine executes and we get two facts generated. The GreenRule fires and generates the fact "go." The PedestrianRule fires and generates the fact "stop."

At this point, the expert system is in a valid state. A fact was entered, inferences processed, and additional facts generated. However, we look at the results and find they are inconsistent. We cannot both go and stop, so the results are not useful.

However, both a strength and weakness of a knowledge-based system is that it can represent this kind of information. An inconsistent result means that we need to refine the rules of our knowledge base to produce more consistent results. We can use the explanation capability of the expert system to see why the inconsistent facts were generated. The explanation for the fact "go" is that the GreenRule fired because the fact "green light is on" was input. The explanation for "stop" is that the PedestrianRule fired because the fact "pedestrian in walkway" was input. Both of those are valid rules; however, they produce conflicting results and have to be resolved.

Conflict Resolution

An additional capability of rule-based systems is being able to *resolve conflicting rules*. There are several ways to manage this. A variety of mechanisms can be provided by the inference engine, and the rule set can then be modified to make use of them.

Removing Conflicting Facts

One engine mechanism that can be used to manage conflict is the ability to remove facts from the working memory. We could take advantage of this by adding the following rule:

- StopRule=IF stop AND go THEN REMOVE go.

This rule states that the fact "stop" has priority over the fact "go." Not an unreasonable rule for a stoplight. If there are indications that you should both stop and go, it is probably better to stop.

::::: Stopping Criteria

An important question in the inference engine, and in particular when resolving conflicts, is the *stopping criteria*: When does the inference engine stop processing rules?

One way is to run until no new facts are added. This works if you only add facts to working memory, but if you can also remove facts you can keep going forever. In the current example, the inference engine will process the PedestrianRule and GreenRule, and add "stop" and "go" to the working memory. Then it will process the StopRule and remove "go" from working memory. This process can continue indefinitely, adding and removing facts.

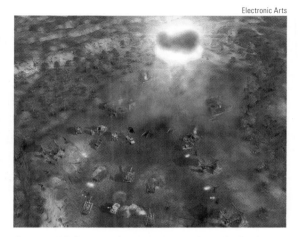
Electronic Arts

Command & Conquer: Generals allows rules to be fired once.

Another way to handle this is to only allow a rule to be fired once. This is simple to implement, and handles the current case nicely. The PedestrianRule and GreenRule fire once. The StopRule fires and we end up with "stop" in the working memory and no more rules to fire. This is simple to implement and guarantees that evaluation will stop at some point, since you can only fire a rule once.

A more sophisticated method is to allow a rule to fire again, but only if one of its input facts has changed value. For example, the GreenRule could fire a second time, but only if the fact "green light is on" was removed and then added to working memory. This method would allow the StopRule to fire multiple times if necessary, which might be useful. If both "stop" and "go" were set, and the rule fired, we would have "stop" set. However, if a subsequent rule set "go" again, the StopRule would fire since the "go" fact had changed value. This would remove the "go" fact again. The GreenRule would not fire multiple times, since the value of "green light is on" never changes. This method has the potential to continue indefinitely, if a number of rules change their respective facts. It may be useful to have a limit on the number of times a rule can change, such as 100, that would cause the evaluation to stop with a warning message.

Finally, a halt operator can be useful. The StopRule could use this:

IF stop AND go THEN REMOVE go AND HALT

This causes the inference engine to stop evaluating rules.

The SAGE engine used in *Command & Conquer: Generals* and *Zero Hour* used two flags to control how rules fire. The first flag indicated whether the rule was enabled. Disabled rules did not fire. Rules could be enabled and disabled by other rules. The second flag was a "Fire once" flag. If this was set, the rule would only fire once. Fire once was the default value. The ability to have rules fire once or multiple times, and to enable and disable rules provided a great deal of control and flexibility. It was not necessary to implement the capability to allow a rule to fire again if its input facts changed after it fired.

Preventing the Addition of Conflicting Facts

Alternatively, we could add a test to the GreenRule:

- BetterGreenRule=IF green light is on AND NOT stop THEN go.

The BetterGreenRule would not fire if the fact "stop" was already in the working memory, thus avoiding the situation with both facts "stop" and "go" in working memory. This raises a problem, however. If the BetterGreenRule fired first, and the PedestrianRule fired second, we would still end up with both "stop" and "go" in working memory. Modifying the PedestrianRule as follows solves the conflict, but it makes no sense in the real world:

- Rule BadPedestrianRule=IF pedestrian is in walkway AND NOT go THEN stop.

This rule prevents the introduction of both "stop" and "go" into working memory, but the BadPedestrianRule effectively says that it is okay to run over the pedestrian if you have already decided to go. This is clearly wrong in the real world. The solution is to ensure that the original PedestrianRule, "always stop if there is a pedestrian," fires before the BetterGreenRule.

Rule Priority

A way to resolve execution order conflicts is to *give the rules themselves a priority.* In this case, we execute the rule with the higher priority first. In simple systems, the priority is that the rules are evaluated in the order they are entered. However, this is a bit inflexible. More sophisticated systems allow priorities to be assigned to rules. We can give the PedestrianRule a higher priority than the BetterGreenRule, so the first fact added is "stop," which then prevents the BetterGreenRule from firing. The result then is that the conflict has been resolved by changing or adding to the rules, and taking advantage of the control mechanisms are provided by the inference engine that specify both the order and number of times rules are allowed to fire.

Forward Chaining Inference

Forward chaining inference (also called data-driven inference) starts from a set of known facts and then processes the rules to derive additional facts. The OPS4 inference engine uses forward chaining. The basic process for forward chaining is to examine the facts in the working memory, fire any rules whose criteria are met by the facts, and repeat with any new facts until there are no more rules to fire.

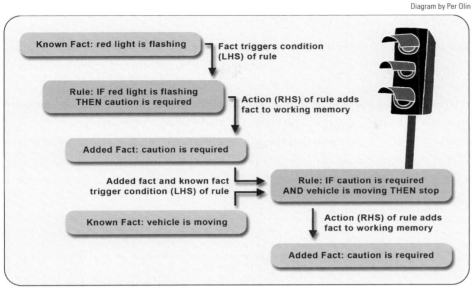

Diagram by Per Olin

Forward chaining processes known facts from left to right and adds new facts to the working memory.

Forward chaining is very useful when we know all the input facts. One example is the XCON/R1 expert system for configuring VAX computer systems. We have the information describing the desired number of disks, amount of memory, and number of IO ports. The expert system then processes all the known facts and should result both in those that are the necessary controllers and configuration to assemble the computer.

Forward chaining is also useful for process control applications. For example, a chemical manufacturing process may have an expert system that handles facts collected from the monitoring sensors associated with the equipment. The system processes these facts, and generates additional facts such as "process within parameters," "operating temperature too low, increase preheating," or "input flow below minimum, shut down and correct."

Forward chaining is useful in game AI applications. It is straightforward to implement and understand, and the facts used in a game come from the game simulation, which is available to the game AI so we do not have only partial information to deal with.

Backward Chaining Inference

Backward chaining inference (also called goal-driven inference) starts from a partial set (sometimes none) of initial facts and works backwards from a possible goal fact. Backward chaining is useful in diagnostic applications. For example, the MYCIN expert system is a medical diagnostic system that uses backward chaining. There are hundreds tests that can be run, and it is not reasonable, or time and cost effective, to run every test on a patient to determine a diagnosis. The known information is thus entered, and then the inference engine works backward from the possible diagnoses to the input facts.

Diagram by Per Olin

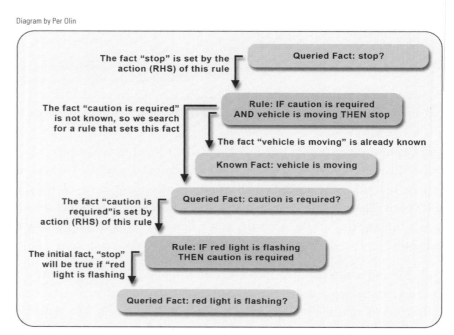

Backward chaining begins with a question about whether a fact is true (in this case "stop"). The search proceeds from right to left in order to find facts that would make "stop" true.

Allows the System to Ask Intelligent Questions

One benefit of working backwards from a goal is that the system can ask questions to determine whether a goal fact is true. The operator may have a suspicion that a certain fact is true and can use the expert system to confirm it. The expert system can do this by asking questions of the operator regarding facts relevant to the goal.

In the stoplight example, we may initially guess that "stop" is true. The operator indicates to the expert system that the goal fact is "stop." By using backward chaining, the inference engine looks at the rules that have a Right Hand Side that involve the fact "stop." The first rule that it looks at is the RedRule, which sets the fact "stop," so this is relevant to the goal. The inference engine examines the Left Hand Side of the rule. The fact "red light is on" would cause the rule to fire and set our goal fact of "stop." However, the fact "red light is on" is not in our working memory. The inference engine then checks rules to see if there are any that have a Right Hand Side involving "red light is on." In our small example, there are no rules with an RHS involving "red light is on." In a more complex rule set, there may be rules several levels deep. In this case, the inference engine would examine those other rules to find conditions that would trigger setting the "red light is on" fact.

When the inference engine reaches a fact that is not present in any other rule's RHS, that fact must be an input fact. In this case, the fact "red light is on" is an input fact. At this point, the inference engine queries the operator: Is it the case that "red light is on?" This way the expert system can direct the operator to gather facts that may justify the conclusion "stop." For the example, the red light is off. The operator indicates this to the expert system and RedRule is abandoned, since it cannot justify the desired conclusion "stop."

The next rule that has an RHS involving "stop" is the YellowFarRule. The inference engine examines the LHS and discovers three facts. Again, none of them occur in the RHS of any rules so they must be input facts. None of the facts are in the working memory, so the inference engine must query the operator. The engine queries the operator on the first fact: Is it the case that "yellow light is on?" In this case, the yellow light is not on. Since the rule requires that all three facts be true to fire the rule, the expert system can stop the examination of YellowFarRule; it cannot justify "stop," so there is no need to query the operator regarding the other two facts concerning vehicle speed and distance.

The final rule that has an RHS involving "stop" is the CautionRule. The inference engine examines the LHS of this rule and finds two facts. In this rule, "vehicle is moving" is an input fact again; however, "caution is required" does occur in the RHS of the RedFlashingRule. The inference engine examines the RHS of all rules and finds "caution is required" in the RHS of RedFlashingRule. Instead of querying the operator, the inference engine examines RedFlashingRule. The fact "red light flashing" is an input fact, so the engine queries the operator: Is it the case that "red light flashing?"

In our case, the red light is flashing and the operator enters that information. The inference engine then enters the fact "caution is required" and the RedFlashingRule can fire, since its conditions are met. Returning to CautionRule, the first condition is met and the second is an input fact. The engine thus queries the operator: Is it the case that "vehicle is moving?" In our case, the vehicle is moving. The expert system returns the answer that "stop" is a valid result. The explanation for this answer is:

```
"red light flashing" -> input fact from operator
RedFlashingRule -> fired because "red light flashing"
"caution is required" -> set by execution of RedFlashingRule
"vehicle is moving" -> input fact from operator
CautionRule -> fired because "caution is required" AND "vehicle is
moving"
"stop" -> set by execution of CautionRule
```

Guides Toward Possible Goals

Another feature of backward chaining is the ability use partial information to guide the operator toward potential goal facts. Let us consider the rule set with one fact set in working memory: "Distance to stoplight is greater than 150 feet." Using forward chaining, we do not get very far. No rules fire and forward chaining finishes processing without producing either "stop" or "go." (This is why forward chaining works better if you have complete information.)

Backward chaining can start working backward from the goal facts and see which goals involve the partial information. In this case, the relevant rule is the YellowFarRule. The fact "stop" is set by this rule, and one of the conditions is met in part by the fact "distance to stoplight is greater than 150 feet." The expert system can notify the operator that "stop" is a possible goal and begin the process of gathering more information to justify the conclusion "stop." In our example, this is not extremely valuable since there are only two goals: "stop" and "go." In the case of a medical diagnosis program where there are hundreds of possible diagnoses, focusing the search toward the diagnoses that are partially justified is a very valuable way to find the correct diagnosis with as few questions as possible. Since a question in this case may involve an expensive and time consuming test, this is important.

Use in Game AI

Backward chaining is not as useful in the game itself as forward chaining. We tend to have complete information in a game, so we do not have to handle partial information. It might be useful if we wanted to ask questions of the player, but that is not a common gameplay mechanic. As we will see later, backward chaining reasoning can be useful offline when developing rules for an embedded expert system that performs control functions in a game.

Let us consider what the absence of a fact means. If RedLightOn is not present in working memory, it means that we do not currently know if the red light is on. We need to explicitly represent a fact and its negation. We would need to have two facts: RedLightOn and RedLightOff. If RedLightOn is present in the working memory, the red light is on. If RedLightOff is present, it means the red light is off. If neither is present in working memory, it means we do not currently know whether the light is on or off. If both are present at once, we have an inconsistent set of input facts, and should have a rule to handle that case. One such rule is: IF RedLightOn AND RedLightOff THEN message "Inconsistent input facts" AND HALT.

Embedded Expert Systems

Stand-alone expert systems deal with facts. Initial facts are specified by an operator who enters them into the system. Then, the results of the expert systems operate an inference engine working on the facts, perhaps using backward chaining, and requesting the confirmation or verification of additional facts present. This results in a set of facts and explanations with regard to why the facts are valid. Rule-based systems embedded in the game work a little bit differently than the standalone expert system in that many facts that are available come from the game's data. The *StarCraft* trigger system is a rule-based system embedded in the game itself. When an expert system is embedded in the game, the actions in the system can either modify facts (as in a stand-alone expert system) or perform actions in the game that change the game state in order to achieve a desired goal.

Courtesy of Blizzard Entertainment, Inc.

StarCraft has an embedded expert system that can modify the game state. One way the system achieves this is by creating additional enemy agents.

Sample Rule Set

This short list of rules could cover one part of an RTS game such as *Warcraft*, *Command & Conquer: Generals*, or *Rise of Nations*:

- Rule1=IF player is novice AND attack is mild THEN the game is fun.
- Rule2=IF player is experienced AND attack is moderate THEN the game is fun.
- Rule3=IF the player is expert AND the attack is intense THEN the game is fun.
- Rule4=IF difficulty is easy THEN the player is novice.
- Rule5=IF difficulty is medium THEN the player is experienced.
- Rule6=IF difficulty is hard THEN the player is expert.
- Rule7=IF two tanks attack THEN the attack is mild.
- Rule8=IF four tanks attack THEN the attack is moderate.
- Rule9=IF eight tanks attack THEN the attack is intense.

Let us assume that the difficulty in the game is selected as medium. The fact "difficulty is medium" is placed in our working memory. We then process the rules using forward chaining. The LHS of Rule5 is true. This results in Rule5 firing, and we add the fact "the player is experienced" to working memory. At this point, forward chaining terminates. Looking at the RHS of the rules, we note an interesting fact: "The game is fun." It seems like this is a good goal for our game. We can use backward chaining from this goal. Rule2 becomes of interest, since the first condition, "player is experienced," is already met. Continuing our backward inference, "attack is moderate" leads us to Rule8. Examining this rule leads us to the conclusion that if "four tanks attack" is true, then "the game is fun" is valid.

Reprinted with permission from Microsoft Corporation

Rise of Nations is an RTS game that fits the conditions in the sample rule set.

Modifying the Game State

If this were a stand-alone system, we could use it to determine whether the game was fun by checking if four tanks are attacking. However, if the expert system is embedded in the game, we can implement actions in the system that change the game state. This allows us to write rules that modify the game state as well as set or

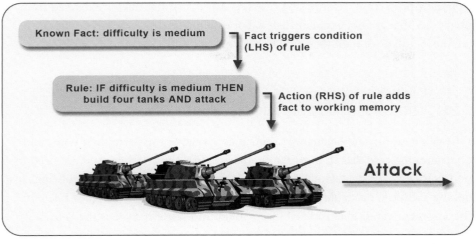
Diagram by Per Olin

An expert system embedded in a game can create and direct game agents as well as add and remove facts from the working memory.

remove facts. Rather than just noting that "if four tanks attack, the game is fun," we can create four tanks and direct them to attack, thus making the game fun. The rule in this case would be:

- RuleB=IF difficulty is medium THEN build four tanks AND attack.

The resulting rule set to create a fun game would be:

- RuleA=IF difficulty is easy THEN build two tanks AND attack.
- RuleB=IF difficulty is medium THEN build four tanks AND attack.
- RuleC=IF difficulty is hard THEN build eight tanks AND attack.

We then move from a rule set that allows us to analyze *whether* the game is fun to a rule set that specifies the *actions to take* in order to make the game fun.

One advantage of this method is that it results in a simpler rule set. The RuleA–RuleC set contains one third of the rules as Rule1–Rule9. In addition, rule set ABC can be processed using a simple forward chaining inference engine. The rule set 1–9 required forward and backward chaining to produce useful results. We can use a small rule set and a straightforward inference engine to process the rules and actions, resulting in game behaviors that make the game fun to play.

A possible problem if we are using rule set ABC is that the rules are derived from other rules that are not explicitly listed. For example, RuleA is based on these rules and the fact that we want the game to be fun:

- Rule1=IF player is novice AND attack is mild THEN the game is fun.
- Rule4=IF difficulty is easy THEN the player is novice.
- Rule7=IF two tanks attack THEN the attack is mild.

If the game tuning and balancing results in a change to the strength of units, and it becomes the case that IF three tanks attack THEN the attack is mild, we need to modify RuleA. This is obvious if we look at rules 1, 4, and 7. It is not as obvious just looking at RuleA, particularly if someone else derived RuleA from rules 1,4, and 7. These sorts of conditions and actions are built into systems such as the *StarCraft* trigger system and the *Command & Conquer: Generals* scripting system.

The designer can use this kind of system to combine knowledge in the form of facts and actions in a sophisticated fashion. For example, the designer can divide up the AI behavior into logical stages. The stages for a RTS may be base building and defense, team building, and attack. Facts in the system can correspond to these stages and can be used to trigger behaviors at an appropriate time in the game. The initial stage can be set as a fact:

IF true THEN set fact InitalBaseBuilding

A series of rules dependent on this fact are written that control the initial behavior:

- IF InitialBaseBuilding THEN Maximize Resource Collection
- IF InitialBaseBuilding THEN Prefer defensive structures
- IF InitialBaseBuilding THEN Prefer defensive teams

The system can then advance to the next stage at an appropriate time:

- IF GameTime >= 4 minutes THEN Remove Fact InitialBaseBuilding AND Set Fact BuildTeams
- IF BuildTeams THEN Prefer Offensive Teams
- IF BuildTeams THEN Research New Weapon Technology

The embedded expert system can be used to manage the facts driving the behavior of the AI, as well as invoking the actions that actually perform the behaviors.

::::: When Good Rules Go Bad

Any expert system is only as good as its rule set and the facts applied to it. As noted earlier, the implicit rules are an area where we can get into trouble. One is the degree of difficulty. The previous example involved the level of difficulty versus the experience of the player. Another few implicit rules that tend to occur in game development are:

IF player is game designer THEN player has vast experience.

IF player has vast experience AND game is insanely difficult THEN game is fun.

If we solve these rules with a goal to make the game fun for the designer, we come up with an insanely difficult game, which triggers the following rule:

IF game is insanely difficult THEN game is not fun for anyone else.

Early versions of *Nanotek Warrior* ran into this problem. The development team's lead tester had no problem playing the game, but no one else could get past the first level. This problem was corrected relatively quickly, but it was a good learning experience for the team.

Virgin Interactive

Courtesy of id Software, Inc.

Prototype versions of *Nanotek Warrior* were frustrating rather than fun due to an extremely high difficulty level.

The *Quake 4* Putrification Center was created with a level of difficulty appropriate to the player, resulting in enjoyable gameplay.

Another area where the problem of game difficulty can creep into games is the crush/burn/vaporize puzzle levels in first-person shooters (FPSs). In these levels, the player walks through/rides on the narrow conveyer/tunnel/cave past a series of moving blocks/saw blades/flame jets/plasma vents that will crush/rip/burn/vaporize him if he does not time his movements just right. Most likely you have encountered at least one case of this type of level that is insanely difficult.

A case in which game difficulty was handled very well was in the Putrification Center level in *Quake 4*. This area is possible to navigate by observing and moving with moderate care. In addition, stopping points are present so the player can pause and survey the timing of the various hazards. The level designers could probably navigate it with one hand tied behind their backs while surfing the Web on their second monitors, but it is still one of the more enjoyable puzzle levels of this type around.

Combining Data-Driven and Rule-Based Systems

In the earlier section on rules, we looked at collapsing a relatively complicated set of rules and some backward chaining into a much shorter set of rules and actions to achieve a particular goal—in this case, the creation of a game that was fun.

Gas Powered Games

Supreme Commander uses data-driven systems to allow rapid modification and tuning of its gameplay.

Similarly, we can combine a data-driven system with some rules to produce one that uses the result of sophisticated reasoning and judgment on the part of the designer, but is captured in a form that can be used by the AI in a relatively understandable system. The system is straightforward and easy to understand and modify both on the part of the programmer and designer.

A good example is the case of base building in an RTS. For the computer player, the base building problem is rather complex and does not have an algorithmic solution to determine what is the best base layout. There are several reasons for this. One is the sheer complexity of the number of possible structures, their location, and the order of construction.

Certain structures are required to build other structures, and all structures have different functions. For example, defensive structures obviously will defend. However, the nature of the RTS is that each different type of structure and defensive unit has a counter on the other side. A well balanced RTS has no one perfect base layout. The game is fun to play using a variety of different strategies. So the problem of optimizing the base layout is intentionally not possible to solve both from a complexity and from a design standpoint. Since you cannot solve this on an analytical level, it becomes a good candidate for a rule-based system.

There are many considerations when building a base. If a structure has defensive capabilities, it should be placed on the outside perimeter of the base. If a structure has no defensive capabilities, it should be placed near the center of the base. If a structure is expensive and has low armor value, it should be closer to the center of the base. If a structure has high armor value, relative to its cost, it can be placed near the perimeter of the base. In addition, there are terrain relative considerations. For example, it is good to place fixed defensive structures along approach routes to the base.

When the AI builds a structure, it is placed it at a particular location on the game map. It is difficult to specify the location with a rule, as we see from the previous multiple considerations.

Structure Location

One way to capture this information is to have the designer actually specify the positions for the base explicitly.

A system that allows the designer to place the base structures on a map can capture the results of sophisticated reasoning on the part of the designer. In addition, it greatly simplifies the implementation of the AI. All the system has to concern itself with is the location of the structures specified by the designer. The designer makes the trade-offs between defensive values, cost, and so forth, and positions the structures.

Electronic Arts

The data-driven base layout in *Command & Conquer: Generals* gives designers precise control of structure locations.

Order of Creation

In addition to the location of the structures, the order in which structures are built is also important. Resource collection is essential, so the first item to be built will often be a resource collection structure such as mine, logging camp, or supply depot. Also important early on are defensive capabilities to prevent an early rush from quickly overrunning the base.

By making the specification of structure locations an ordered list, the designer can determine the order in which the structures will be built, as well as their positions.

Electronic Arts

It is important in *Emperor: Battle for Dune* that the construction yard and refinery be built before other structures. The construction yard is a prerequisite for all structures, as is the spice processed by the refinery.

Additional Base-Building Rules

One of the initial goals in an RTS is to avoid cheating. Thus, a rule that is valuable is: If a technology is lacking for a particular structure, then do not build the structure. Continue on to the next one in the list. This ensures that the AI is not allowed to build structures for which the player does not have the resources to build just because the structures were entered out of order in the build list for the AI.

The previous rule is intended to avoid accidental cheating on the part of the AI. A designer may enter a nuclear missile silo into the build list before the technology center, and according to the game rules, the technology center is a prerequisite to the missile silo. Either the designer forgot, or the prerequisites may have changed during game development. This rule causes the AI to build the technology center first, followed by the missile silo. In some cases, it is desirable to allow the AI to cheat. For example, a script command that is "build structure X now" allows the designer to break the rules if necessary by an explicit command to do so, rather than accidentally doing so.

Similarly, if construction agents such as a "dozer" (*Command & Conquer: Generals*) or a "peasant" (*Warcraft*) is required, the AI waits until a construction agent is available in order to start building a structure.

Combining rules with data allows the creation of sophisticated AI systems that would be extremely difficult to build with rules alone, or with data alone. A list of structures, with locations, combined with two rules results in a flexible base building system. Implementing the same system using rules alone would require 30 or more rules. This technique is applicable to other game areas. One game prototype used a similar system of rules and data to control a day/night cycle; instead of sequencing the building of AI structures, the system modified the lighting and environment.

Expert systems are commonly used in industry and science, and are excellent tools for developing game AI as well. They require the knowledge of an expert to develop the rule set, but can capture multiple kinds of knowledge, ranging from analytical results, data collected by observation, and intuitive knowledge. In the case of game AI, the lead designer and lead AI programmer function as the experts. The game AI has access to the complete game state, so forward chaining is the primary method for inference in game expert systems. In some cases, combining expert systems with data can simplify the rule set and produce sophisticated AI systems.

Expert systems, scripting, and state machines can be combined to create sophisticated game AI. However, the reasoning and control happen inside the game code, and are not always apparent to the player. A key aspect to allowing the player to appreciate the quality of the AI is exposing the AI's reasoning and behavior to the player. We will examine techniques to do this in Chapter 8. Before we get to that, we will take a look at one of the more common problems in AI programming: getting from point A to point B, or *pathfinding*.

:::CHAPTER REVIEW:::

1. Add rules to complete the stoplight example. Handle the case of a flashing yellow light (proceed with caution). Handle the case of a power outage (caution is required).

2. Add rules to handle a broken stoplight control mechanism. For example, what if both the green and red lights are on?

3. Add rules to handle invalid input facts. For example, the facts red light is on, and red light is flashing are both in working memory.

4. Add a command, list *input facts*, to the interactive mode. This command lists all facts that only occur in the Left Hand Side of the rule set.

5. Modify the evaluation of rules so that the order of rules in the data file is a true priority evaluation. Currently, if there are 10 rules in the list, the inference engine will examine rule 1, then 2, then 3, and so on. If rule 3's conditions are not met, the inference engine will proceed to 4, 5, and so on. If rule 5 adds a fact to the working memory that meets 3's conditions, a true priority implementation will immediately fire rule 3. The current implementation would test rules 6–10 before starting at 1 again.

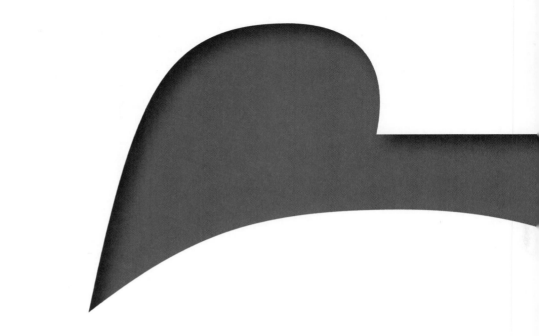

CHAPTER

Pathfinding

allowing agents to properly find and follow paths

Key Chapter Questions

- What is a path network?

- What are the advantages of a manually generated path network versus an automatically generated network?

- When would you search for a path but not know the final destination?

- What search algorithms are appropriate when you know the final destination?

- When would pathfinding involve moving other agents?

This chapter delves into the complex problem of *pathfinding*, which continues to be one of the most challenging areas of artificial intelligence (AI) programming, and the bane of both programmers and designers. However, by designing multiple solutions that fit together, it is possible to create a pathfinding system that produces good results.

Pathfinding Systems

Although a number of references and comments from AI programmers have indicated that problems related to pathfinding have been solved, issues related to poor pathfinding are still being uncovered by game designers and players alike. Pathfinding does not involve one simple operation; in fact, a total of four operations need to be correctly performed in order to successfully produce good quality pathfinding: path node definition, path planning, pathfinding, and path following.

Pathfinding in modern video games is performed by searching a network of connected points, or nodes, in the game world. The network is generated before pathfinding operations are performed, since the creation of the network is time-consuming. The network can be generated manually, with markers placed at each location by a designer in the game level editor, or generated automatically. In some cases, a semi-automatic method is used with some nodes being placed manually and others generated automatically.

Pathfinding Networks

A pathfinding network consists of a set of *path nodes*, each one corresponding to a point in the game world. In addition, each node has a link to each adjacent node. By following the links, an agent can build a path to other nodes in the network. Regular networks of equally spaced nodes are often used when automatically generating networks. Arbitrary custom networks are often generated by hand.

Regular Grids

Regular grids, either rectangular or hexagonal, can be used to automatically generate pathfinding networks. The regular spacing makes them easy to both generate algorithmically and determine the connectivity of the nodes. In fact, the connectivity is essentially trivial and does not have to be stored as arbitrary mesh.

Diagram by Per Olin

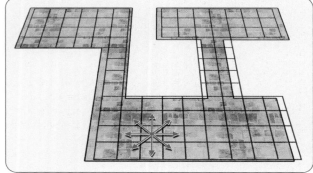

The rectangular structure is a little easier to deal with from a programming standpoint, since a simple two-dimensional array maps exactly to the rectangular mesh, and the coordinates of the mesh positions can be trivially calculated from the row and column indices of the nodes in the two-dimensional array. The hexagonal grid is a little more complicated to deal with, since the computation of the node

In a square grid, the agent can move to one of eight adjacent nodes.

positions involves an offset that changes every other column. However, the hex grid has the advantage of the six adjacent nodes each being equidistant from the current node. Thus, when doing pathfinding the calculations are a bit simpler. The other advantage to using the hex grid is that the grid is visible due to agents being in exact grid positions and moving between grid points. In this case, the movement visible to the player along hex tiles tends to be more regular because each of the tiles is equidistant from the other tiles. Thus,

Diagram by Per Olin

In a hexagonal regular mesh, the agent can move to one of six adjacent nodes.

if the movement along the grid is visible to the player, the hexagonal movement is often more visually pleasing than the rectangular grid. The path resulting when an agent is moving from one position to another on a rectangular grid tends to have a "stair-step" appearance (se diagram below). An agent following the grid from **Start** to **Goal** would move along the yellow squares.

In many 3D games, however, the movement is not locked to the grid. The agent would actually move directly from the goal to the end position, following the straight blue line, since the agent can move arbitrarily in the world and is not constrained to stay on the squares when moving between locations. This movement requires additional processing, since the pathfind search returns the yellow path. It is necessary to perform additional checking along the blue path to make sure that the agent does not clip any obstacles when moving from **Start** to **Goal**. For example, it would not be possible to move directly from **Start** to **Goal2** since the path would intersect an obstacle.

The advantage of the regular grid is that it can be used to automatically generate the pathfinding network. This saves design work because the designer does not have to specify the position of path nodes in order for agents to be able to move. Generally, the information required to create a regular grid is extracted from the level and the mesh is created automatically. This allows a map or level to be tested rapidly and immediately once the basic structures are laid out and the agents are placed into the map or level. This also allows activities such as building

Diagram by Per Olin

An agent can move directly from **Start** to **Goal** following the straight blue line representing the optimized path. When moving from **Start** to **Goal2** the agent cannot follow the dashed line, as it would run into the obstacle.

Warcraft III uses a regular grid for pathfinding.

structures and walls or fences that are barriers to path-finding as part of the strategic gameplay, which requires that the game engine partially rebuild the pathfinding network during play.

The disadvantage of the grid approach is that you end up with a lot of data to process. For example, if you have a large open space, there may be hundreds of positions in the open space that are not particularly interesting but have to be available for pathfinding , consuming memory and increasing processing time during pathfinding.

Arbitrary Grids

The arbitrary mesh nodes are usually placed by hand, which requires that the designer add the nodes to the map or level after the structures have been placed. Systems like the Unreal Engine used in games such as *Unreal 2* and *Swat 4* automatically generate the node connectivity links from the level data. However, the designer may have to add additional connections or forbid certain connections. If the structures are modified, path nodes may have to be modified as well.

Diagram by Per Olin

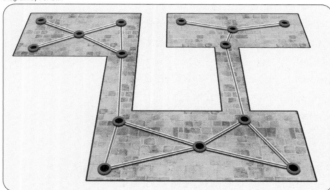

The arbitrary mesh allows nodes to be placed only at important locations, such as in doorways or near cover points.

The advantages of the arbitrary node are two-fold. One advantage is that the position of the nodes can be placed exactly where a path following movement is desired. For example, the center of a doorway is a good spot to put a node. If you have a regular grid, that node may not lie exactly in the center of the doorway. AI agents would tend to move to one side or the other when moving through the door. If you place the nodes manually, the node can be placed exactly in the center. AI agents will tend to move exactly through the center of the doorway.

Another good spot for a node is behind a crate that is good for cover. The designer can specify exactly where that position is behind the crate. In addition, it can be marked as a "cover node" in that it is good for hiding from the player. The second advantage of the arbitrarily place grid is that there is generally less data than a regularly spaced grid. Only the points that are necessary for navigation are specified. This results in a much smaller data set for pathfinding.

Epic Games

Electronic Arts

Unreal Tournament 2007 and *Medal of Honor: Pacific Assault* use an arbitrary grid for pathfinding. The grid is created manually by the level designer.

The drawback of the arbitrary grid is that the node positions and some of the connectivity have to be specified manually by the designer. This means that once a level is created, an additional amount of work needs to be done to insert the pathfinding nodes before the level can be used or tested. Subsequently, the pathfinding nodes may have to be corrected and debugged if the pathfinding behavior produced is not the behavior desired. A hybrid method is to automatically generate an arbitrary grid. This is a much more difficult programming problem than generating the regular grid, since the algorithm must derive the position of interesting nodes, create them, and put them into the map.

The automatically generated grid will not be as accurate as a hand placed grid, so it is necessary to also have tools to adjust the automatically created grid by hand for optimal node placement. Depending on the amount of time for development and programming resources, it may be more efficient to use a manual system for node placement, rather than implementing an automatic system, and a manual system for tuning the automatic placement. For example, Guerilla's *KillZone* creates an arbitrary path mesh automatically. However, the gameplay resulting from the automatic mesh alone is not compelling.

The Challenge of Pathfinding

Pathfinding is a great example of a more mathematical challenge. You look at the room, you look at the character, and how he or she should move through that space is obvious. But put eight of those characters in a room with lots of obstacles and you have a very challenging programming task if you want the game to look good. It's all too easy to turn eight bloodthirsty monsters into a college cheerleading squad that pursues the player in a way that resembles a homecoming parade instead of a ravenous attack.

—*Don L. Daglow (Chief Executive Officer, Stormfront Studios)*

Path Planning

Path planning is the process of determining a destination for an agent. This operation involves examining search algorithms to find the best path from node A to node B in the pathfinding network. In order to do this, we have to provide the search algorithms with node A and node B. Node A is often easy to come up with, since it is usually the node closest to the current location of an agent in the game. Node B is where the agent needs to go. There are two primary requirements that should be handled by path planning. The first is to keep the agents from stacking up at one location, and the second is to minimize the amount of movement required by the agents to reach the goal location.

In most games, agents are not supposed to stack up at the same location or the game would appear to be broken. We need to have some mechanism for representing that a node is occupied by an AI agent (and that no other agents should occupy that same location). There are a variety of mechanisms that can be done in this way. Generally, space is reserved to store in the node information concerning whether an agent is currently positioned at this node.

Marking a location in the pathfinding network "occupied" when an agent is positioned there, and not permitting other agents to move there, prevents the AI from stacking agents up.

Illustration by Per Olin

Stacking agents at the same location is unattractive and confusing to the player.

However, this question arises: If a node is blocked, which node should be used as an alternate destination? The node closest to the agent is the best choice. The agent can follow a shorter, direct path to the closer node. The agent will have to follow a longer path to the node past the blocking agent—if it is possible to get around the blocking agent—and will have to turn sharply to get there. In an RTS game, many agents are unable to fire while moving. Thus, getting to the destination more quickly and being able to fire right away is an important issue for choosing a destination.

Another issue arises when multiple agents are given move orders, either by the AI or by the player. The orders can either be given simultaneously or over a period of time, but are given quickly enough that the movement is not complete before the final order is given. For example, agents 1 and 2 are given an order to move to node A. At the time the order is given, there is no agent at node A. Using our current information, both agents are given an order to move to node A. Agent 2 arrives first, and agent 1 arrives shortly afterwards, stacking on agent 1.

This problem can be solved by adding more information to the pathfinding grid beyond the agents that are occupying the grid. Additionally, an agent can mark a node as its destination that it is moving toward. Agent 1 first marks node A as its destination. Agent 2 executes its path planning and, noting that agent 1 has occupied node A, will choose node B as its destination, using the rule established earlier ("choose the closest empty node"). Good path planning at this point can improve the apparent intelligence of the agents by addressing the following problem:

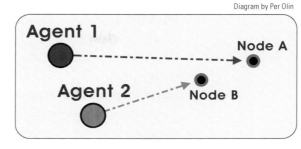

Diagram by Per Olin

Agent 2 selects an alternate destination, node B, to avoid stacking on agent 1.

Agents 1 and 2 are again given the order to move to node A. As before, agent 1 chooses node A, and agent 2 chooses node B. However, in this case agent 2 is in front of agent 1 and will reach node B first. Agent 2 stops and agent 1 runs into agent 2. Agent 1 is not permitted to move through agent 2, so it must stop, turn left, move up, turn right, move, turn right, and move again to get around agent 2. This sequence is slow and awkward in appearance. Agent 1 reaches its final destination much later than agent 2, and all the unnecessary turning around looks awkward. However, if agent 2 moves to node A and agent 1 moves to node B, the result will be a quicker, smoother movement, and both agents will arrive at the same time.

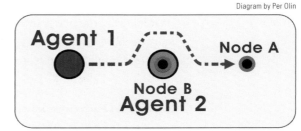

Diagram by Per Olin

Agent 2 stops at node B, forcing agent 1 to turn four times to reach node A.

This occurs when a squad or group of agents are controlled as a group, and directed to move to a destination by the player or AI. A solution to this problem is to sort the agents by distance from the destination. In this case, agent 2 is closer to the goal than agent 1. Agent 2 reserves node A, and agent 1 then selects node B as the destination. Both agents are then able to move to their respective destinations without blocking each other.

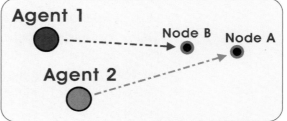

Diagram by Per Olin

Both agents are able to follow a direct path to their respective goals.

Path Searching

At this point we have a network. Now we are able to consider *path searching*, finding a path between two nodes. At this point, one agent is at one node and either the game or the player has indicated that the agent has to move to another node in the pathfinding network. How do we find the best path through the pathfinding network? In order to answer this, we need to define what we mean by "best." Frequently, "best" is considered either the shortest *distance* (if the agent generally moves at the same speed) or the shortest *time* to cross the path (if the agent has different speeds depending on different aspects of the map). Terrain can sometimes affect an agent's speed; for example, muddy terrain causes the vehicles to move more slowly than they do on pavement. A soldier may be able to swim, but much slower than he can run on land. Thus, the shortest path may be measured in distance or time, depending on what the design of the game indicates is the best choice. Given that we want the best path and we have decided whether it is the fastest or the shortest path, how do we find it?

Table Lookup

The most efficient way to find the shortest path is to do a *table lookup,* where we have a table for all the nodes in the game level. Table lookup is appropriate for relatively static levels with less than 1,000 path nodes. First person levels with manually placed path nodes fall into this category. We will look at a small network with eight nodes.

Our eight-node network would require an 8 × 8 table. Each node in the mesh would have an entry for the other eight nodes that would contain the node that should be moved next in order to reach the goal node.

In order to get from node H to node B, for example we would look at node entry FROM H TO B. This entry is node A, so the path is from H to A. (Note that the entry in FROM H TO A is A.) Next, we would look at node entry FROM A TO B. This entry is node C, so the path is H to A to C. Looking at FROM C TO B, the entry is node B, and we have arrived at the end of the path. From the table lookup, we can access the complete path from node H to node B:

```
H -> A -> C -> B
```

Diagram by Per Olin

The complete pathfinding information for a path network with eight nodes can be stored in an 8 × 8 table.

The advantage of using the table lookup is that it is extremely fast—potentially hundreds of times faster than doing a search through the network to find the path. The table can be generated using *Dijkstra's algorithm*, described later in this chapter, once for each node in the network.

There are two drawbacks of the table lookup method. First, the table size is the square of the number of nodes in the pathfinding grid. This is of reasonable size if there are 250 or fewer nodes, taking about 64k of memory. However, 2,000 path nodes would require 8MB of data, which may be excessive. Large RTS maps with auto-generated grids can have up to 80,000 nodes. The table for a grid this size would be several gigabytes in size, so the table lookup is clearly unsuited for such large auto-generated grids. This problem could be addressed by using a hierarchical data structure with fewer nodes in the top level network, so that even with a large number of nodes, the table lookup may be applicable at the hierarchical level.

To From	A	B	C	D	E	F	G	H
A	X	C	C	C	C	H	H	H
B	C	X	C	C	C	C	C	C
C	A	B	X	D	E	D	D	A
D	C	C	C	X	E	F	F	F
E	C	C	C	D	X	D	D	C
F	G	D	D	D	D	X	G	G
G	H	H	H	F	F	F	X	H
H	A	A	A	G	A	G	G	X

This table contains the pathfinding information for the eight-node network.

The second drawback is that the table must be pre-computed; it takes too long to generate the table interactively. It is best done in the level editor before saving the level; this way, it does not impact level load time. Efforts are in progress to use streaming to minimize or eliminate load times, so it would be counter-productive to add additional computation. For this reason, the pathfinding network has to be relatively static. The straightforward implementation of this requires that the game design does not need the pathfinding grid to change at all. It is possible to extend this so that several pre-computed tables are generated and saved with the level. This would allow the pathfinding to change once or twice. For example, a level could contain a blocked-off area that is revealed, producing a second pathfinding mesh. Perhaps a third area could also be revealed, producing a third pathfinding mesh. It would then be necessary to perform a total of three table generation operations and to store three pathfinding tables, which may be practical.

Gameplay involving frequent or player-controlled modifications to the pathfinding grid make the use of the table impractical. In a strategy game such as *Kohan II*, the player can build structures throughout the game. The structures would then block of an area in the pathfinding grid and change the node connectivity, invalidating the table data. Many games, such as *Half-Life 2* and *Halo 2*, do not include a way to build structures or other methods that permit the player to affect the pathfinding network. In these cases, the pathfinding network is relatively static, and pre-computing the network connectivity may be a good mechanism to have available for pathfinding.

Diagram by Per Olin

Pathfinding: allowing agents to properly find and follow paths

chapter 6

In *Kohan II: Kings of War,* structures built by players throughout the game may block off areas in the pathfinding grid, thereby changing node connectivity. In *Half-Life 2,* players are not able to build structures and cannot affect the pathfinding network.

An issue that can preclude the exclusive use of the table lookup is the existence of events that can temporarily modify the pathfinding network. One example would be doors that can be opened or closed. A few doors could be handled by pre-computing multiple tables, but as the number of doors increases, this solution becomes unworkable. A second condition is when other agents block the process of an agent. For example, if two or three allied, enemy, or neutral agents are occupying a corridor, it may not possible for the player character to pass through the corridor. The path using the table would take the agent through this corridor, when in this case it would be preferred to find a path around this corridor. One solution is to use a combination of the table and a search algorithm. If the path from the table is open, use it. If it is blocked, perform a search. The A* search described later requires a good estimate of the shortest path to the goal, and the table can be used to provide a very accurate estimate.

Search Algorithms

There are several criteria we require from *search algorithms* used in pathfinding:

1. If a path exists, the algorithm must find it.
2. If multiple paths exist, the algorithm must find the best path.
3. If no path exists, the algorithm should terminate and return that information rather than searching forever.
4. The algorithm must be efficient.

Considering the path network shown in the accompanying diagram, we would expect the following: There is a single path from node I to node K. When searching for a path from node I to node K, the algorithm would return the path:

I → J → K

Multiple paths exist from node B to node G. Let us look at three possible paths:

Path 1: B → C → A → H → G
Path 2: B → C → D → F → G
Path 3: B → C → D → E → C → A → H → G

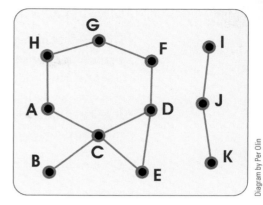

This network contains two connected sub-networks: nodes A through H, and nodes I through K.

Paths 1 and 2 are acceptable paths, but path 3 is unacceptable. Even though path 3 does successfully go from node B to node G, it loops through the same node (C) twice and is much longer than paths 1 and 2.

Let us examine the following search algorithms:

- *Breadth first search* is straightforward, but it is not efficient, nor does it always return the best path. As such, it is not suitable for use in games.
- *Dijkstra's algorithm* is a modification of breadth first search that always returns the best path. In some cases with video games it is the best algorithm to use, but it is not always the most efficient algorithm.
- *Best first search* is a very efficient algorithm, but it does not always return the best path. Best first search works well with convex obstacles, and can be used if the game design restricts the shape of obstacles.
- *A* search*, when used with an appropriate heuristic, will perform a more efficient search and will always return the best path.

Breadth First Search

A good search algorithm to start with is known as a *breadth first search*, which tends to find a short path because it examines nodes closer in the network first. (*Depth first search* examines distant nodes first, which tends to find the longest path possible, rather than the shortest.) Breadth first search is implemented using a *queue data structure*. A queue is a first in, first out list. By adding nodes A, C, and E, the queue consists of ACE. By removing the first node, the queue is CE. After adding D and F, the queue contains CEDF.

Diagram by Per Olin

Marking Nodes

The pathfinding network is a graph with cycles, rather than a tree. A cycle means players can traverse the network and end up back where they started. As we have noted earlier, a path with a loop in it (the B → C → D → E → C → A → H → G path above) is not desirable. So we will want to avoid cycles in our search. This can be done by marking nodes as "visited" in the search. Unvisited nodes are normal text, F, and visited nodes are bold italic, *F*.

The breadth first search is as follows:

```
Mark all nodes as not visited.
Mark startNode visited.
Add the start node to the queue.
WHILE (queue is not empty)
BEGIN
 Remove currentNode from queue.
 FOR EACH nextNode connected to currentNode
 BEGIN
     IF (nextNode is not visited)
     BEGIN
         Mark nextNode visited.
         IF (nextNode is goalNode) TERMINATE WITH SUCCESS
         Add nextNode to queue.
     END
 END
END
TERMINATE WITH FAILURE
```

Successful Search

A successful breadth search from B to G would work as follows:

At the start, ABCDEFGH queue is empty.

After adding start node to queue A*B*CDEF, queue *B*.

The first time through the loop, we remove B from the queue and examine B's neighbors. The only neighbor is C, and it is not visited, so it is marked "visited" and added to the queue.

A*BC*DEFGH, queue *C*

The second time through the loop, we remove C from the queue and examine C's neighbors. A is not visited, so it is marked "visited" and added to the queue. B is visited, so it is skipped. D and E are both not visited, so they are marked "visited" and added to the queue.

*ABCDE*FGH, `queue` *ADE*

The third time through the loop, we remove A, and add H.

ABCDEFGH, `queue` *DEH*

The fourth time through the loop, remove D, add F.

ABCDEFGH, `queue` *EHF*

The fifth time through the loop, remove E, add nothing.

ABCDEFGH, `queue` *HF*

The sixth time through the loop, we remove H. After examining H's neighbors, we find that A is already visited, so it is skipped. G is the goal node, so we have succeeded in finding a path to G.

Unsuccessful Search

Searching from node B to node J will be unsuccessful, as there is no path in the network. This search will be the same as the search from B to G for the first five iterations through the loop, resulting in:

ABCDEFGH, `queue` *HF*

The sixth time through the loop, remove H, add G.

ABCDEFGH, `queue` *FG*

The seventh time through the loop, remove F. Both F's neighbors, D and G, have been visited, so add nothing to the queue.

ABCDEFGH, `queue` *G*

The eighth time through the loop, remove G. Both G's neighbors, F and H, have been visited, so add nothing to the queue.

ABCDEFGH, `queue` empty

At this point the queue is empty, and the result of the search is that there is no path between B and J.

Returning the Path (Parent Link)

After the successful search, we will want to return the path. We can do this by storing at each node a parent pointer as we do our search, and walking backwards to find the path. The algorithm is modified as follows:

```
IF (nextNode is not visited)
BEGIN
    Mark nextNode visited
    Set nextNode's parent to currentNode
    IF (nextNode is goalNode) TERMINATE WITH SUCCESS
    Add nextNode to queue
END
```

Using the lowercase letter to indicate a parent node: node B with a parent node C would be Bc. In the successful search above, the network and queue would be:

```
A B C D E F G H queue B
A B Cb D E F G H queue Cb
Ac B Cb Dc Ec F G H queue AcDcEc
Ac B Cb Dc Ec F G Ha queue DcEcHa
Ac B Cb Dc Ec Fd G Ha queue EcHaFd
Ac B Cb Dc Ec Fd G Ha queue HaFd
Ac B Cb Dc Ec Fd Gh Ha queue Fd
```

We would then start with node G and work backwards. Gh takes us to Ha, which takes us to Ac, which takes us to Cb, which takes us to B. We have our path backwards, GHACB. Reversing it gives us the final path, BCAHG.

Evaluation

Breadth first search is a good starting point, since it is a straightforward algorithm and meets *some* of our criteria. Let us revisit the four search algorithm criteria:

1. *If a path exists, the algorithm must find it.*
2. *If multiple paths exist, the algorithm must find the best path.*
3. *If no path exists, the algorithm should terminate and return that information rather than searching forever.*
4. *The algorithm must be efficient.*

Breadth first search meets criteria 1 and 3, but not 2 and 4. The algorithm does gain some efficiency by stopping the search as soon as the goal node is encountered. Stopping before we traverse the entire network reduces the amount of computation required. Although the first path to the goal node found in breadth first search requires the fewest steps through the network, it is not necessarily the shortest path. Consider the network illustrated in the accompanying diagram.

In this network, the breadth first search from node D to node G will return D → F → G. This is the path with the fewest number of network connections. However, this path is actually longer than path D → C → A → H → G, even though it takes four network connections, rather than two. This disparity in connection distance can arise easily when nodes are placed by hand. Even in automatically generated square grids, the diagonal node distances are longer than the orthogonal node distances. In addition, terrain can change the effective cost of following one path over another. If there is swampy ground that prevents the use of a vehicle in a game, the "longer" path around the swamp may be the lowest cost path. In order to be sure that there is not a shorter path that we will encounter farther along in the search, we must continue searching after having found a path to the goal node.

The distance between nodes is variable; the distance from G to F is more than twice as far than the distance from G to H.

Dijkstra's Algorithm

Dijkstra's algorithm is a variation of breadth first search that has the additional property that the first path found to a destination node is guaranteed to be the best path because there are no shorter paths possible in the network. At this point, we can then stop the search, knowing that there will be no better path possible.

We will implement a variation of Dijkstra's algorithm by making two modifications to the breadth first search algorithm. First, Dijkstra's algorithm uses a *priority queue*. A simple queue, as we discussed earlier, returns elements in the same order in which they were added, but a priority queue associates a value with each element and returns either the smallest value or the largest value among the elements in the queue. In this case, we will use the smallest value for our priority queue. The value assigned a node is the sum of the distance (cost) of the links taken to get to the node.

```
Mark all nodes not visited
Mark startNode visited
startNode.dist = 0
Add startNode to priorityQueue
WHILE (queue not empty)
BEGIN
    currentNode = RemoveSmallest(priorityQueue)
    IF (currentNode is goalNode) TERMINATE WITH SUCCESS
    FOR EACH nextNode connected to currentNode
     BEGIN
     curDistance = Distance(currentNode, nextNode)
     IF (nextNode is not visited) THEN
        BEGIN
        Mark nextNode visited
        nextNode.dist = curDistance + currentNode.dist
        nextNode.parent = currentNode
        Add nextNode to priorityQueue
        END
     ELSE
        BEGIN
        if (curDistance+currentNode.distance<nextNode.distance)
        THEN BEGIN
            nextNode.dist = curDistance + currentNode.dist
            nextNode.parent = currentNode
            END
        END
     END
END
TERMINATE WITH FAILURE
```

We will extend the notation used with the breadth first search to include the distance. Ac15 is node A, with a parent node of C, and the total distance to A from the starting node is 15 units.

At the start, the nodes are marked as "not visited," with no parent node, and the queue is empty.

```
A B C D E F G H I J K
```

The starting node, G, is given a distance value of 0, marked "visited," and added to the queue.

```
A B C D E F G0 H I J K, queue G0
```

The first time through the loop, G is removed from the queue and is currentNode. The nodes connected to G are examined. G is examined first, and is nextNode, and the distance from G to F is 20, so curDistance is 20. F is not visited, so F is marked "visited," its parent set to G, F.dist set to curDistance + G.dist, or 20+0, resulting in Node Fg20. F is added to the priority queue.

A B C D E *Fg*20 *G*0 H I J K queue *Fg*20

The other node connected to G (Node H) is examined. H is nextNode, and the distance from G to H is 8, so curDistance is 8. H is not visited, its parent is set to G, H.dist is set to curDistance + G.dist, or 8+0, resulting in Node Hg8. H is added to the priority queue.

A B C D E *Fg*20 *G*0 *Hg*8 I J K queue *Hg*8 *Fg*20

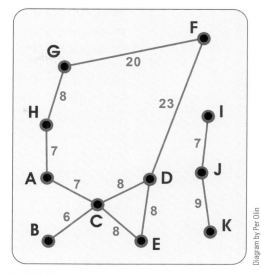

Each link in the network has a distance value. Dijkstra's algorithm uses the distance values to find the shortest path.

Note the first difference between Dijkstra's search and breadth first search. The priority queue returns the node with the smallest distance value. So Node H is in the front of the queue, although it was added after Node F.

The next time through the loop, H is removed from the queue and its neighbors are examined. Node A is examined first. A is nextNode, the distance from H to A is 7, so curDistance is 7. A has not been visited, so its parent is set to H, A.dest is set to curDistance + H.dist, or 7+8, resulting in Ah15. Node A is added to the queue. Again, note the behavior of the priority queue in that A is at the front of the queue even though it was added after F.

*Ah*15 B C D E *Fg*20 *G*0 *Hg*8 I J K queue *Ah*15 *Fg*20

Node G is examined second, so nextNode is G. The distance from H to G is 8, so curDistance is 8. Node G has already been visited, so we execute the ELSE, and compare curDistance + H.dist to G.dist. Basically, we are comparing the length of the path GHG to the path G. The test fails, as the 15 is not less than 0, so we make no change to node G. The network and queue are unchanged.

The next time through the loop, A is removed from the queue and its neighbors examined. Node C is examined first, and has not been visited. Since curDistance from A to C is 7, C.dist is set to A.dist+curDistance, or 15+7, and C is marked visited, its parent is set to node A, and Ca22 is placed in the queue.

*Ah*15 B *Ca*22 D E *Fg*20 *G*0 *Hg*8 I J K queue *Fg*20 *Ca*22

Node H is examined, but it has already been visited, and the curDistance+currentNode.distance<nextNode.distance test fails, so no change is made to node H.

Next, F is removed from the queue. Node D is examined first. Although D is the goal node, we do not stop at this point (unlike the previous breadth first search). The parent node is F, which would result in a path GFD, which is not the shortest path. So we mark D "visited," set D.dist to F.dist+curDistance, or 20+23, set the parent to F, and put D in the queue.

*Ah*15 B *Ca*22 *Df*43 E *Fg*20 *G*0 *Hg*8 I J K queue *Ca*22 *Df*43

Node G is examined, but it has already been visited and the distance test fails. No change is made.

The next time through the loop, node C is removed from the queue and its neighbors examined. A is examined first. It is already visited, and the distance test fails. B is examined next. B has not been visited, so it is marked, its parent is set, and B is placed in the queue.

*Ah*15 *Bc*28 *Ca*22 *Df*43 E *Fg*20 *G*0 *Hg*8 I J K queue *Bc*28 *Df*43

D is examined next, so nextNode is D. The distance from C to D is 8, so curDistance is 8. Node D has already been visited, so we execute the ELSE and compare curDistance + C.dist to D.dist. Effectively, we are comparing the length of the path GHACD to the path GFD. In this case, curDistance+C.dist, or the length of GHACD, is 30. This is less than D.dist, which corresponds to the length of the path GFD. In this case the IF test succeeds, so we set the parent of node D to C, rather than F. D.dist is also set to curDistance+C.dist, or 30. This behavior, combined with the use of the priority queue, is how Dijkstra's algorithm guarantees that the shortest path will be found. The resulting network and queue are:

*Ah*15 *Bc*28 *Ca*22 *Dc*30 E *Fg*20 *G*0 *Hg*8 I J K queue *Bc*28 *Dc*30

Node E is examined last, and it is added to the queue.

*Ah*15 *Bc*28 *Ca*22 *Dc*30 *Ec*30 *Fg*20 *G*0 *Hg*8 I J K queue *Bc*28 *Dc*30 *Ec*30

Next, B is removed from the queue. The only neighbor, C, has already been visited and fails the distance comparison, resulting in:

*Ah*15 *Bc*28 *Ca*22 *Dc*30 *Ec*30 *Fg*20 *G*0 *Hg*8 I J K queue *Dc*30 *Ec*30

Finally, node D is removed from the queue. At this point, we can stop the search since we have found the shortest path from G to D. We also have the length of the path, 30. By following the parent nodes, we go Dc Ca Ah Hg G. Reversing the order, the final path is GHACD. The length of this path, 30, is shorter than the earlier path encountered (GFD, which was 43 in length). Note that we can stop searching, even though there may be additional possible paths from G to D. There is in fact another path, GHACED. However, due to the use of the priority queue, we know that any additional path will be at least 30 or longer, as node D would not have reached the front of the priority queue otherwise.

Using Dijkstra's Algorithm to Build a Path Table

There are several useful properties of Dijkstra's algorithm in addition to finding the shortest path. First is that it also provides the length of the path. In addition, it is possible to use Dijkstra's algorithm to find the shortest path to any node in the network from a given starting node. This is done by continuing the loop until the priority queue is empty. When this is complete, each node visited will contain the shortest distance to the starting node, and the shortest path can be determined by following the parent links to the starting node. This produces a row of data for the path table, so repeating the algorithm once using each node in the network will produce the entire pathfinding table.

Evaluation

Dijkstra's algorithm meets the first three criteria perfectly. 1: If a path exists, the algorithm will find it. 2: If multiple paths exist, it will find a shortest path. 3: If no paths exist, it will terminate and indicate this condition. It is reasonably efficient, in that we can stop searching as soon as we get a goal node from the queue; it is not necessary to continue searching. Dijkstra's algorithm is the best choice for searching in several situations in video game AI programming. The first situation is when we do not have a specific location for a goal, but rather a condition that the goal must meet. An example of this situation is when an agent is low on health and is pathfinding to the nearest health pickup. Dijkstra's algorithm can be used to search, and the first node from the queue that is adjacent to a health pickup provides the agent with the shortest path to that pickup. The second situation in which Dijkstra's algorithm is the best is when teleportation is possible. The only requirement of Dijkstra's algorithm is that the length of connections between nodes be non-negative. So a teleportation device that creates a link to a distant receiver, effectively zero distance, is valid for Dijkstra's algorithm, and it will still find the shortest path, taking teleportation into account.

Improving Efficiency

If we know our destination, and agents are not allowed to teleport instantaneously from one place to another, we can use this information to improve the efficiency of Dijkstra's algorithm. Let us take a look at a larger search using Dijkstra's algorithm. We will use a rectangular grid network, similar to what would be used in a real-time strategy (RTS) game such as *Warcraft III*. In this case, we know the starting and ending points for the search.

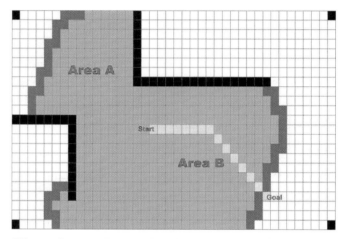

This search was performed using Dijkstra's algorithm with SmallSampleMap.txt

Square Grid Networks Using Pathfind.exe

The previous diagram of a search of a square grid network using Dijkstra's algorithm was produced by Pathfind.exe, which is included on the companion DVD. Pathfind.exe performs Dijkstra's algorithm, best first and A* search interactively. The previous example is done using the SmallSampleMap.txt data file. You can perform different search algorithms using the searching menu. Different start and goal nodes can be selected using the mouse. Click the start node, hold the mouse button down, and drag to the end node. Releasing the mouse button will start the search. The speed of the interactive search can be controlled using the draw speed menu. Additional documentation and the source code are available on the DVD. Notation: The white nodes are nodes that are clear, and can be traversed. The black nodes are walls that block agents. Green nodes are visited nodes. Blue nodes are nodes in the queue. The start and goal nodes are yellow, and when the path is found the path is marked yellow as well.

Looking at the results of Dijkstra's algorithm, we see three interesting results. First, it found a shortest path to the goal, of length 14. Second, it terminated before exhaustively searching the network. Of 920 nodes, it visited 489. This is better than a search of all 920 nodes. However, 489 nodes is a large number of nodes through which to search for a path of length 14. In particular, since Dijkstra's algorithm examines nodes based only on their proximity to the start point, a number of nodes are examined above and left of the start point in Area A. As noted before, Dijkstra's algorithm works with any network and correctly handles exceptional conditions such as teleporters. However, if the network corresponds to a real-world network, such as series of locations on a map, we can tell intuitively that the nodes in area B are more likely to be on the shortest path as they are closer to the destination than the nodes in area A.

The next two search algorithms are based on our ability to quickly estimate how close a node is to the goal. In the case of a two- or three-dimensional grid, the straight line distance serves as a good estimate. If an agent is standing at a location 100 feet from the goal, the path to the goal will be at least 100 feet long (and longer if there are obstacles in the straight line path). We can use the straight line distance as a *heuristic* to estimate the distance to the goal.

Best First Search

Best first search uses the estimated distance to the goal instead of the distance from the starting point. This results in a very efficient search, since the nodes closest to the goal are examined first, minimizing the number of nodes examined. However, obstacles can cause the best first search to double back, returning a zig-zag path that is clearly not the best path. This occurs primarily when concave obstacles are present. A room with a door is a concave obstacle, so best first search is not suitable for a game taking place in a building. Best first search may be suitable in cases where extremely efficient searching is required, such as on a hand-held game with limited processing power. In this case, the game design can be constrained to avoid convex obstacles. The resulting paths returned by best first search are reasonable, if not the best possible. Dijkstra's algorithm sorts nodes based on the actual distance from the start. Best first search sorts nodes based on the estimated distance to the goal. It is possible to combine the actual distance and the estimate to search efficiently, and find the best path.

A* Search

The A* (the asterisk is pronounced as "star") algorithm is a combination of Dijkstra's algorithm and the best first search that results in an algorithm that meets all four of our requirements. The first path A* finds is the shortest path, allowing the search to terminate immediately without examining additional nodes. Early termination of the search increases the efficiency of the search considerably. A* also uses a distance heuristic to push the search toward the goal. This results in a more efficient search than Dijkstra's algorithm.

The A* algorithm is similar to Dijkstra's algorithm, but uses slightly different terminology. The priority queue is referred to as the open list. Nodes that are visited but are not in the open list are placed in a list called the closed list. The set of nodes in either the open or closed list are the same as the visited nodes in the preceding adaptation of Dijkstra's algorithm. The closed list is a simple list that allows insertion and removal of elements.

The A* algorithm uses the same information as Dijkstra's algorithm, plus the estimate of the distance to the goal used by best first search. The value used in the open list (priorityQueue) is the actual cost to get to the current node from the start node, plus the estimate of the distance to the goal node.

The Estimate (node, goalNode) estimates the cost from node to the goal node. In this example we will use the Euclidean line length, sqrt(sqr(deltax)+sqr(deltay)) as the estimate.

```
startNode.distFromStart = 0
startNode.estimateToGoal = Estimate(startNode, goalNode)
Add startNode to priorityQueue.
WHILE (priorityQueue not empty)
BEGIN
 currentNode = RemoveSmallest(priorityQueue)
 Add currentNode to closedList
 IF (currentNode is goalNode) TERMINATE WITH SUCCESS
 FOR EACH nextNode connected to currentNode
    BEGIN
    curDistance = Distance(currentNode, nextNode)
    IF (nextNode not in openList AND nextNode not in closedList) THEN
        BEGIN /* Section 1 */
        nextNode.dist = curDistance + currentNode.dist
        nextNode.estimate = Estimate(nextNode, goalNode)
        nextNode.totalCost = nextNode.dist + nextNode.estimate;
        nextNode.parent = currentNode
        Add nextNode to priorityQueue using nextNode.totalCost
        END
    ELSE
        BEGIN /* Section 2 */
        if (curDistance+currentNode.dist<nextNode.dist)
        THEN BEGIN
        nextNode.dist = curDistance + currentNode.dist
        nextNode.parent = currentNode
                nextNode.totalCost = nextNode.dist +
                                        nextNode.estimate;
```

```
      IF (nextNode is in openList)
          Remove nextNode from openList
      IF (nextNode is in closedList)
          Remove nextNode from closedList
      Add nextNode to openList


          END
      END
    END
END
TERMINATE WITH FAILURE
```

A* Details

The companion DVD contains a step-by-step description of the execution of the A* algorithm, as well as the example program that performs A* interactively. The source code of the A* implementation is available as well.

Evaluation

A* is a search algorithm that combines the efficiency of the best first search while also guaranteeing to find the shortest path (similar to Dijkstra's algorithm). In the following example of SmallSampleMap.txt, Dijkstra's algorithm searched 552 nodes to find a path of length 30. Best first search only examined 164 nodes; however, the path found was of length 40. A*, in the accompanying diagram, found a path of length 30, but it only examined 170 nodes. This is more efficient than Dijkstra's algorithm, but still finds the best path.

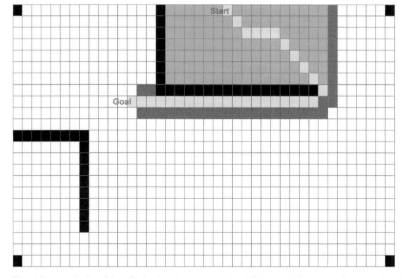

The A* search algorithm finds the shortest path while examining a smaller number of nodes than Dijkstra's algorithm.

We use an estimate of the distance from a node to a goal node in A*. The accuracy of the estimate will vary depending on the layout of the network and the method we use to make the estimate. One good question is whether A* will always find the shortest path. The answer is yes, if the estimate meets certain requirements. Otherwise A* may not find the shortest path. Estimates that meet the condition are called admissible. The requirement that estimates for A* must meet is that the estimate of the distance between any two nodes must be less than or equal to the actual distance of the shortest path between the nodes.

One simple admissible estimate is 0. This is always shorter than the actual path. If we use 0 for the estimate, A* has the same behavior as Dijkstra's algorithm, which is also guaranteed to find the shortest path. It is also no more efficient than Dijkstra's algorithm.

The Euclidean line length is admissible if we are considering the shortest physical distance. In the absence of obstacles this is a good estimate. When concave obstacles are present it is not as good an estimate, and A* will search more nodes, although it will still find the shortest path.

An estimate that is exactly equal to the path length will result in an extremely efficient A* search. In general practice, that requires pre-computing a path table. As we discussed earlier, the size of the node network may preclude this, in which case the line length estimate is preferable. The line length estimate does not work in the case in which there are teleportation pads. In this case, either a pre-computed path table must be generated, or Dijkstra's algorithm must be used.

Path Following

Once we have chosen a goal location and performed a search, our agent has a path to follow. The major challenge with path following is other AI agents present and moving in the environment. The reason is that the pathfinding node networks cannot take moving agents into account when finding a path. The pathfind code is aware of where agents currently are, but has no way of knowing where they will be in the future. So it is possible (and in many games likely) that when an agent is moving, either another stationary agent will have blocked its path, or two agents may both be moving and will collide.

In most games, an agent is not allowed to move through another agent. It tends to ruin the illusion of a real 3D world.

Ships overlapping each other break the appearance of a realistic world in *Age of Empires III*—while agents block a path in *Warcraft III*.

This is not an absolute rule, depending on the game. For example, the *Age of Empires* series allows the agents to move through each other when going to a particular location. But in many cases, particularly with games that use more visual realism (such as *Command & Conquer, Warcraft,* and most first-person shooters such as *Half-Life 2* and *Halo 2),* it is not acceptable for agents to move through one another. As a result, it is not uncommon to have an agent blocking a path.

Agent 1 wishes to move to node C, but is blocked by agent 2. Normally agent 1 would move from node A to node B, then node C. The agent cannot move through agent 2 at node B, so we have to do something different. There are several techniques that can be used to address this.

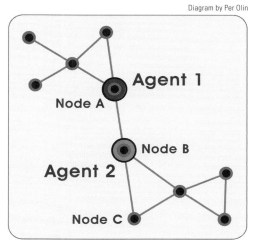

Agent 1 is blocked by Agent 2 on the way to node C.

Leave Space Between Agents

The easiest solution is to space our pathfinding nodes sufficiently far apart so that there is enough room for an agent to go around an agent at a particular node. This can be very effective in the case where the game consists of agents that are of a relatively fixed size and are reasonably small. For example, if the agents are humanoid it is reasonable for them to stand spaced apart, not touching shoulder to shoulder. In this case there is enough room for the agents to move between or around other agents.

When the agent is moving from node A to node C, the agent can move around the agent at node B and get to node C. In this case it is very simple and straightforward from the pathfinding standpoint in that node B is still passable, even though there is an agent there and we cannot use it as a goal location. The agent can use node B; we just need to keep track of whether there is another agent occupying it. Agent 1 can adjust its path by curving around the node; it will not run through agent 2 at node B.

This solution is dependent on the design of the game. If there are relatively small agents whose spacing can be made reasonably broad so that other agents can move in between them this works extremely well. It works well with human agents; even in a crowded nightclub, there is enough room to move between people. It does not work well in cases where you have larger agents—tanks or cars, for example. Spacing tanks far enough that you can drive another tank in between them looks odd, and makes it very difficult to get the tanks into firing range to attack an enemy structure. The tanks need to line up relatively close together in order to get into a firing arc. With most vehicles, the extra spacing is not acceptable.

Diagram by Per Olin

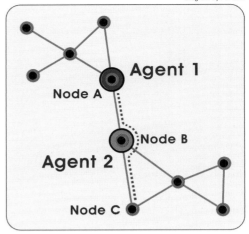

Agent 1 can follow the dashed path around agent 2 if there is enough space.

Electronic Arts

The tanks in *Command & Conquer: Generals* are spaced close together to maximize the firepower that can be applied to the target.

Path Around Other Agents

A method that works in the case where you cannot leave enough space between agents is to have additional pathfinding nodes in the area so that there are multiple paths through an area. The node that is occupied by the other agent can be marked as impassable, causing the path search algorithm to find a path around the agent.

Problems arise with this scheme, however, when there are more then a few agents. For example, if you have got a squad-based party with five agents, one player, and four non-player characters (NPCs) or a real-time strategy game where you have a squad of tanks, even with multiple path nodes around a particular area it is not difficult to get an area blocked off by a number of agents.

Agent A wishes to get to path node B in order to pick up a crate. The crate contains a level up, gold, or another object that the agent needs. Or, in the case of the player the player wants to level up his character. All of the available nodes to get to the path are blocked by agents. How do we get to this crate?

Assume No Path Exists

A solution of last resort is to simply treat the path as blocked. The pathfind fails and the agent cannot get to the destination. If the squad is player-controlled, the player is required to move one of the other agents out of the way, and then try again. In the case of an AI agent, the move fails, and with luck the AI waits and tries again later, after one of the blocking agents has moved.

Request Agents to Move

A solution that results in a better player experience is to request that one of the agents blocking the path moves out of the way. The advantage of this is that the player or AI agent's request to move succeeds. The disadvantage is that additional coding is required and this behavior complicates the pathfinding quite a bit. First, in order to know that we need to move an agent out of the way to get to our goal we have to determine that the path goes through the agent. In order to do this we can no longer simply consider a node that is occupied as blocked. If it is blocked then the path will not go through it and we will not know we need to move the agent in order to get through there. So we have to modify our pathfinding to allow movement through agents.

At the same time if there is a path around the agent, we do not want to go through it. So one mechanism that we can use for this is to make an adjustment to the cost to move through the occupied node rather then making it blocked. Setting the cost approximately three to five times the normal cost to move through the node will allow the agent to move around the blocking agent if there is room to either side. However, if the path is blocked and there are no alternative paths, the shortest path will be the path through the blocking agent. The A* search will eventually find the path through the agent, although it will search other possible paths first because we have artificially raised the cost of this node.

At this point, the path search has returned a path, and we can examine the path and note that the path goes through agent 2. At this point, we can direct agent 2 to move out of the way. It is useful to pass agent 1's path to agent 2 so that the latter moves far enough to be off the path. It would not be very useful if agent 2 moved to node C.

When an agent moves from its position so that another agent can pass, it seems that it might be a good idea to move it back after the first agent has passed by. However, this tends to be a bad idea because you have the potential for setting up a perpetual "bumble bee dance" activity where one agent will request that another agent move. When moving back, the second agent may need the first agent to move. It may take three or four movements before all agents settle in their destinations. This appears chaotic and is not expected by the player. If a player needs the moved unit adjusted back, the player can move it. If the AI needs the agent to be in a different position for attacking or other reasons, the AI will generate that request as well as subsequent updates.

Moving blocking agents requires you to be careful when the agent being moved is doing something important. When an agent is attacking and firing a weapon it is inappropriate for another agent to direct the attacking agent to move out of the way. It disrupts the attack, causes the other agent to take damage, and is generally a problem. Therefore, another important polishing and tuning behavior needed for the AI is to determine when it is appropriate for an agent to request another agent move out of the way. In *Command & Conquer: Generals,* the AI was implemented so that if the other agent was idle or guarding a particular spot it could be requested to move. When the agent was actively attacking or performing another task the AI would not ask it to move out of the way because it would disrupt the agent from performing its task. Building structures was another task where it was important that the agent not be interrupted. In these cases, if an agent needed to get through the agent building structures it would fail. It was more important that the blocking agent complete the task that it was performing.

Bad pathfinding is obvious, with the game stuttering and agents moving oddly or failing to get where they are going. Good pathfinding does not bring attention to itself. The agents move smoothly where they are supposed to go, and none get "stuck." Good pathfinding requires several systems. First, it requires a network so that the agents have somewhere to go. Next, it requires an appropriate search algorithm to find short paths through the network. Finally, good pathfinding requires a system to take the player and other agents into account so that they do not get stuck when a route is blocked. All three need to work well together to create high quality pathfinding. Some games, with large networks, many agents, or both, may require the use of additional techniques to achieve high quality pathfinding. We will look at some of those techniques in the next chapter.

:::CHAPTER REVIEW:::

1. A useful feature in a game is the automatic generation of an arbitrary mesh. This is a challenging problem. One technique to overcome this problem is to create a regular mesh and then remove redundant nodes. Specify a set of rules for removing redundant nodes. Would your rules create a minimal set of nodes? Is there any situation that would cause your rules to remove a necessary node?

2. In this chapter's examples both Dijkstra's algorithm and A* use the distance between nodes to find the shortest path. In some games it may be preferable to follow a longer path along a road around a field, rather than taking the shortcut across a field. However, if the destination is in the field, or there is no road, the agent can move through the field. What would be a way to adjust the distance values used in the searches to cause the search to follow the road instead of cutting across the field? Would this still allow the agent to find a path to a node inside the field?

3. The table lookup method cannot be used if the path network changes—for example, if a door is closed, or a hallway is blocked. The A* algorithm can find paths in a dynamic network, but it works best with a good estimate of the distance to the goal. Design a system where a table is used to generate a good estimate of the distance to the goal for the A* algorithm. Would this estimate be admissible?

4. In some cases, such as hand-held games, processing and memory are extremely limited. The best first algorithm is very efficient in both areas. Design a layout of obstacles that would produce reasonable pathfinding using the best first algorithm. What types of games would be able to use this sort of layout in order to maximize efficiency?

Part III: Advanced Topics & Applications

Bigger Is Better

Large, complex pathfind networks are a part of modern video games. Although consoles and personal computer hardware are much faster than they were a few years ago, cutting edge games always push the hardware and programming to their limits. It is important to avoid delays and unexpected pauses in the game. Pre-computing zone information allows us to quickly avoid path searches that are both time-consuming and ultimately unsuccessful. Zone equivalency arrays allow us to store this information efficiently for multiple terrain types, such as water, ground, and cliffs. This information quickly tells us whether agents with different capabilities, such as boats, infantry, or hovercraft, can reach a particular location.

Often multiple agents will have to move to the same location. Sharing the same path search is very efficient, but can lead to undesirable behavior, such as antlining. Creating offset paths can correct this behavior, but the path search must consider the spacing of the path from obstacles.

Dividing long paths into a series of shorter paths is a technique that reduces the amount of time spent pathfinding and spreads it out in small pieces. This can be done using waypoints provided by the game designers or by using hierarchical data to divide long paths. Hierarchical data can also be used to reduce the scope of data used in a given path search. This greatly reduces the time required for long distance path search operations.

Handling complex pathfinding problems well gives the player the impression of quality AI. Expert systems, scripting, and state machines can be combined to create sophisticated game AI. However, the reasoning and control happen inside the game code and are not always apparent to the player. A key aspect to allowing the player to appreciate the quality of the AI is exposing the AI's reasoning and behavior to the player. We will examine techniques to do this in the next chapter.

:::CHAPTER REVIEW:::

1. A game has three types of terrain that affect movement: water, ground, and ground occupied by a building. The game also has three vehicle types. Boats can move on water, jeeps can move on ground, and hovercraft can move on ground and water. How many zone equivalency arrays are required to determine whether paths exist between two points for each of the three vehicle types?

2. A helicopter is added to the game. It can fly over water or buildings, but can only land on ground. Is another zone equivalency array required? Why or why not?

3. An AI player in a game will be directing agents to move long distances. What are two techniques that allow agents to move by following a series of shorter paths to their destination? What are the advantages of either method?

4. The game in question 3 may have an automatic random map generation feature. How would this affect the two options?

5. What types of games could benefit from a group pathfinding feature? For each type, what are some of the potential problems with such a feature? Under what situations would it be preferable to find paths individually?

6. What are two ways that hierarchical data can be used to improve path search performance? Consider an agent approaching another agent that is moving. In this case, which method would be more efficient? Why?

CHAPTER

8

Looking Smart

maximizing the perception of intelligence

Key Chapter Questions

■ What are two types of cues that can be used to make the "intelligence" of the AI apparent (visible or audible) to the player?

■ What are three techniques for optimizing the AI that preserve the player's perception of the AI's intelligence?

■ What types of behaviors cause the AI to appear mechanical, rather than intelligent, to the player?

■ When should cues be used to simulate an intelligent behavior, instead of creating an AI system to perform the behavior?

■ Varied strategic choices indicate intelligence to the player. Why may the AI appear less intelligent if it always chooses the best strategy?

The major difference between computer science and game artificial intelligence (AI) involves the *perception* of intelligence. The effectiveness of game AI depends on whether the player perceives that the AI is behaving in an intelligent fashion; on the other hand, the effectiveness of computer science AI depends on whether there is an intelligent operation happening within the code, which is a much more difficult standard to meet. Game AI can take advantage of the ELIZA effect, whereby players attribute intelligence to a computer agent when the agent performs appropriate behaviors that the player can see or hear. The player cannot tell whether the behavior is the result of intelligent reasoning, a script provided by a designer, or random luck. Game AI can take advantage of any or all of these to give the impression of intelligent agents. The key is that the behaviors need to be apparent to the player. An agent's movement, animation, and speech (or sound cues) are all ways the AI system can present behaviors to the player.

The Appearance of Intelligent Behavior

The fact that game AI is judged on perception is a double-edged sword. On one hand, it makes the problem more challenging because we could be using correct algorithms (such as A*), finding the shortest path, sending our agent along that path, and having our agent successfully navigate to the goal. When the scenario is ready, the executive producer plays it, looks at it, and says, "Okay, the troll goes around the right side of the mountain every time, and it never goes around the left. It looks dumb. It looks like the AI is not smart enough to try different sides." Even though the algorithm is correct and the behavior is correctly coded, the resulting gameplay is such that it is perceived to be poor AI. This judgment is correct, since the *perception* of the AI is the final goal. Even though our coding is correct, the AI programmer must go back and modify it to produce the desired behavior.

However, the benefit of the perception factor is that human beings are often willing to ascribe more intelligence to agents that simply exhibit the *appearance* of intelligent behavior. We see an appearance, and we are often willing to assume that there is substance behind the appearance. This effect is common in movies and television as well. You have probably seen the commercial in which an actor whose character is a doctor in a medical television show says, "I'm not a doctor, but I play one on television." The actor then proceeds to recommend a cough syrup. Clearly the actor is not a "real doctor," and he even says so. Yet his pitch is effective on some level, because he *looks* like a real doctor. In some cases, a fictional doctor on television looks more like a doctor than one in real life!

"Flanking It"

A memorable "head fake" (behavior that makes players think that the AI is really smart when in fact it was just "faking it") showed up on one of the fan forums. The AI liked to distribute its forces for defensive purposes, as well as use some for attacking, and when forces became engaged, this increased the priority to send in reinforcements. If an attack force encountered the enemy, this rule applied as well. Depending on the map topology, the reinforcements may end up picking another direction to move in. Occasionally, this would be from the opposite side of the enemy. One of the fans thought the AI was doing planned "flank" attacks, when it was really just a result of the circumstances.

—*Denis Papp (Chief Technology Officer, TimeGate Studios)*

The ELIZA Effect

The program ELIZA was written by Joseph Weizenbaum in the 1960s to carry on a conversation with a human. The program had no knowledge of humans or psychology, but it was able to parse sentences and create simple leading questions in response to statements based on a script provided by Weizenbaum. As far as actual knowledge, ELIZA was a little less capable than the grammar checker software available in Microsoft Word. If it did not recognize any of its scripted cues, then it "responded" by asking a generic leading question, such as, "Can you think of a specific example?"

The following is a transcript of an ELIZA session from *Computer Power and Human Reason*, by Joseph Weizenbaum. The person's input is in normal type, and ELIZA's response is in capitals. ELIZA is running a script designed by Weizenbaum that mimics a Rogerian therapist performing an initial interview with a patient. This implementation was the most common; people often thought of ELIZA as an AI therapist!

```
Men are all alike.
IN WHAT WAY
They're always bugging us about something or another.
CAN YOU THINK OF A SPECIFIC EXAMPLE
Well, my boyfriend made me come here.
YOUR BOYFIREND MADE YOU COME HERE
He says I'm depressed much of the time.
I'M SORRY TO HEAR YOU ARE DEPRESSED
It's true. I am unhappy.
DO YOU THINK THAT COMING HERE WILL HELP YOU NOT TO BE
UNHAPPY
I need some help, that much seems certain.
WHAT WOULD IT MEAN TO YOU IF YOU GOT SOME HELP
Perhaps I could learn to get along with my mother.
TELL ME MORE ABOUT YOUR FAMILY
My mother takes care of me.
WHO ELSE IN YOUR FAMILY TAKES CARE OF YOU
My father.
YOUR FATHER
You are like my father in some ways.
WHAT RESEMBLANCE DO YOU SEE
You are not very aggressive but I don't think you want me
to notice that.
WHAT MAKES YOU THINK I AM NOT VERY AGGRESSIVE
You don't argue with me.
WHY DO YOU THINK I DON'T ARGUE WITH YOU
You are afraid of me.
DOES IT PLEASE YOU TO BELIEVE I AM AFRAID OF YOU
My father is afraid of everybody.
WHAT ELSE COMES TO MIND WHEN YOU THINK OF YOUR FATHER
Bullies.
DOES THAT HAVE ANYTHING TO DO WITH THE FACT THAT YOUR
BOYFRIEND MADE YOU COME HERE
```

People were very willing to pursue the conversation with the computer, even though the computer really did not have any idea what was going on in the conversation. A number of people actually told ELIZA some very personal information about their lives and what was going on with them as a result of the interaction with the computer performing a simple question-asking technique!

This effect of "seeing more than what is really there" even happens to people within their areas of expertise. For example, let us look at a technique often used in first-person shooters (FPSs) that would be quite familiar to a programmer specializing in this game genre. One of the tasks that is challenging in first-person games is to get the interaction of characters to work correctly when one character is touching another. All of the hand movements are controlled by animations; a character's animation, particularly when controlled by the human player, varies considerably. When there is an operation such as a medic applying a bandage, getting the associated animation showing the doctor's hands moving to the position to apply the bandage on the soldier is very difficult.

Electronic Arts

A medic treats a squadmate in *Medal of Honor: Pacific Assault.*

One way to attempt to approximate this is by using a technique called *inverse kinematics (IK)*, which calculates the positioning of the joints in an animation skeleton to get the hands, for example, to move to a particular location in game space. It is a difficult problem and, in the general case, IK does not always result in a solution. An additional wrinkle is getting the correct orientation of the hand. If a character is shaking hands, the hand is oriented generally with fingers forward, thumb up and palm to the left. If the character is pushing another character, the palm is forward, fingers up and thumb to the left.

Both position and orientation are important details, as well as avoiding the appearance that the character has a broken wrist. Doing this is quite difficult, and doing it well is not often achieved. This is one of the reasons

Illustration by Per Olin

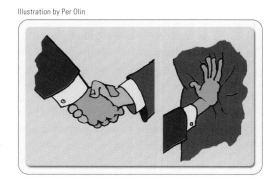

why a medic in a game might use a hypo spray, for example, that does not actually have to have contact with the other character to work, or the medic might just wave his or her hands in the general direction of the character, as in *Pacific Assault.*

A programmer familiar with IK saw a demonstration of a wrestling game involving two player characters. A sequence of moves showed two characters coming together, grappling, and then one character throwing the other down and pinning him. The movements were extremely precise, and the character's hands lined up exactly on the opponent's body. One character would grab the other correctly without either going too deeply into the model and having his arms go through the other character or leaving too much space so that he appeared to be levitating the other character by remote control. The characters moved correctly into position and performed the wrestling move.

Wrestling moves in *Def Jam Vendetta.*

The programmer looked at that and said, "Wow! That's amazing! The developers must have done some incredibly complex IK work to get that particular behavior to work."

In reality, there was no IK done in that particular game. Instead, the developers switched animations from two separate animated models, one for each player model, to a combined animation—a single animation that controlled both player models. The hands and body movements were all done manually by the animator, rather than using IK.

When observing something that looks impressive, even people in the industry will assume that there is more background and depth to the effect than there is in reality. We can use this to our advantage with game AI by making it look more intelligent than it is, thus convincing the players that the behavior is more intelligent than it really is.

There are several tasks that must be done to make the AI look great to the player. The first task is that the AI must perform a variety of behaviors correctly. These are the tasks performed by the techniques examined in earlier chapters, such as state machines, pathfinding, and modular design. However, as we have noted, good AI is not in the code. It is in the mind of the player. Therefore, in addition to good code and correct behaviors, there are several additional guidelines to consider when creating great AI, such as:

- make the AI visible to the player
- only implement AI that the player can detect
- avoid behaviors that appear mechanical
- show the player AI that makes choices
- give the player reason to see more than is really there

Let us take a closer look at these guidelines.

::::: *Tony La Russa Baseball*: Do Not Make the Artificial Intelligence *Too* Accurate!

Electronic Arts

When we created *Tony LaRussa Baseball,* the Cardinals' manager (then managing the Oakland Athletics) spent days and days with us working to help make the AI work properly. The game would simulate the way Tony manages a team, and a menu system allowed you to change settings to have it mimic the style of different managers. An easy example of this is that La Russa rarely uses sacrifice bunts to advance runners, but (assuming he has the right players at bat and on base) uses the hit-and-run play much more often than most managers. Players could set their own level of manager AI for how much they preferred bunting vs. calling the hit-and-run, and the AI would combine an evaluation of the situation with that player AI setting to govern strategy.

One story from *LaRussa Baseball* proves the maxim that "sometimes having the game's AI be too accurate is a problem, not a feature": If you are at a baseball game and see a pop-up to shortstop with a runner on first, watch what the players do. There are some variations based on details, but most often the third baseman will back up the shortstop and the left fielder will come in behind the third baseman as another backup. On the field no one notices because lots of players are moving and you just watch the shortstop circle under the ball until he catches it. In a game, however, our eye looks at the screen differently. The third baseman and the left fielder lining up behind the shortstop jump out at you, especially if the camera angle foreshortens the perception of distance on the field. When we implemented the fielders' AI accurately they looked like dancers in a music video, moving into a line. Offsetting it by a few pixels did not help.

The final solution was to make the AI do the wrong thing in such a way that the defense could still recover quickly from an error. We moved the third baseman toward the shortstop and somewhat behind him, but not so close as to draw the user's eye. We brought in the left fielder in a traditional back-up position, but left him farther back. It looked "right" compared to the way you watch sports on TV, even though it was *wrong*. The compromise meant that if the shortstop dropped the ball the other players were only slightly slower in getting to it, and we sacrificed mathematical accuracy for perceived visual accuracy.

—*Don L. Daglow (Chief Executive Officer, Stormfront Studios)*

Make the AI Visible

When we have AI algorithms in place that are doing actual work, one of the key requirements is that we make these operations visible to the player. If the player cannot tell what is going on in the AI, the player will not be able to appreciate the things that the AI is doing. A corollary to this is that the AI should not do things that are not visible to the player. We will examine this area later.

Some of the AI operations, such as pathfinding, are relatively easy to make visible to the player. When the agent follows the path that was generated, a player can see that the path is being followed by the agent. If the path was correctly calculated and is a reasonable way to get from point A to point B, the player will be able to see it.

Other operations, such as the AI searching for and finding the player using a visual mechanism, are more difficult because the player cannot see them. The game *No One Lives Forever 2* contains a number of stealth elements. The player can hide in shadows while enemy agents are patrolling and looking for the player. The state of the agents is made apparent to the player by a combination of animation and audio cues. Enemy agents will play an animation to indicate the search behavior (looking around, shading the eyes). They also play some audio cues indicating what the agent currently perceives. When an agent is unaware of the player, it will be silent or will occasionally play an "All Clear" announcement. If the agent has "heard" a sound and knows that the player is somewhere in the area, then it will play "I know you are here." If the agent "sees" the player, the agent will say, "I see you now!" and begin moving to attack the player.

F. E. A. R. (also developed by Monolith) uses similar audio cues to inform the player what the AI is "thinking." Radio chatter is used to tip off the player that the AI is planning an ambush, and when an AI agent "sees" the player, the agent shouts out, "Movement Detected!" to warn his squad mates. Of course, the player is the actual target of all these messages that are "overheard."

Reprinted with permission from Microsoft Corporation

Brute Force uses animation and audio cues to show the player than an AI agent is searching for the player, and whether the agent has seen the player.

Reprinted with permission from Microsoft Corporation

Perfect Dark Zero uses audio cues to let the player know what the enemy agents are thinking and planning.

The combination of audio and animation cues addresses two important goals. First, it helps the AI appear more intelligent to the player. Second, and more importantly, it improves the gameplay experience. The goal of the game is for the player to ultimately defeat the enemy agents. Allowing the player insight into what the AI is "thinking" helps the player choose good tactics, and it gives the impression that the player is facing an intelligent opponent.

Eliminate Invisible AI Activity

The corollary to making the AI visible to the player is avoiding AI activity that the player cannot see. The reason for this is two-fold: it increases efficiency and reduces confusion on the part of the player. By avoiding work in game, the CPU demands of the AI are reduced. This also decreases the amount of code development required and speeds up the development of the game. Finally, avoiding hidden behavior makes the behavior of the AI clearer to the player, improving the gameplay experience.

Game Performance Efficiency

The first gain in efficiency is game performance. There are never enough CPU cycles to go around, so reducing the amount of computation the AI performs is always valuable. There are a variety of techniques that can be used to improve the performance of the AI.

100 Percent Optimization

The way to get 100 percent optimization is to eliminate the agent altogether. Many first-person games have intentionally limited visibility with walls and other obstacles, so the actual area a player can see is small. This is done to improve rendering efficiency, and it should also be used to improve AI efficiency. This can be accomplished simply by creating the AI agents out of sight of the player as soon as the player approaches the location.

:::::Smoke & Mirrors vs. Simulation

In current generation video games, we have enough computing power to consider doing some moderately complex simulation in the AI. For example, we can have a squad of AI agents guard a house with front and rear entrances. Depending on how the player chooses to enter the building, the squad of defenders will react in a different fashion. The front entrance has a balcony, and a sniper could deploy there. The rear entrance is near the kitchen, where there are tables and counters for cover.

At first glance, it appears that a simulation would be the best way to get "realistic" behavior. The squad places two agents on the front balcony and two agents behind counters in the kitchen. Four more agents would be distrib-

Activision

Call of Duty 2 features battles where the player faces many enemies in a scene, but only a few are interacting with the player at any one time.

uted through the house to support the point agents in the front and back. The player enters through the front door. The agents on the balcony see the player and start firing. The other agents in the house hear the noise and begin moving. The closer two agents arrive quickly and attack the player. The player has killed the agents on the balcony at this point, or the player has been killed. The other two agents supporting the attack arrive, and finally the two agents that were stationed in the kitchen hear the noise of the gun battle and arrive from the kitchen.

This sounds all very realistic, and the programmer and designer can tweak realistic sounding values like "hearing range" and "reaction time." However, there is a better way to handle this. As the player approaches the front door, spawn two agents on the balcony. A few seconds later, spawn two more around the corner in a hallway, and have them attack the player. Repeat for the next four agents.

The player sees the same behaviors. However, we only have two to four agents active at any time, since the player is killing the agents as they are spawned. Thus, we get the same gameplay with half the agents in the world at a given time. Due to the ELIZA effect, particularly if we hear some sound effects from the nonexistent reinforcements, the player will perceive that there is more going on than in reality.

One issue related to achieving 100 percent optimization is what to do with the dead agents. They are not moving, so they do not use much CPU compared to active agents, but they tend to pile up after a while and clutter the landscape. This tends to reduce the frame rate as well. Destroying the agents solves these problems, but having them "pop" out of existence is very distracting to the player.

Electronic Arts

Epic Games

Command & Conquer: Generals and *Unreal Tournament 2007* both dispose of dead agents quickly to improve game performance.

Command & Conquer: Generals has dead agents sink into the ground over a span of ten seconds or so. This effect is gradual, allowing the agent to be "popped" out of existence after it is beneath the ground and invisible to the player. *Unreal Tournament 2007* has another optimization. As soon as the player turns away from the dead agent, and the dead agent is out of view, the AI "pops" it out of existence. This is extremely efficient, since the gameplay in *Unreal Tournament 2007* is such that it is unlikely a player will stand around looking at a dead agent, and it simply avoids the problem of seeing the agent pop out of existence.

Partial Optimizations

Other game styles are not as amenable to the technique of only creating agents when needed. Open world games allow the player to see relatively long distances, so it may be possible to see agents that are outside of the immediate area. Repeatedly creating and destroying agents is expensive as well, so it is not a good idea to create and destroy agents as they come into and out of view. Real-time strategy (RTS) games have a different challenge. The view of the player is somewhat restricted, but the game is a simulation and battles are going on whether the player is looking at the agents or not. So it is not at all possible to delay the creation of agents.

In both cases, there are partial optimizations that can be done. One way is to use a *distance based control*. In open world games, the player can see agents that are quite a distance away from the player. Small details are often not relevant at that point. The game *Far Cry* contained a distanced based *level of detail (LOD)* for the AI characters.

It would perform simple behaviors and animations or no animations at a far enough distance to reduce the computational demands on the system. As the player moved closer, the agents would perform more complex AI behaviors so that what the player could see close up was complex, but at a distance where she could not really perceive the details, the AI would not bother to actually perform the behaviors.

Unreal Tournament 2007 and *Command & Conquer: Generals* both provide levels of detail in their simulations. In cases where the player can see the small details, a detailed simulation is performed. When not visible to the player, a faster, more limited simulation is performed.

Unreal Tournament 2007 uses an IK system for the characters' feet. This ensures that the feet touch the floor and ramps when a player is running. This avoids having a character's feet sticking into the ramp or floating above the ramp. It also adjusts the angle of the foot so that it matches the slope of the floor or ramp. This is a relatively expensive operation to compute, but the effect is subtle. The player has to be relatively close to the agent to see whether her feet exactly line up with a ramp. If the agent is at a sufficient distance that the detail of the foot is not visible to the player, we can skip the calculation, once again not performing operations that are invisible to the player. *Command & Conquer: Generals* modified the detail of the simulation depending on whether the agent was visible to the player or not. The core details of the simulation had to be performed at all times: position, movement, weapon firing and damage calculations. Other aspects were only performed if the agent were visible. The roll and pitch of a tank chassis were calculated using a multiple spring physics simulation, taking into account the speed and turn rate of the tank as well as the ground slope. This produced realistic movement, but it was expensive to calculate. When the tank was not visible, the position and speed were calculated, but pitch and roll were not calculated. Similarly, if a rocket damaged a tank and the tank was visible, the impact would calculate the damage, apply it to the tank, and spawn a particle system. If the tank was off screen, the impact would calculate the damage, but not spawn the particle system. Similarly, tanks visible on screen would produce dust particle effects when moving, but not when off screen.

Game Development Efficiency

Avoiding unnecessary AI behavior improves game development efficiency as well as game frame rate. Another way of eliminating work that is not visible to the player is to avoid complex internal states that cannot be perceived by the player. For example, in an FPS, a player may come to an area that is defended by a squad of enemy agents. There may be a setting maintained inside the AI allowing the agents to have different levels of aggressiveness. It is easy enough to make the aggressiveness setting a percentage so that the value is between 0 and 100; however, this is a case of adding too much detail that the player cannot perceive. Consider the difference between 47 percent and 46 percent aggressiveness, for example. If this difference is not apparent to the player, then it is a case of too much detail, and it is not really a good design.

A system that represents aggressiveness with a value between 0 and 100 should be replaced with a system that has a few discrete levels that can be recognized and understood by the player. A better choice would be a system with a three levels of aggression; neutral, aggressive, or afraid. These three levels of aggression can be tied to animations and behaviors that make the agent's "state of mind" apparent to the player. For example, an agent in the **Aggressive** state would tend to advance, taking cover, and quickly moving forward and attacking the player. Agents in the **Neutral** state would take cover and pop out from cover and fire at the player. Finally, the agents in the **Afraid** state would drop their weapons and run.

These three states can be made obvious to the player so that players can recognize that a particular AI agent is either aggressive, neutral, or afraid. This is particularly useful if the player can affect the AI's "state of mind" by specific game actions, such as killing the AI's squad leader. This makes the AI agents' behavior seem reasonable and intelligent as opposed to random and confusing.

Avoid Behavior That Looks Mechanical

As we noted with the ELIZA effect, people will see more intelligence in a game's behaviors given the right cues. However, there are several behaviors that people immediately recognize as artificial or mechanical. Behaviors such as inappropriate repetition and inappropriate synchronization break the spell, so to speak, and it is important to avoid them.

Inappropriate repetition happens when one or more agents repeat the same behavior in an inappropriate fashion. The key here is inappropriate repetition. Some behaviors are repeated because there is only one way to perform the behavior (or one correct way). For example, a squad of riflemen will raise their rifles and fire using the same movement and hand positioning. Similarly, a character shoveling coal into a train boiler will repeat the same movement to shovel the coal. The shoveling only becomes inappropriate if the coal loader repeats the identical movement indefinitely. A real person would stop after a number of times, stretch a little, take a breath, and then resume shoveling. Adding this kind of break keeps the repetition from becoming inappropriate.

Repetitious audio cues can appear mechanical as well. Brothers and sisters often discover this effect by repeating what you say back to you. A computer agent that always says the same thing can easily become irritating and mechanical. We noted that it is helpful for the AI to provide audio cues that give information to the player. It is good to have several different cues that have the same meaning. For example, when an agent detects the player, it could say one "Enemy Sighted," "Perimeter Breached," or "Intruder Detected" as appropriate for the agent's character. This gives players the same information that they have been detected, without repeating the same phrase over and over.

:::::Using Cues to Add Personality

Red Alert 2 takes advantage of the need to vary audio cues to add some personality to the game agents. In an RTS game, an attention cue is played when agents are selected and ready to receive orders. The agents play several "ready" cues to avoid mechanical repetition. One agent, the tesla trooper, has an electrical weapon that produces artificial lightning. The agent uses the following audio cues to add personality and humor into the game, in addition to notifying the player that the unit is ready to receive orders:

Ready to begin electro shock therapy
It will be a shocking experience

Electronic Arts

The *Red Alert 2* tesla trooper uses a series of tongue-in-cheek responses to demonstrate personality and style to the player.

One Minute of Brilliance

Often in sports games we give computer players a set of simple, logical, fast process directions: stay between this opponent and the goal, run towards a fumble, block out opponents for rebounds in a zone based on the length of the shot. That gets you football, soccer, or basketball teams that move somewhat well on the field or court. Players tend to be in the right places, but also look "dumb" because once you think about it there are all sorts of holes in their defense and failures in their offense. The AI is then tuned for each kind of player until those shortcomings are filled in a way that the CPU can handle. It is much less of an issue now than when we had 6502-based consoles. Here's what I saw happen over and over in these games. After you had the base AI running, and before you added the layer of sophistication, some players in some situations would always look perfect. A linebacker with a 60 percent chance of blitzing on long 3rd down would seem to read the defense perfectly for an entire game. A center would be standing in the perfect place for five straight rebounds. The game AI looked brilliant...for one whole minute! Then reality set in, the player did something dumb, and we had to go back to work.

—*Don L. Daglow (Chief Executive Officer, Stormfront Studios)*

Provide AI That Makes Choices

AI agents appear more intelligent if they give the impression that they are making choices. As we noted before, the AI code may or may not actually be making choices; the value lies in behaviors that cause the player to *perceive* that the AI is making choices.

Provide Multiple Options

In early video games such as *Space Invaders*, the AI agents displayed a single behavior. The aliens all moved in the same pattern and dropped occasional rockets on the player. As games became slightly more complicated, there were multiple agents, each demonstrating a single behavior. In *Asteroids*, the asteroids had one behavior and the spaceship had another, but that was the extent of it. With a single behavior, there were no choices to be made. To give the impression of choice, there must be *multiple options*; the AI must be able to perform more than one behavior.

Minimize Random Behavior

It is possible to have strictly *random behavior*. For example, in *Tetris* the game pieces drop in random orientations. This is not at all intelligent, but it can be fun. An agent appears more realistic to the player is if there are small, random variations in its behaviors (e.g., an engineer shoveling coal that randomly takes a brief break). However, a series of random, apparently unrelated behaviors tends to give players the impression that the AI is not very intelligent, so it is important to avoid behaviors that appear random to the player.

Provide Strategic Choices

Strategic choices demonstrate high-level intelligence to the player. Let us consider a squad of AI agents attacking the player. The AI would appear more sophisticated and intelligent if there was a squad leader that directed the squad's strategy as it attacked the player. As we noted, this must be made apparent to the player so that she can appreciate the AI's choices.

Define Multiple Strategies

The first task in creating strategic choices is to *define multiple strategies*. If we only have one strategy (rush the player, for example), then there can be no element of choice. For this example, let us consider two strategies: aggressive and defensive. Since one of the main goals is to have the player see the choice, the strategies must be sufficiently different than is obvious to the players, whether they are encountering the aggressive or defensive strategy. For example, consider a squad of five commandos attacking the player in a large room such as a warehouse. The warehouse has various cover points. One set of strategies would be as follows: The defensive strategy has four of the commandos take cover and shoot at the player. One commando rushes the player. Another commando rushes the player when the first commando is killed. The aggressive strategy sends two commandos at a time at the player. This difference is pretty subtle, and the player may not realize that it is a strategic choice on the part of the AI. Exaggerating the difference as follows may make it more obvious to the player: The defensive strategy sends all squad members behind cover, and they lean out to shoot at the player. The aggressive strategy involves two squad members rushing the player immediately, and the other three rush the player as soon as the first two are killed. This difference in behavior would be hard to miss, even in the heat of battle.

An additional way to exaggerate the difference is to add audio cues, such as those used in *Half-Life 2*. Cues such as "Take cover!" or "Keep your heads down!" can be used to emphasize that this is a defensive strategy. Alternatively, cues such as "Advance by numbers!" or "Flank him!" let the player know that the squad is taking an aggressive posture, and to get ready for a rush attack.

Half-Life 2 uses audio cues to tell the player the type of strategy that the AI has chosen.

Implement the Strategies

After multiple strategies are defined, we must *implement* them, which may or may not involve employing a squad AI. Tyrion is a goal-based AI framework used in *S.W.A.T. 4* and *Tribes: Vengeance*. It supports high-level squad goals, as well as lower-level agent goals. In the case of Tyrion, there is an actual AI system corresponding to the squad AI. In this case, we would implement two attack goals, one using the aggressive strategy, and the other using the defensive strategy. Activating the first goal would cause the squad AI to execute the attack using the aggressive strategy. A free form battle encounter, such as a skirmish game in *Command & Conquer: Generals*, would also require an actual implementation of a strategic AI behavior.

Free-form skirmish battles in *Command & Conquer: Generals* require the creation of a strategic AI system to control the enemy units. The linear nature of *Perfect Dark Zero* allows strategic behaviors to be scripted by a level designer.

However, as we have noted, it is only necessary that the player perceive the existence of squad leader intelligence. It is not necessary that there actually be a corresponding AI system. In a linear FPS such as *F.E.A.R.*, it is possible to script the behavior of the individual agents so that in one instance they perform the defensive strategy, and script another set of behaviors in another part of the game that perform the aggressive strategy. We can then create the appearance of a squad level strategy by directly controlling the individual agent behaviors, rather than implementing an AI system that controls the squad.

Choosing a Strategy

Once multiple strategies are implemented, we must choose between them. The mechanism for performing the choice will vary depending on the type of game and implementation. A key detail is that the choice of strategy must vary. If the AI always chooses the aggressive strategy, it will appear to the player that there is no choice at all and that the AI is in fact only capable of one behavior.

Designer-Scripted Choice

One method of choosing a strategy is to script the choice. This method is suitable in a linear, story driven game such as *Half-Life 2* or *Medal of Honor: Pacific Assault*. In the case that we are simulating choice by scripting the individual agent's behavior, this is the only method available.

© Valve Corporation. Used with permission.   Electronic Arts

Half-Life 2 and *Medal of Honor: Pacific Assault* have a relatively linear story, requiring that the player experience a series of scenes in order. The designer can choose the AI's strategy for each scene.

The designer can vary the strategy from encounter to encounter. This level of control allows the designer to make the choice for the AI. As we have noted earlier, this can give the impression of very sophisticated AI if used in conjunction with the level design. The designer can also ensure that the player encounters the variety of strategic behaviors, which will give the impression of sophisticated AI behaviors.

Programmed Choice

In the case in which there is an actual squad level AI system, the choice can be made via code or code in conjunction with designer scripting. If the game is linear, then the designer-scripted choice is a good solution.

Electronic Arts

Firaxis Games Inc.

The Lord of the Rings: The Battle for Middle-Earth and *Civilization IV* allow the player to vary the location and order when building structures and units. The AI's strategy evolves during gameplay, rather than being preset.

Games that lack a linear path are not as amenable to a scripted solution. A skirmish game in *The Lord of the Rings: The Battle for Middle-Earth* against a computer opponent does not have fixed encounters with predetermined agents. Similarly, gameplay evolves in *Civilization IV* as the players' technology grows. In cases such as this, the strategy has to be handled by AI code.

There are several methods for accomplishing this. Cycling randomly is actually a good choice, since it presents a variety of behaviors to the player. In many cases, there is not a clear advantage to one strategy over another, and varying the strategies makes for interesting gameplay. In some cases, there may be situations in which one strategy is preferable due to the terrain, for example. It may be useful to have the AI recognize these situations. However, it is important to be careful to avoid instances in which the player runs into a series of these situations in a row. The AI may start to fall into what appears to the player as inappropriate repetition of the same strategy.

In situations where we are programming the AI's choice of strategy, there is the temptation to base the choice on the player's behavior. We know that random behavior is not intelligent. It seems that having AI that reacts to the player would seem more intelligent. Unfortunately, there is a very strong likelihood that basing the AI's strategy on the player's choices will actually make the AI seem less intelligent. In many cases, consciously or unconsciously, a player develops a gameplay style. In first-person games with ranged (rifles) and melee (fists & knives) weapons, a player may choose to use the ranged weapons almost exclusively. RTS players tend to have a preferred mix of units for their squads, emphasizing armor over air power.

Basing the strategy on the player's choices often results in a player seeing only one strategy. Player A tends to emphasize attack over defense, and the AI always chooses the aggressive strategy. Player B likes to use defensive structures that cannot be easily attacked, so the AI avoids aggressive strategy in this case. The AI programmer may (incorrectly) consider that this is the most intelligent behavior, as the AI is correctly choosing the best strategy for each situation. However, the end result is that the individual players see the AI as predictable and inflexible, since it always chooses the same behavior. Another problem is that if the game always chooses the more effective method, it can make the game frustrating to play for the player. The game will be more interesting if the AI uses a variety of tactics.

Use Cues That Imply Intelligence

We have examined a variety of cues to expose the intelligence of the AI to the player. If the player cannot see and appreciate the work, it is wasted. Another use of cues is to make the player think that the AI reasoning is present, when it actually is not. As noted with the ELIZA effect, people will assume intelligent reasoning if they see behaviors that appear to support that assumption. They will also assume a complex system if the cues are present, such as the IK system, on the part of the game programmers. One option is to provide the cues without actually implementing the AI system that supports them. This can be done using several techniques, ranging from simple scripting, to creating a system whose purpose is to play the cues at appropriate times.

Scripting

In some cases, we can just script the cues. This can be done in a relatively straightforward fashion in heavily scripted games that have a relatively linear gameplay, such as *Quake 4*. These games could actually have a squad level AI and use the cues to expose the actual system behavior. Alternatively, the squad level strategy audio cues can be played using time and location triggers, without the need to actually implement a squad level AI.

Courtesy of id Software, Inc.

Quake 4 has linear gameplay that allows scripted control of AI cues.

Simple Systems

Another method that can be used is to create a simple system whose purpose is to generate the audio and animation cues. *The Lord of the Rings: The Battle for Middle-Earth* contains a system to manage emotions in AI agents. The system supports three emotional states: **Afraid**, **Taunting**, and **Celebrating**.

The triggers are relatively simple. If an agent sees enemy agents of similar strength, it enters the **Taunting** state. This involves playing a taunt animation and an audio clip. The agent in the taunt animation waves a shield and shakes a sword at the enemy. If the agent sees a much more powerful enemy unit, it plays a fear animation. For example, trolls can easily destroy swordsmen. If swordsmen see a troll nearby, an animation plays that indicates fear, usually involving the swordsmen cowering behind their shields and the sound of armored knees knocking together. Finally, the **Celebrate** state is triggered in two situations. The first situation is when an allied hero unit arrives (e.g., Gondor units celebrate if Gandalf arrives). The second situation is when no enemy agents are nearby, and there are more dead enemy agents than dead allied agents. Thus, if a battle has ended and more enemies were killed, the agents will celebrate.

At first glance, because of the ELIZA effect it appears that emotion is deeply tied into the AI system of the game. However, the emotion system is actually separate from the AI and does nothing more than play animations and sounds. It bases these on the **World** state, so the reactions are appropriate and relevant to the game, but it actually has no impact on the AI of the game. There are several reasons for this. First, it makes the system much easier to create. Since the emotion system does not interact with the AI, the emotion system is much easier to develop and debug. Second, having the emotion system interact with the AI has the potential for interfering with gameplay. An initial plan for the emotion system was that a unit that was suffering from fear would be unable to attack. However, standard RTS behavior dictates that an agent directed to attack will do so until the target is destroyed or the agent itself is destroyed. Allowing an emotional state to interfere with the agent's behaviors is more irritating than realistic, and that approach was discarded. By playing an animation and audio cue at appropriate times, agents appear to have a realistic emotional response, but at the same time they follow the orders issued as expected.

> A simple "he's over there" said by an AI guard about a player is a very effective audio cue alerting the players that more AI units are likely banding together and heading their way.
>
> —Frank T. Gilson
> (Senior Developer,
> Wizards of the Coast)

Animation and Audio Cues

A programming example is included on the companion DVD that demonstrates the use of animation and audio cues in conjunction with AI systems. In one case, the cues are used to expose the processing performed in the AI state machine. In another case, an animation is used to imply additional AI not actually present in the code.

::::: *The Lord of the Rings: The Battle for Middle-Earth:* Using Animation and Audio Cues for Emotion

Electronic Arts

Using animation and audio cues to create the sense that the soldiers and creatures in *The Lord of the Rings: The Battle for Middle-Earth* were emotional-based organic creatures was a big win. We worked hard to create a sense that the "units" in the game were "emotional individuals" that understood what was happening on the battlefield and responded accordingly. Since we could track the results of skirmishes, super weapon attacks, and the rest of the fighting going on in the game, we could tell the game units to cheer when something good happened around them, or yell in fear as something scary was about to happen. These simple cues really added a new dimension to people's perceptions about the soldiers or "units" you play with in RTS games. When you see a game without the same level of "emotional" cues, it feels flat and a bit old fashioned.

—*Mark Skaggs (Chief Executive Officer, Blue Nitro Studios)*

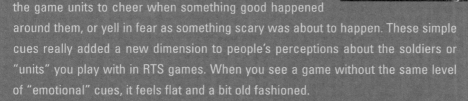

::::: *Utopia:* Using an Audio Cue
as a Distraction

Mattel, Inc.

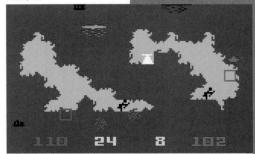

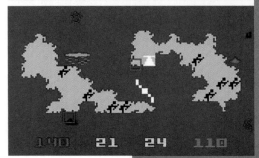

Machines are so fast today that if we depict a machine as thinking it is usually a ruse to give the player time to think. The AI does not need the extra seconds. When I wrote *Utopia* for Intellivision in 1981, I took a lot of kidding from the other designer-programmers because it was a turn-based sim game. When the computer calculated the score based on the happiness of your people, the GI1610 microprocessor would hesitate for almost a second before updating the score. All of our games were supposed to run at 30 frames a second to mimic movies and TV, but with a turn-based game we realized that requirement was irrelevant. The Intellivision ran at a little less than 1 MHz in speed, so the computer on which I'm writing this has a processor that is over 2,000 times faster than the 1610. The delay was not long enough to call for an "I'm thinking" audio cue, but I did cheat and create an audio tone that played 60 percent of the way through the calculation. The user heard the tone that meant "Here comes the updated score!" with a sound duration of a portion of a second, and then the screen update with the score followed. The perception was that the time before the tone was the delay, when in fact the tone was a distraction to make you stop thinking it was a delay. The joke on the team was that I was the only video game programmer in history ever to write five pages of code that displayed absolutely nothing on the screen. In the arcade game era of the early 1980s the team enjoyed nagging me about that "world record."

—*Don L. Daglow*
(Chief Executive Officer, Stormfront Studios)

David Javelosa on the Use of Audio in Artificial Intelligence :::::

David Javelosa is a composer/technologist and game industry specialist based in Santa Monica, California. Previously, he worked with Yamaha Corporation of America as an evangelist for their game audio technology. David is currently an instructor at Santa Monica College's Entertainment Technology program, teaching game development and digital audio, and composing music for the Internet and live performance. He has created soundtracks for most of the major game consoles and has been involved with digital media since its inception. David's interests include vintage synthesizers, remixing pop bands and sci-fi soundtracks, skydiving, biking, and raising his three kids. Also known as "David Microwave," he began releasing recordings in 1979 with his bands Los Microwaves and Baby Buddha, representing fusion of synth-pop ballads, vintage analog sound, "lo-fi" game music, and experimental techno grooves. His recordings have included veteran musicians Robert Williams of Capt. Beefheart, Knox Chandler of the Psychedelic Furs, and Steve Berlin of Los Lobos, among others. His game music background includes audio director positions at Sega and Inscape, as well as credits on titles from Disney Interactive, Microsoft Network, Sony Online, Crave, Psygnosis, Marvel Interactive, and Voyager.

David Javelosa (Professor of Interactive Media, Academy of Entertainment & Technology at Santa Monica College)

As an early adopter of Microsoft's Direct Music engine, the goal has always been to create context specific music that would re-arrange itself to the user's actions in the game. This goal was accomplished in the mainstream release of Marty O'Donnel's interactive score for *HALO* on Xbox. The goal of the interactive sound designer is to give an appropriate voice to the "artificially intelligent" character.

Working with triggers set by the programmers, conditional and randomized musical responses need to be composed to be played back in all possible combinations. This creates a perceived AI in that it sounds like the music is being arranged on the spot to match the actions of the player.

Stephen Superville on Improving the Player Experience through Artificial Intelligence :::::

Stephen Superville
(AI Programmer,
Epic Games)

Stephen started in the industry in 2000 working for the Department of Defense on *America's Army*. His role on development teams has been to design, implement, and iterate on systems the player will interact with. He most recently completed a large part of the AI work in *Gears of War* for the Xbox 360.

One of the most important skills in game programming is spending time on features that improve the experience of the player. An obvious corollary: it is important to avoid spending time on features that have little or no impact. AI development is an inherently iterative process. Striving to make something fun and interesting is always going to be more art than science; it's nearly impossible achieve the "feel" you are looking for the first time. You'll need to make time for iteration and make sure you are spending that time wisely. The difference between a good and great player experience can often be reduced to how effectively time distributed to polish features.

If they can't see it, it's not in the game

If the player cannot perceive your AI performing an action, that action does not exist. The role of any AI system is to provide the player with a stimulus to respond to. This creates the gameplay loop: The agent decides what to do and communicates that action to the player, the player responds to the AI, the agent decides what to do next, and the cycle repeats. Whichever job your agents perform, the result must be communicated to the player in some way; anything that exists outside this core loop is wasted effort, both in terms of your implementation time and CPU cycles. Much like an ostrich sticking its head in the sand to avoid danger, players who can't see your agents working are not affected by them. The only person appreciating your smart AI is you, and that's never very satisfying. Bottom line: If you are going to put a feature in, make sure it is visible.

If they can't see it, cheat!

If the player cannot perceive your AI, then you are free to break all the rules of "good" behavior. This is helpful in two ways. First, you can do whatever you would like to get your AI into an interesting position for the next encounter with the player. Second, you simply use less processing time by cheating. The natural tendency is to want our creations to behave correctly all of the time, but remember, our mission is to create an enjoyable player experience. To achieve our objective, it is often better to create two sets of rules. When in view of the player the agent should display correct, natural behaviors that produce good results. When hidden from the player, the agent should have no behavior! Use the time and cycles to figure out the best, most interesting results, and just put the AI in position. Always remember, your job is to make the experience for the player fun and interesting. Not to produce the most sophisticated (read: pointlessly complicated) AI in the world.

Implying an AI Behavior

Cues can be used to imply an AI behavior as well. Gameplay may require that an agent perform similar actions repeatedly. In order to break up the sequence of repeated actions, different behaviors can be inserted. The purpose of these behaviors is to give the agent's behaviors some variety. A way to do this is to simply have the AI pause and play one of a variety of different animations. A soldier may check his rifle or stretch. Although the AI is just waiting for the animation to complete, the animation can give the impression that a more significant activity is taking place.

Illustration by Per Olin

This animation sequence implies that the agent is placing the coin in his pocket.

The preceding animation gives the impression that the agent is picking up the coin and putting it in her pocket, when in fact as far as the AI code is concerned, there is no coin or pocket. This demonstrates the use of cues to give the appearance of more intelligent behaviors on the part of the AI.

Creating AI that appears intelligent is important when building game AI. Writing sophisticated game AI code and systems is valuable, as long as the results of the code and systems are apparent to the player. Animation and audio cues can be used to make sure that the player can see and appreciate the quality of the work.

It is also important to present cues to players that lead them to believe that there is more to the AI than is actually coded. As we see with the ELIZA program, people, given the right kinds of cues, are willing to interact with a computer program as if it were a human being. Presenting these kinds of cues, while avoiding other cues that "break the spell," so to speak, maximizes the player's perception of the level and quality of the game's AI.

In the next chapter, we will examine the process of building AI for a game. The tasks range from system design to debugging. In addition, we will look at career issues for video game AI developers.

:::CHAPTER REVIEW:::

1. Consider a scenario in which the player attacks an AI squad of five human agents. Player and agents are using ranged weapons, such as rifles. What are cues (audio, animation, and movement) that would indicate that the agents in the squad are communicating and working together, rather than acting as five isolated agents?

2. Creating a squad AI is difficult, expensive, and time consuming. What are ways that the cues in question #1, such as timers and area triggers, can be produced that do not require a squad AI system? Describe a scene using these techniques, and the cues presented to the player.

3. What gameplay and game design issues would require the creation of a squad AI? What behaviors would the squad AI perform to address these issues?

4. A rich AI sysem has been created for a game. All agents in the game use the same AI currently. During play, the player interacts closely with three to five agents, and another twenty agents are in the nearby area. Perhaps ⅓ of the nearby agents are visible at any given time. Analysys has indictated that the AI is using more CPU time than was budgeted, and is impacting the frame rate. What are several possible ways to reduce the cost of the AI in this situation, while minimizing the impact visible to the player?

5. Consider several different game styles. List multiple strategies for each style the AI could use to vary its behavior. Create one or more rules for the use of each strategy. Consider whether the player will see all of the strategies in action. Would any rule or game design changes or restrictions be needed to ensure that the player saw multiple strategies used?

CHAPTER

9

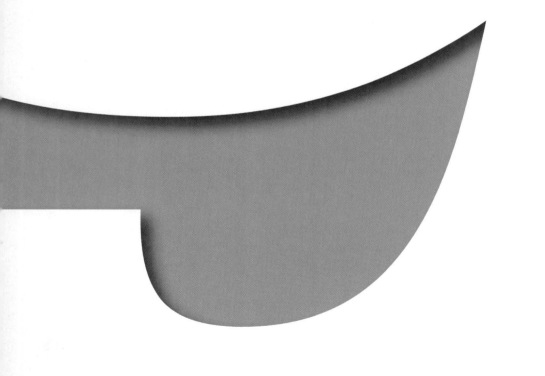

Putting It All Together

designing and building quality game artificial intelligence

Key Chapter Questions

- What types of games use virtual players, AI agents, or both?
- What are four steps in the development of the AI portion of a video game?
- What are the benefits of iterative development? How can it be applied to a video game project?
- What are the responsibilities of an AI programmer and designer, and what experience is required for each role?
- What is the future of game artificial intelligence?

Different games require different types of artificial intelligence (AI) behaviors and systems. Some games have sophisticated virtual players, while others have autonomous agents. Creating AI begins with the game's initial design. The design determines which AI behaviors will be needed. The required behaviors determine the necessary AI systems. At this point, the AI development team can design the AI systems and begin the implementation. An iterative development process is useful in creating high quality video game AI. Programmers and designers work together to create compelling AI behaviors.

The AI development is often done by an AI programmer and an AI designer. On small teams, one person may perform both roles. Larger teams may have a lead AI programmer, a lead AI designer, and several additional designers and programmers. There are a variety of types of education and experience that can be used to prepare for a career as an AI programmer or designer.

Game AI Requirements

A wide range of AI systems and behaviors are used in various games. A game's style and play will determine which type of AI is appropriate. A racing game will have detailed control of tires, engine speed, braking, and distance to adjacent cars, but little or no pathfinding if the race course is pre-determined. A first-person shooter (FPS) may have detailed AI control of aiming a laser sighted rifle, but only simple control of agent spawning and movement, with the bulk of the orders provided by game designers rather than the AI.

Each game has different AI requirements, and that is where the AI design process starts. Once the game design takes shape, the AI behaviors can be specified, and the AI systems designed.

Simple Agents, Smart Virtual Players

The agent AI will be relatively simple in some games. This is often the case when a player controls a number of agents in the game, such as strategy games. It is the player's job to develop and execute a plan, and the individual agents "just follow orders."

One example is *Civilization IV*, in which the agents essentially correspond to pieces in a board game. The agents (such as cannons, horsemen, and tanks) are relatively limited in their autonomous behaviors. The player directs the movement of the pieces. Agents can move through each other and stack up at any location. Combat is resolved through a system of modifiers to the unit's basic armor value and attack and defense attributes. The coding required for the behaviors is relatively simple. The major activity of agent AI is computing the combat resolution. This is done in a straightforward fashion, using an evaluation of the unit health and attack and defense factors. For the individual agents, there is not a lot of complex AI coding, nor are there many complex systems.

There is a lot of AI development in the virtual player in this game, since a human plays against several virtual players on the map. Rather than an individual agent such as a rifleman having much in the way of intelligent behavior, the other virtual players in the game demonstrate the intelligent behaviors.

Firaxis Games Inc.

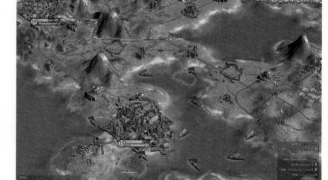

In *Civilization IV*, the agents correspond to pieces in a board game.

The virtual players have to make intelligent decisions. Areas of expertise on the part of the virtual players include construction, such as determining which structures to build in the cities. They also attack and defend, determining the quantity of units to build to defend their cities, and how many units are needed to successfully attack and conquer an opposing player's cities. The virtual player will also have to make reasonable decisions in situations such as determining when to expand, when to attack other players, and when to build defensive structures such as walls when his cities are vulnerable.

The area of the virtual player, in this case, is where most of the interesting AI work is done. The AI engineer works on the virtual player, creating systems that support the decision-making process of the virtual player so that it can emulate the intelligent decisions of a human.

Smart Groups of Agents

Other games have complex individual agent behaviors. Often, the player controls a single character in these games or inhabits the character, in the case of first-person games. The enemy agents have intelligent individual behaviors. In addition, they may coordinate their behaviors using military style squad attack movements.

One such game is *F.E.A.R.*, an FPS in which the player character moves through a series of environments. The primary objective is to shoot the opposing enemy agents, who are primarily either guards or combat soldiers. This type of game does not have a virtual player. The agents themselves perform complex behaviors. The AI programmer focuses on creating systems that support intelligent behavior on the part of the individual agents.

Unlike the agents (such as riflemen and tanks) in *Civilization IV*, the agents in *F.E.A.R* have complex individual behaviors. They use cover, talk to each other, and attack the player in a coordinated fashion. In this environment, the AI programming is more concerned with the intelligent behavior of the individual agents. Rather than dealing with strategic decision making, as in *Civilization IV*, the AI programming is concerned with low-level tactical decisions and basic behaviors such as using the weapon and cover effectively. In *F.E.A.R.*, the player is attacked by squads of agents that have coordinated behaviors. The AI programmer may create a squad level behavior system that allows the designer to coordinate the behavior of the individual agents in squads. This allows the agents to successfully emulate military squad tactics when they are attacking the player.

Reprinted with permission from Microsoft Corporation

First-person shooters such as *Perfect Dark Zero* do not have a virtual player.

Solo Agents

Other games place more emphasis on the individual agents rather than squads. The gameplay is such that the enemy agents are more concerned with attacking the player than performing coordinated squad movements.

Doom 3 is designed as an FPS (like *F.E.A.R.*). However, in this case, the enemy agents in it are primarily demons, who are relatively solitary, anti-social creatures. They tend to be single agents or small groups that are not particularly cooperative. Therefore, AI development for games in the style of *Doom 3* focuses on the individual agent. *Serious Sam* is another FPS that has very similar AI requirements.

Courtesy of id Software, Inc.
Courtesy of Take-Two Interactive Software, Inc.

First-person shooters *Doom 3* (left) and *Serious Sam* (right) focus on solo agents.

FPS games *Doom 3* and *Serious Sam* both focus on solo agents. The AI programming also supports the level-specific scripting of the games so that designers can create and control agents at specific locations. The AI code allows the designer to trigger the creation of agents at particular times or events in the levels. The AI also allows the designer to specify and customize the behaviors of the enemy agents—demons, in this case. Finally, the AI programming focuses on the movement and attack behaviors of the individual monsters in response to the player's actions.

An important method for creating quality AI that appears intelligent is by capturing information from the designer. In the case of *Civilization IV*, information is captured, either as rules or scripts, in order to control the behavior of the virtual player. In *F.E.A.R* and *Doom 3* information is captured regarding placement of the agents in the levels, controlling pacing to make the game interesting and triggering the agents' behaviors.

Agents and Virtual Players

Another option is to have agents with some degree of intelligence and virtual players that control them as well. Real-time strategy (RTS) games tend to have moderately intelligent agents and also virtual players.

In a game such as *The Lord of the Rings: The Battle for Middle-Earth*, we have some intelligence on the part of the individual units, such as the tanks, infantry, and helicopters, and we also have a virtual player. In this environment, the AI programmer creates basic behaviors for the individual units. A tank or infantry has to be able to determine a location that is within range of its target and move using pathfinding to get within range of its target and fire its weapon.

However, compared to an FPS such as *F.E.A.R.*, the attack behavior is less complex. The attacking units do not use cover to hide from the enemies. Line of sight calculations are made to make sure that there are no blocking structures in the way. This prevents agents from firing through buildings or allied units.

Electronic Arts Reprinted with permission from Microsoft Corporation

Attack behavior in *The Lord of the Rings: The Battle for Middle-Earth* (left) is less complex than in *Perfect Dark Zero* (right).

Although attack behavior in *The Lord of the Rings: The Battle for Middle-Earth* involves pathfinding behavior in order to move within range and fire, it is less complex than in an FPS such as *F.E.A.R.*, where attacking units may use cover to hide from enemies. Some units have automatic behaviors, such as resource gathering or harvesting. The AI programmer will spend considerable time working on systems for the individual agents. Each individual agent's behaviors are simpler than combat behaviors in an FPS. On the other hand, the number of different agent types in an RTS ensures that there will be plenty of work for the AI programmer writing agent behavior.

> Artificial intelligence design and implementation for games should be concrete and specific, created to solve certain problems within the current project, and should provide end users with a more fun gameplay experience.
>
> —Frank T. Gilson
> (Senior Developer, Wizards of the Coast)

These types of games also have a virtual player as well that issues the commands to the enemy agents in a similar fashion to that of *Civilization IV*. In addition to the individual unit behaviors, the AI programmer also has to support higher level strategic decision making in the virtual player AI. This involves creating systems to support the virtual player. The AI programmer may create a scripting interface combined with a rule-based system to allow the designer to specify the information necessary to control the behavior of the virtual player in a game. In the interests of re-using code, these systems can also be used for specifying the behaviors of the individual agents.

> I believe we will be experiencing more realistic and less predictable behaviors in non-player characters (NPCs), as well as seamless interactive music and sound in gameplay.
>
> —David Javelosa
> (Professor of Interactive Media, Academy of Entertainment & Technology at Santa Monica College)

A Hypothetical Case Study—*Titanium*

Titanium is the code name for a fictional game. We will examine the process of defining and creating the AI systems and behaviors for the agents in *Titanium*.

The *Titanium* development team was organized so that the AI was created primarily by two people: the AI designer, Dustin, and the AI programmer, Martin. Dustin was also lead designer for *Titanium II*. Dustin had worked as a designer on four games previously and was familiar with AI behaviors. Martin was an experienced programmer who had extensive experience in C++ programming, and had implemented the AI for *Titanium I*.

Both Dustin and Martin had worked together on *Titanium I*, an FPS with a complex back story. Numerous scripted scenes were used to advance the story along with the action. The challenge for *Titanium II* was to bring new elements into the game while retaining the elements that made the first game popular. *Titanium II* was targeted for the next-gen console hardware. This provided challenges and opportunities.

Reprinted with permission from Microsoft Corporation

Titanium I is a first-person shooter that is similar to *Perfect Dark Zero*.

The AI Core

Now that we're seeing multiple cores in a single processor, I can see a core being devoted to AI. Right now, I'm often hamstrung by the amazing amount of calculations AI must go through in order to make smart decisions. Once we have a processor devoted to it, we can crunch the numbers even more. With that, like most things in the industry, you'll start seeing the AI teams grow and the AI systems getting smarter simply because the hardware we run them on can handle it.

—John Comes (Lead Designer, Gas Powered Games)

Processing Power & Customization

First of all, I think that the incredible increase in processing power allows teams that are willing to take the time the opportunity to tune and individualize on-screen character behavior to wonderful levels. You no longer have to worry about dragging the frame rate if you code efficiently, and it's more likely that schedule and budget will limit innovation. Secondly, I think the greatest promise of AI in the future is making games react individually to individual players. Some of this is customized content, some is tuning difficulty level to individual play style to avoid frustration, some is looking for the ability to "surprise" the player in a way that works for that particular user.

—Don L. Daglow (Chief Executive Officer, Stormfront Studios)

Game Development Environment

Game AI does not drive the choice of a game engine and environment, but it is an important part of the decision. The engine and environment chosen, and tools available in that environment, have an impact on how the AI is developed. Dustin and Martin were involved in the early meetings to determine the development environment for *Titanium II*.

The decision was challenging. The team had the engine for *Titanium I,* which was familiar to the development team, stable, and well suited for the *Titanium* gameplay. However, it would have to be ported to the next-gen console. Commercial game engines were becoming available, but were still under development. If the development team did not already have an engine in place, the obvious choice would have been a commercial game engine. As it was, the team decided to stay with its current engine and upgrade it for next-gen hardware. There was agreement that either method—upgrading the *Titanium I* engine or licensing a commercial engine—would work. It was decided that there was a slight advantage to using familiar technology.

Initial Game Design

The design of a game defines the world and data for the AI, and it also creates certain expectations regarding behaviors that might exist in the AI. It is important that the designer work with the AI engineer to make sure that the design can be built.

One of the keys to good AI is that the designer works with the AI programmer to make sure that the design is achievable, given the available resources and time that have been allocated for the project. Dustin and Martin knew that they needed to push the envelope and go beyond what had been done before. Their goal was a set of AI features that were aggressive but achievable. If they put too many new features in the game the result would be that *Titanium II* was incomplete and late, rather than being new and interesting.

One of Dustin's goals for the design of the game itself, and the AI in particular, was to create a game that was both fresh and familiar. This has been the model for a number of successful games. A fresh game is new and interesting, but including elements that are familiar to the player makes the game more accessible. This way, the game is easy to learn and play. This is the recipe for success when making a high-quality game sequel such as *Titanium II*, which maintained common elements of the previous version of the game that were familiar to the player, while adding enough new content and gameplay so that the game was fresh.

Dustin knew that familiar elements can be superior to fresh elements. In some cases, the familiar gameplay mechanism turns out to actually be the best way to play, and does not necessarily signify a lack of imagination on the part of the game development team. For example, in the game *Halo*, the final level design was relatively linear. Many preceding FPSs, such as *Doom* and *Half-Life*, also had a very linear data level design.

It may appear that the developer just decided to follow the familiar path and not innovate in this area. In fact, the *Halo* team experimented with a non-linear level design that was more open, and

The final level design in *Halo* was relatively linear.

they built several sample levels, which were focus tested with a variety of players. They found that the non-linear levels allowed players to wander off and have a hard time finding their way back to a place where something interesting was going on. The linear nature of the level made it easier to play the game. In the case of *Halo*, the familiar linear layout was a better way to implement the level design and gameplay than trying a new mechanism. Dustin felt that it was important to make sure that the new features of *Titanium II* were better, not just different.

Since *Titanium II* was a direct sequel, the design started with the *Titanium I* feature set: first person weapons and small squads of enemies that appeared to attack cooperatively. The step to next-gen hardware meant that the quantity and quality could be increased, meaning better models for characters, larger levels, and more enemies in a battle. Dustin decided to add two completely new features that would impact the AI. First, the game levels would be streamed, providing a seamless experience to the player as the player moved through the world, rather than a series of "LOADING" screens. The second feature was the addition of a teammate for the player. This feature would have the most impact on the AI, as the AI would control the teammate's behavior.

Dustin discussed the teammate concept with Martin, and they considered many options. They settled on a single teammate, with the option for a second player to control the teammate either in a cooperative mode using split screen or two consoles networked together. This would be new work for the AI group, as *Titanium I* had no concept of cooperative play. All the AI agents were enemies of the player, and their behaviors involved attacking the player.

Putting It All Together: designing and building quality game artificial intelligence

chapter 9

An open question was whether the player had any direct control of the player's AI teammate. Dustin and Martin considered three scenarios. In the first, the teammate was completely autonomous. The teammate would accompany the player, but move and choose targets without player input. The designers could script actions for specific situations. A second scenario would require the player to direct the teammate. The player would direct the teammate where to go, and select targets for the teammate to attack. This was quickly discarded as being too much busy work for the player, given the run-and-gun style of *Titanium I*. The third scenario considered was a combination of the first two, in which the teammate would move and attack autonomously by default, but the player could optionally direct his teammate to move to a particular location or attack a particular enemy. Dustin and Martin decided that they would evaluate the first and third modes and defer the decision until they could play test both modes.

Define the AI Feature Set

The first step to building the game AI is to specify the feature set for the AI. As we noted earlier, this is heavily dependent on the game style and specific design. Once Dustin had completed the initial game design, Martin could define the AI feature set. One way to start the AI design is to divide it into two phases. The first part is the familiar portion of the AI, and the second is the fresh part. Along with being familiar, the first part of the game AI is frequently the minimum acceptable behavior that has been established by preceding games. In this case, it included the *Titanium I* feature set. Martin had the advantage that he had the code as well, making the process easier.

Familiar Features

Martin began by specifying the minimum feature set that was familiar and well-established. This began with the *Titanium I* features: multiple AI enemies attacking the player and using a variety of weapons. Next, Martin added features that were expected in the game genre. AI agents in competing games were making sophisticated use of cover. Martin added the ability to locate, duck behind, and shoot from behind several kinds of cover. The initial three types of cover were short walls, corners, and certain kinds of furniture.

Fresh Features

After the minimum set of familiar features were specified, Martin went to work specifying the new features that would be used to extend the gameplay. The new features required more work than the familiar features, particularly since the *Titanium I* code base already supported many of the familiar features. In addition, Martin didn't know for certain whether his team could implement the new features, and, if it could, whether the features would improve gameplay. Martin spent some time investigating the details of the new features and breaking them down into tasks to get a better idea of the amount of work required. This was not generally necessary with familiar features.

At this point, Dustin and Martin got back together to analyze the relative difficulty of the new features versus the value. For example, *Titanium II* had a feature, "duck behind cover," "pop up and shoot," and "duck back behind cover," that did not exist in the *Titanium I* engine. Martin made a rough guess regarding the level of difficulty of the implementation. At this point, the estimates were not exact, but they were reasonable and indicative of the relative cost of the features.

During one session, three new features (Cover, Long Distance Pursuit, and AI Teammate) that would enhance the gameplay were considered. Cover was the ability of agents AI agents to automatically use and shoot from behind cover. Long Distance Pursuit was the ability of AI agents to chase the player from one area to another. The AI Teammate was an AI controlled ally that accompanied the player. Dustin specified a relative value regarding each feature's effect on gameplay. The AI Teammate feature was key to the gameplay, and would occur at all times in the game. The value of the AI Teammate was judged to be 9 on a scale of 1 to 10. The Long Distance Pursuit was rated a 6, and Cover a 5. Martin looked at those features and determined how much work was involved with each feature. If two features appeared to have the same difficulty, Martin might suggest implementing them in order of design importance.

The AI Teammate feature was judged to be important, and would be implemented first. However, the Cover feature appeared to be much easier to implement than the Long Distance Pursuit, from a programming perspective. The existing engine supported some cover features, so extending the engine to implement the Cover feature was straightforward. The Long Distance Pursuit was not supported by the engine. After discussion with Martin, Dustin decided to defer the Long Distance Pursuit feature in favor of the Cover feature, as Cover would require less engineering work than the Long Distance Pursuit feature.

Design the AI Systems

Once the game design and AI features had been specified, Martin needed to design the AI systems. When specifying the systems, Martin worked closely with Dustin. The design of the AI systems determined how Dustin and the other designers would have to work with those systems. Wherever possible, it makes good sense for the AI programmer to design systems that are familiar to the designer's way of thinking.

Black Box vs. White Box Design

An important choice that Martin needed to make was to decide which parts of the AI systems would be Black Boxes, and which would be White Boxes.

The most common situation concerning White or Black box is between the AI programmers and AI designers. The systems used by the designers can be self-contained, Black Box, or more complex White Box systems. In the case of *Titanium II*, the early design contained a Black Box/White Box question for the player as well. The AI Teammate could be a Black Box system, and operate autonomously, or it could be a White Box system and respond to player commands.

The AI in *Gears of War* control the players's teammate Dominic with no input from the player. In this case, the AI teammate is controlled by a Black Box system.

The player's AI teammates in *Tom Clancy's Ghost Recon Advanced Warfighter* respond to a number of commands issued by the player: stealth or aggressive behavior, movement directives, and attack orders. The resulting White Box system gives the player a great deal of control over the teammates, but it required that the player spend time directing the teammates' behavior.

Data-Driven Systems

All systems, whether Black or White Box, should be made data-driven. Nine times out of ten, even with a familiar behavior, a designer or producer will want to make an adjustment to the behavior. Accessible data values allow them to quickly try changes, and either improve the gameplay or discover that it was not such a good idea after all.

Black Box Systems in Titanium II

Automated systems tend to naturally fall into the category of Black Box systems. Martin decided to use an automatic path node generation system for *Titanium II*. An automatic path node system has several advantages. First, it supports quick generation of pathfinding data for game levels. As a result, automatic path node systems are faster for the designer to use. It can also support a user modifiable game level. An automatic path node system supports changes to the level, such as building additional structures and walls. If the game level changes, the automatic system can be used to update it.

The automatic method is not without its drawbacks. Automatic systems tend to be harder to control than manual systems. Since the nodes are placed by code, they may not have ended up exactly where Dustin and the designers expected. This is often addressed by allowing the modification of the pathfinding nodes after they are created, and it can lead to a problem when additional changes to the level require the regeneration of the path node data. This results in the loss of the manual adjustments. In this case, much of the speed advantage of the automatic method can be lost.

The quick results received by the designer are also offset by the fact that it takes much more programming work to create an automatic path node generation system. The automatic system usually requires continuing programming support as the game is built. The automatic system will produce quick results, but it will often require tuning. Since the placement is done in code, this tuning is done by an AI programmer familiar with the path node generation.

Before finalizing the decision to use an automated system, Martin and Dustin considered the manual system that had been used in *Titanium I*. Manual placement has its advantages as well, which mirror the disadvantages of the automatic system. The designer can place the nodes in the exact position desired. Changes to the nodes can be made easily in the level editor. It is very easy to adjust and tune in a manual system. Once the system is in place, it does not require any additional engineering support. These features are useful in a controlled, highly detailed environment. The relatively linear FPS genre fits this model.

The manual method's drawbacks again mirror the advantages of the automatic system. It takes time to place nodes after a level is created, and gameplay testing cannot be done until the nodes are added. Changes to the level require that the affected nodes be moved by hand. Finally, the manual method is hard to use in cases where the player can modify the level arbitrarily.

A third party AI toolkit provided support for automatic path node generation, which reduced the development time for this system. Dustin pointed out that designers spent a lot of time adding path nodes to levels during *Titanium I* production, and that this delayed level testing. As a result, Martin decided to use automatic path node generation in *Titanium II*. Martin added the feature of "seed nodes" to the system. This allowed path nodes to be specified in the editor, which in turn allowed a few critical nodes to be placed by hand, while generating the majority of the nodes automatically.

:::::: Real-World Path Node Systems

The Kynapse AI middleware (developed by Kynogon and used in a number of games including Eden Games' *Alone in the Dark 360* and Ascaron Entertainment's *Sacred 2*) supports the automatic generation of pathfinding nodes. Using a middleware tool reduces the amount of programming required to support automatic node generation. Game-specific tuning of the automatic system is still required. It is recommended that an AI programmer be available to support the designers' needs with respect to automatic path node generation. This system precomputes the path nodes using a batch process. Using this system speeds the designers' creation of playable levels.

Courtesy of Atari Interactive, Inc

The Kynapse AI middleware, used in games such as *Alone in the Dark 360,* supports the automatic generation of pathfinding nodes.

Command & Conquer: Generals also used automatic path node generation. In this case, the system was a custom system developed for the SAGE engine and required considerable programming work for its development. This system also provided fast turnaround for designers, who were able to playtest their levels immediately. In addition, this system supported dynamic pathfinding. Players and the AI virtual player could build structures and walls that blocked movement and destroy them later, restoring the movement. Since players could build on any area of the map, it was not possible to pre-compute pathfinding data. The automatic system allowed the re-computation of the data in real time during gameplay.

Games such as Epic's *Gears of War* allow the designer to manually place the path nodes. This allows the nodes to be placed exactly at particular locations in the level for gameplay reasons. In addition, attributes can be specified for the path nodes. For example, the designer can specify that the agent should crouch from a particular location and lean to the right to be able to fire around an obstacle. The game design for these games is such that the detailed positioning and information provided support the behavior of the agents, and it is worth the time necessary for the designers to place the nodes individually.

Epic Games

Gears of War allows the designer to manually place the path nodes and specify attributes for them.

White Box Systems in Titanium II

White Box systems are useful when the person using the system wants or needs to provide a lot of information to the system in return for precise control over the behavior of the system. Most of the White Box AI systems in *Titanium II* were for the use of Dustin and the other the game designers building the game. In addition, *Titanium II* had the possibility of presenting a White Box system to the player via the interface to the AI teammate. By allowing the player to specify stealth, movement, and targeting parameters, the AI teammate acted as a White Box system that the player could control with a high degree of detail.

One important goal when developing White Box systems is to provide the required degree of detail, while avoiding *micro-management*. For the player, micro-management occurs when the player must perform detailed operations in situations where no operation should be necessary. One example of micro-management would be if the AI Teammate in *Titanium II* blocks a corridor the player is trying to walk through. The micro-management occurs if the player has to stop, move back, order the teammate to move, then walks through the corridor. The expected behavior would be that either the teammate would not stop in narrow corridors or would move out of the player's way.

Micro-management for the designer occurs when the designer has to specify a large number of repetitive values each time a behavior is used. The preferred operation of the system would provide reasonable defaults for the values, saving the time to enter the same values over and over.

Agent Strategic and Squad Behavior

Dustin wanted to try a variety of strategies for the AI's behaviors and give the player the impression that the enemy agents were well coordinated squads. This was a new feature, and the details were still unclear. Martin designed this system as a White Box to give Dustin maximum flexibility and the ability to try different variations. The control code for the strategic "brain" that controlled whether the agent would advance, retreat, flank, or hold position was controlled using a set of rules, so Dustin could modify it without having to rebuild the game. The rules could be modified by timers, so Dustin could modify the behaviors over time as well. The area trigger capability common in many games was included so rules, behaviors, and timers could be triggered by the player entering or leaving an area.

These capabilities were straightforward for Martin to develop and allowed Dustin to try various behaviors. Playing the game is the best way to evaluate AI behaviors, and this system gave Dustin the ability to try a variety of possible behaviors.

Agent Spawning

Martin designed the agent spawning system as a White Box system. Dustin wanted to avoid giving the player the impression that the player was fighting the same battle over and over, so the spawning system gave the designers complete control over when and where agents would be created in the missions. This required that the designers place positioning information for each agent in the level and write a script to control when the agent would be created.

In order to minimize micro-management, Martin created a default script that would spawn the agent when the player approached to within 200 feet of the agent's spawn location. This allowed the designers to quickly place agents in a level and playtest the levels. Subsequently, the designer could go back and adjust the script as needed for the specific situation in the level.

White Box vs. Black Box

In some cases the choice between White Box systems and Black Box systems are obvious. Martin felt that a system provided by the engine or a third party that performs a well known function, such as path node generation, was an excellent candidate for a Black Box. This allowed the development team to avoid spending time re-inventing the wheel.

A few systems in *Titanium II,* such as event control in solo play missions, were obvious candidates for White Box systems. The designers needed to customize each mission, so it was valuable to give the designers detailed control in this area. These systems are often customized for a particular game, and the White Box model generally requires less programmer time.

In other cases, the choice was less clear. Either approach would work, with both having different advantages and disadvantages. Martin had to consider these in the context of the game feature set and the staff available for *Titanium II.* Black Box systems tend to require more AI Programmer time during development, and White Box tend to require more designer time. Martin's goal was a balance so that neither group would be overloaded during the game's development.

Capturing Information

One area Martin considered during the design of the AI systems was the ways information would be captured for the AI. An important function of the AI system during game development is capturing the information necessary to generate the desired AI behaviors in the game. Part of the AI design is determining what information will be captured and how it will be represented in the AI system. Much of the information comes from the game designers and is captured directly by the AI programmers in code, or captured by systems such as script systems or rule systems created by the AI programmers. Martin and Dustin met to discuss how they were going to handle this in *Titanium II*. Their goal was to make the process as efficient as possible for both the AI programmers and the AI designers.

Coding

As a programmer, Martin instinctively understood that a significant amount of information is represented as C++ code in the AI systems. The Black Box systems tend to be mostly C++ code. These systems require primarily AI programmer time, although it is also helpful if the designers can provide a detailed specification of the expected AI behaviors. C++ code is time-consuming to write and modify. It is best to use C++ for systems that are well-defined, such as the path node generation system in *Titanium II*.

Data

Without even thinking much about it, Martin made all the parameters to the AI systems data-driven. This had been established in previous games as a good idea, and there was no reason to do otherwise. The values for AI agents controlling attributes such as vision and hearing range, peripheral vision angle, speed, reaction time, and aiming error were specified in well labeled data files. This allowed Dustin and the other designers to easily modify these values and create and test various enemy agents in the game.

Script

Martin's AI design used scripts to control the agent spawning. This allowed the designers to write arbitrarily complex scripts to control spawning in the game, which in turn allowed them to achieve Dustin's goal of making each battle unique for the player.

Rules

The strategy rules captured the information that controlled the agent's choice of strategy. This allowed Dustin to develop and tune various strategies. By using multiple rule sets, Dustin could have different agents use different strategies.

Level Editor

The level editor was used to collect the location information for the agent spawning system and the scripts that controlled the spawning. The level editor is the best tool for collecting position and movement information for the AI.

Real-World AI Data Capture Methods

A variety of data capture methods have been used to capture AI data in video games. *Command & Conquer Generals: Zero Hour* used a graphical user interface (GUI) that expanded on the concepts used in *StarCraft*'s GUI based trigger system. This system was already familiar to most of the designers working on the game, and provided a productive environment for controlling the agent behaviors. Using familiar constructs allows designers to enter the required data more efficiently.

Electronic Arts

Courtesy of Blizzard Entertainment, Inc.

Command & Conquer: Generals   *StarCraft*

Data-driven systems are commonly used to capture AI data. This gives the designers, artists, and producers an opportunity to provide input into the systems. *Supreme Commander* uses a data-driven system to allow Chris Taylor and the other designers at Gas Powered Games to quickly prototype and tune the AI. The Kynapse AI system used in a variety of games including *Medal of Honor: Airborne* uses XML data files to configure the AI.

A scripting system can be used to capture AI information, as well as other game data. *Civilization IV* and *Earth & Beyond* use Python scripts to control and define AI behaviors. *Earth & Beyond* was a massive multiplayer online role-playing game, and the scripting was used by the game designers on the server. *Civilization IV* made the scripts available to players so that the players could easily create mods.

Scripting languages can also be used to perform complex AI control, event handling, and state machine implementation. The UnrealScript language is used in this fashion in a variety of games, including *SWAT 4*, *Tribes II*, *Gears of War,* and *Unreal Tournament 2007*. In this case, creating this type of script can require the programming skills of an AI programmer. One fairly useful development methodology in this case is to have the AI programmer write the initial scripts. Once the scripts are written, they can be modified by the designers in order to adjust the behaviors. This allows the designers to make modifications without requiring designers to have advanced programming skills.

Epic Games

UnrealScript is used in *Gears of War* to handle complex AI.

Rule-based systems are also a way to capture information from the designer. Rule sets are a powerful means to represent the reasoning needed by the AI agents in a game. Rule sets can be particularly valuable when creating virtual players for strategy games. The rule-based model is powerful and flexible, which makes it well-suited for controlling the strategic behavior of a virtual player in order for it to make reasonable decisions.

Resolving Issues

The design phase is a good place to resolve questions regarding the use of manual vs. automatic systems. After Martin completed the initial AI design, he met with Dustin to review the design and make sure that it would meet the needs of designers. In the case of the automatic path node generation system, Martin was using a third party package. This would allow it to be added to *Titanium II* quickly, and the system could be evaluated at that time. The cover system was going to take a long time to finish, as it was a new system that would be created from scratch by the AI development team. Martin and Dustin decided to implement a very simple manual cover system initially. This could be done in a short time, and would allow designers to place cover points on the map manually. This would allow the designers to prototype levels while the automatic cover system was being implemented. In addition, it gave the team a fall-back position if serious technical difficulties became apparent during the development of the automatic cover system. In that case, the manual system could be enhanced and expanded, allowing the game to be completed without the automatic cover system if necessary.

Implement the AI Systems

Once Martin and Dustin had finalized the AI design, Martin and the other AI programmers began implementing the AI systems. They had two goals for the implementation. The first goal was to leverage the *Titanium I* code base to provide a base level of AI functionality as quickly as possible. The second goal was to create the new systems, such as the automatic cover system, as quickly as possible.

A development method Martin used in *Titanium II* was to have a successful *daily build*. This meant that every day the game engine would be functional. The game would run, and previously created levels would load into the game. New features would be added, but the existing functionality of the game would be preserved. This allowed other team members, designers, and artists to work in parallel during the AI and other C++ development.

Leveraging Familiar Features from *Titanium I*

The first phase of development for *Titanium II* AI development was adapting the *Titanium I* code base so that designers could start building prototype levels as quickly as possible. The *Titanium I* code base provided a substantial amount of the functionality required, so the development team could start work immediately.

The plan was for the AI developers to complete an initial AI implementation during the eight weeks that the engine was being ported to the next-generation consoles. At the end of this time, the engine with some basic AI would be running on the target console platform. At this point, designers could begin prototyping levels and evaluate gameplay using the initial AI systems. The AI programmers would continue developing and expanding the AI systems in parallel with the designers' initial prototypes. Information learned from the initial prototypes would be used to further improve the AI systems.

Low-Level Behaviors

Martin used a state machine system from *Titanium I*. The system was functional and already included implementations of useful low-level AI behaviors, such as pathfinding, weapon selection, aiming, firing, and reloading.

Martin considered extending the state machine system to use a scripting interface such as Lua. This was discarded, as the AI programmers were already comfortable programming in C++, and Dustin's design team did not have much experience in Lua programming. Adding a script interface to low level behaviors did not fit the team's needs at this point in time.

One of the tasks for *Titanium II* was to get the engine running on next-generation consoles. A small programming team was given the task, and it set to work on a separate copy of the engine. The task took approximately eight weeks. The changes involved were significant, and parts of the game were broken while this team worked on changes to its copy. The rest of the team used the working *Titanium I* code during this time. Once the engine was working on the next-generation consoles, the whole team spent a few days merging all of the work that had been done on both copies of the engine for the past eight weeks.

High-Level Behaviors

The principal high-level behaviors *Titanium II* required to support Dustin's design were the automatic cover system and cooperative squad behaviors. The new cover system was going to be implemented using the state machine system as well. The cover system was designed to function automatically without special input from the designers. Implementing them in C++ using state machines was a reasonable method for the AI programmers.

The cooperative behavior of the AI agents in *Titanium II* was created by designer control of the agents, rather than an automatic system. Designers triggered audio cues and initiated attack behaviors directly using scripts and triggers in the level editor. *Titanium II* used these methods with the addition of the sophisticated spawn system to allow the designers more flexibility when spawning agents.

A Player's "Best Friend"?

I think the future of game AI over the next five years includes a making the "actors" seem more emotional and lifelike—first by simple audio and animation cues, then possibly by having emotional state machines that modify basic behaviors and actions of an actor on screen. I also think that in a larger sense, game AI will continue to evolve around the lines of making the game world feel real and welcoming to the player. Imagine for a moment a "meta AI" that starts learning about the player the instant the game is started. This "meta AI" would be responsible for ensuring all the things that need to happen to make a player feel welcome and comfortable in the game world, according to the skills, abilities, and play style of that individual player. In effect this would customize the game experience for the player, and with that customization would come an emotional tie from the player back to the game. After all, how fun would it be if the characters, game world and even the functioning of the game itself felt like they were your "best friend"?

—*Mark Skaggs (Chief Executive Officer, Blue Nitro Studios)*

Preparing the Foundation for New Features

The new features were the most time consuming part of the AI development process. The process would take several months, and the schedule for new features is often imprecise. Rather than making Dustin and the designers wait for the completion of the new features, Martin opted for a phased approach. The manual path node system from *Titanium I* was included in the initial builds of *Titanium II*. This allowed the designers to build small prototype levels for testing while the automatic system was being implemented. Similarly, a simple manual cover system was implemented first and given to the designers. Again, they could use it to build small prototype levels and experiment with the cover behaviors.

The phased approach involves some duplication of effort, and some work that will be discarded. The manual cover system would likely be discarded when the automatic system was completed. However, the phased approach allowed the development team to be more productive overall. The use of the manual cover system allowed the designers to evaluate scenarios in the game, and this gave the team a better idea of what it needed from the automatic cover system. The team's productivity was higher, as was the final quality of the game.

Initial Implementation Complete

At this point the initial implementation was complete, and designers could begin prototyping levels in the engine. The cover system remained to be completed, with the simple manual system available for prototyping. The AI programming team spent a few days with the design team, fixing problems and adding a few minor features that had been overlooked in the initial design. The team was ready to move forward with the game development.

Iterate Details and Design

Once the basic systems were in place, it was time to begin the process of iterating the details and, where necessary, modifying the design of the AI system. From their experience with previous games, Martin and Dustin knew that the initial implementation would likely contain some flaws that would only become obvious in actual gameplay. They wanted to correct these as soon as possible. This is a key reason why it was important to get basic functionality into the designers' hands quickly. Without this, it is impossible to evaluate the quality of gameplay.

Development Iteration

The *Titanium II* team used an iterative development methodology to create the game. The first iteration was during the development of new AI systems. In some studios, this work is called *preproduction*, as the team is creating the tools and systems that will be used to produce the final levels or missions in the game.

Diagram by Per Olin

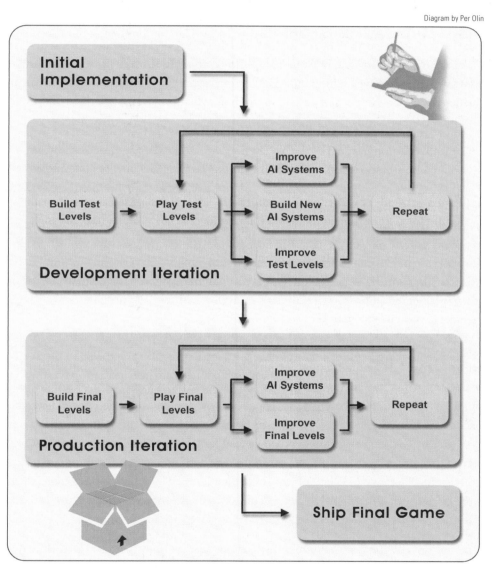

The *Titanium II* team used an iterative development process to create the AI. Prototype test levels were used initially to evaluate and inprove the systems.

In a perfect world, Martin and Dustin would make the correct design decisions the first time. They could follow a very simple production process with respect to the AI: Design AI Systems → Implement AI Systems → Build Final Levels → Ship Game. This is not possible in the real world. One reason is that Martin and his team learned a great deal when implementing new features. Lacking knowledge of the future, what worked well was to make reasonable decisions quickly and correct problems as soon as possible. As a result, it was necessary to go back and modify some portions of the design when it became obvious that there was a problem or a potential improvement.

Once the design is correct, the details need to be adjusted. In some cases where the controls are data-driven, either a designer or programmer can make the changes. In the case of spawn scripts, the designers can make the changes in the editor. Martin provided a set of sample scripts, so the designers could in most cases copy and paste to produce the required behaviors. Where necessary, AI programmers create new scripts.

> Any software development process that requires knowledge of the future is doomed to failure.
>
> —Ahlquist's Last Law of Programming

Additional design needs may also cause changes in the design and implementation. This should be expected, and be part of the plan and schedule. Creating a complex new video game is not a straight line journey from Point A to Point B It is normal to learn important details during the implementation process. The iterative development process provides a way take advantage of that learning.

Often, while iterating through design and implementation improvements, it becomes apparent that a *hybrid solution* is required to get the level of quality required for a particular game. In *Titanium II*, this was the case for the cover system. The automatic cover system was completed during the development iteration cycle. The team used input from the designers gathered from prototype levels using the manual cover system. The resulting system worked very well most of the time. However, there were a few instances in specific levels where the resulting cover behavior was not quite right. There were certain objects in the game, such as a glass topped table, that were large enough that the system recognized them as providing cover. However, the designers felt that it looked wrong for the AI to try to use them for cover.

One option would have been to eliminate these types of objects from the world. Because the art team had worked hard to get the visual effect of reflection and translucence working, this was discarded. The option used in *Titanium II* was to add an area marker to the cover system. Areas marked were off-limits to the automatic cover system, and the cover system would not look for potential cover points in these areas. This allowed the designers to flag these areas, eliminating the awkward behaviors. The automatic cover system handled the rest of the cases. The use of a hybrid system allowed the designers to customize the behavior in a few special cases. In the majority of cases, the hybrid system handled cover automatically, reducing the amount of work required on the part of the designers.

The optimal situation is to continue the development iteration process until the required systems are completed and the resulting behaviors are of the desired quality. The other common situation is to iterate until the team runs out of time. *Titanium II* had a target schedule for shipping the game. This fixed the date for the completion of the development iteration process. The team would have preferred another iteration, but the AI systems were all completed on schedule.

Production Iteration

The final phase of the AI work occurred during the production iteration of *Titanium II*. At this point, most of the AI agents were completed and working in the game. Major parts of the levels had been prototyped and playtested. It was easy to visualize the behaviors of the AI agents in *Titanium II* and see how the behaviors were working.

At this point, the major AI activities were tuning, polishing, debugging, and minor extensions to the AI. The major system and feature development had been completed during the development iteration process.

Now that actual levels were approaching completion, Martin was periodically called to take a look at cases where the frame rate was too slow. In some cases, there were operations that could be optimized, and the code was rewritten to improve the frame rate. In other cases there was simply too much data. Sometimes adjustments were made, such as increasing the spacing between path nodes or decreasing the level of detail. In other cases, the only option was to simplify the level by removing agents.

Polishing the AI behaviors was done on a case-by-case basis in each level. The spawn scripts were adjusted so that the player never saw an agent pop into existence, and there were no straggling AI agents in an attack sequence. The spawn locations were adjusted so that the cover points chosen by the automatic cover system made sense, and did not result in an enemy squad bunching up.

A few minor extensions were made to the AI systems. The team noted that in some cases the AI agents would take cover in a doorway. It was possible for the player to move to a position at an angle to the doorway such that the agent was no longer protected by the doorway. The team added code to detect this situation and automatically moved the agent to the other side of the doorway.

Much of the work at this point was done on specific agents in specific levels. Global changes to the systems were avoided, as this had the potential to break levels that were already working. Changes to an agent's scripts were the safest way to make a localized change, as well as specific changes to a level. In some cases, the programmers analyzed the internal data structures and identified changes to the level, such as adjusting the width or height of a wall that could correct specific problems with the AI movement. Localized changes were safer than making changes to the AI systems at this point in the development.

Martin, Dustin, and the development team completed and shipped *Titanium II* to an appreciative fan audience. The new features, coupled with the level of polish made possible by the iterative development process, resulted in an exciting and entertaining game. There were a few spots that could have been improved given more time, but overall the game was high quality and received good reviews. The team took a couple of weeks off to bask in the glow of a successful development cycle, and shortly afterward went back to work on *Titanium III*.

Careers in Game Artificial Intelligence

There are two primary careers in game AI development. They are the AI programmer and the AI designer. The programmer focuses on C++ programming, which involves creating the systems that support the AI and implementing behaviors that are built on a low level in the application. The AI programmer creates the Black Box behaviors in code. The AI programmer will build automatic systems to support the AI and will integrate and support scripting languages.

The second career is the AI designer, who specifies behaviors and gameplay. These define the desired behavior of the AI agents. The designer then builds the level-specific or instance-specific data that create specific instances of the agents and behaviors. The line between AI programmer and AI designer is fairly flexible. In some cases, AI programmers will also do design work. In other cases, some AI designers will do a fair amount of programming. But in general, the programmers focus more on the code than on the level design and specific agent behaviors, and the designers tend to be concerned more with the design and level creation aspects than the C++ coding aspects.

AI Programmer

The specific focus of the AI programmer will vary, depending on the game and genre. For example, the strategy game *Civilization IV* does not have a lot of individual agent AI, but it does have a rather sophisticated virtual player system. In this case, the AI programmer will be concerned with systems to support the virtual player. In an FPS such as *F.E.A.R.*, the AI programmer does not have a virtual player at all to deal with. However, the AI programmer deals with the behavior of the individual agents in a 3D world and would be concerned with aspects such as cover points, visibility in the 3D world, and access paths to a destination that may be covered from enemy fire rather than open to fire.

Responsibilities and Tasks

The AI programmer is a C++ programmer familiar with the development and use of pathfinding systems and scripting systems. The programmer will maintain systems that are used to create AI behaviors, and either assist designers in creating the AI behaviors or do the actual creation of the behaviors. Senior AI programmers design the AI systems and evaluate and select commercially available AI toolkits.

AI System Design

The senior AI programmer will be in charge of the AI system design. As discussed earlier in the chapter, system design involves determining what systems will be required to support the AI behaviors needed for the gameplay. A part of this involves specifying the data definitions that will be used to control behaviors and which are available to designers. An important design concern is determining where a scripting or user interface will be made available to the designer to control or define a particular behavior.

C++ Programming: System and Behavior Creation

The AI programmer will spend a significant portion of time programming compiled code. Generally, in modern video games, the coding is done in C++. The first activity in C++ will be to build the systems, which are the basic building blocks of the AI. The systems may vary, depending on the game. Pathfinding systems allowing the agents to move through the game world are common. Scripting systems support scripting various operations in the AI. State machine frameworks support building behaviors using state machines.

In addition to the systems, specific behaviors will often be created in C++. A common process is to create low-level behaviors using state machines implemented in C++. Behaviors such as movement to a location and firing the weapon are often implemented using C++ code.

Scripting

AI programmers are often involved with scripting languages. One task is to interface a scripting language to the engine. This may involve interfacing a scripting language, such as Lua or Python, to the game engine. Another task is to provide utility functions to the scripting system that can be used by designers or other scripters. For example, there may be a function to direct a unit to move to a particular location. The script function would be implemented in C++ code by an AI programmer, and it would be the programmer's task to interface the function to the script system.

The AI programmer may also spend some time writing scripts, depending on the complexity of the scripting interface. Some scripting implementations are strictly a high-level control mechanism, and there is not a lot of actual programming that is done in the script language. It is used just to set parameters and initiate actions. The AI programmer may create the initial scripts and allow the designers to modify and maintain them.

In some cases, substantial programming may be done in the scripting system. The Unreal scripting language, UnrealScript, is actually a full-featured programming language with Java-like syntax. Substantial parts of the programming for the game can be done using the UnrealScript language. In this case, the AI programmer may spend most of the time writing scripts as well as programming in C++.

Data Definition

The AI programmer will often do initial setup on data-driven systems to get the first implementation working and available to the designers. From that point, the designers can make modifications to data files. The initial setup can be done more quickly by the AI programmer, who is familiar with the code underlying the data-driven systems.

Debugging

Debugging is an important activity for the AI programmer. AI systems are large, complex software projects in modern video games. Agent behaviors are complex, and unexpected situations show up in games that are difficult to anticipate. Simple coding errors are impossible to eliminate. As a result, debugging is always necessary.

The AI programmer is the key person responsible for doing debugging in the AI gameplay area. Although errors can be introduced in scripts, and problems may emerge in the data, it is often difficult for the designer to isolate and identify these. The designer normally only has access to the higher-level script and data—not the C++ code in the engine.

It is helpful and often necessary to have access to the C++ code. The AI programmer can access the C++ code, as well as any scripts or data, in order to determine the exact source of the problem. In some cases, the problem will be in C++ code. In some cases, it may be in script code. Since AI programmers have access to all parts of the application, they are generally best qualified to do the final debugging.

Animation Control

AI programmers may spend a fair amount of time doing animation control. The animations are a good way of displaying the internal AI states to the player and to giving the player the impression of intelligent behavior.

Part of the job of the AI programmer is to make sure that the appropriate animation is played at the right time. This can be done using a direct or indirect system. In a direct system, the AI code will play the animations directly. Code in state machines may choose the animation appropriate to the behavior and start it playing at the appropriate time. In this case, the AI code is in control of the animations being played by the system. The code, written by the AI programmer, drives the animations system directly.

An indirect system decouples the specific animation from the AI code. This involves creating an animation selection system that interprets information from the AI state and possibly other game systems such as the physics system. The AI must make the necessary information available to the selection system. The AI may set flags that indicate that it is firing a weapon, for example, or that the AI is opening a door. The selection system interprets those status flags and plays the appropriate animation.

Education

A computer science degree is recommended for AI programmers. General computer science training is good to both learn the techniques of programming and to give you a broad understanding of computer science. Current video games are complex software projects. The new hardware on consoles includes multiple processors, making multi-threaded programming relevant. The graphics hardware on both console and PC is very sophisticated. A computer science degree is useful in order to deal with the complexity of the systems.

General computer science AI programming concepts are good to know. As we have noted, game AI is not the same as computer science AI. However, some of the areas, such as expert systems, do provide a useful basis for systems in video games. The general concepts are helpful as a background, even if they are not specifically applicable to games.

C++ programming and object-oriented design are important skills for the AI programmer. Modern game engines use these, and creating new behaviors is well-suited to object-oriented design. Training in 3D graphics is very useful as well. Most modern video games are rendered in a 3D world, and the AI operates in a 3D simulated environment. AI operations often involve visibility and collision calculations. The 3D graphics training—particularly involving modeling, ray-casting, and collision—is very helpful in order to perform some of the lower-level operations that are required to do AI programming in a modern video game.

Experience

In addition to having a computer science degree, the best training for video game development is to actually build a video game. One obvious question is, "How do I get experience building a video game if I am trying to get a job building video games?" The answer is that there are actually quite a few ways to build a video game outside of the game industry.

Gunman Chronicles (a *Half-Life* mod) impressed Valve so much that the company helped the developers finish and publish the game.

Modding

Many PC video games support modification to the games. You can take the game, modify it, and produce a variation of it by changing the scripting, story, gameplay, data, and possibly assets in the game. It is possible to build a new game (mod) using the commercial game as a base. The new game has its own gameplay, but uses the commercial game engine and its assets. This is one way get experience in the process of building game AI. *Gunman Chronicles* was built as a mod of *Half-Life* by a group that was not professional developers at that point. It was impressive enough that Valve (creators of *Half-Life*) helped the developers finish and publish the game.

Free Downloadable Game Engines

There are also game engines available for free. The older versions of the Quake engine can be downloaded for free from the Id software Web site. It is possible to create a game using that version of the game engine. It does not include the latest rendering techniques, but many of the AI concepts are still valid. Being able to program in an actual video game engine environment is a very powerful asset, as far as getting a job.

DirectX

It is also possible to build a small 3D game from scratch using DirectX on the PC. The DirectX SDK provides a variety of tools and support for building games and rendering them. In some cases, students have done an independent computer design project and built a limited video game using the DirectX SDK. This is an advanced project, more difficult than making a mod, but has been successfully performed by a five-student team in the course of a two semester independent design project.

"Indie" Game Engines

There are low cost game engines that are available for license. The Torque engine from Garage Games is available for a nominal license fee to independent developers. In this case, independent being defined as not for sale. It is possible to get access to a relatively sophisticated engine and scripting environment, and use that to build a sample game. All of these are good ways to get experience in actually building a game. In order to get a start in the video game industry, the best way to get a foot in the door is to actually have some experience building a game. AI programming is a technical position that requires attention to detail. Creativity and good communication skills are a plus as well. Creating behaviors in video games can be a fascinating and engaging occupation.

AI Designer

The tasks that the AI designer performs in his day-to-day job also vary depending on the game time. In a heavily scripted FPS, they will tend to focus more on the placement and triggering of behaviors in the individual enemy agents and level. In strategy games, AI designers often spend a fair amount of time focusing on the design and tuning of the virtual player. There are some game- and genre-specific tasks.

Responsibilities and Tasks

The designer creates the instance specific data for the behavior of the AI. An agent may follow a patrol path to guard an area. There is code written by the programmer to allow the agent to follow a patrol path. However, the specific patrol path is placed into the level and positioned by the designer at a specific location. The designer also creates the trigger or script that is set up to control when the agent begins to follow that particular patrol path. The designer usually handles any manual placement resulting from AI design. For example, if path nodes are placed on a level by hand, it will generally fall to the designer to place the path nodes. The designer specifies the necessary flags and indicates whether they can be used for cover.

The AI designer is involved with the tuning of the AI. Usually the AI will have a number of parameters that can be set to control the behaviors. Items such as vision range and unit speed, which affect how soon a unit will react and how quickly it will move once it observes the player, can be set and tuned by the designer. Attributes such as aggressiveness are often made parameters in the AI. The designer can tune these values to create the appropriate gameplay experience at a specific part of the game.

The AI designer helps with debugging as well. The tasks for the designer when debugging are somewhat different than for the programmer, because the designer does not have access to the C++ code. As a result, the AI designer is not generally responsible for isolating and determining the actual bug. However, one task that the designer often performs is producing a test case that demonstrates the bug on a small-scale example. The programmer, stepping through the C++ code, runs the game about 100 times slower than the designer does when he is running the game without using a debugger.

It greatly helps the programmer debug if the designer can provide him with a very small test case of a few agents that demonstrate the problem, rather than a full-scale level with 10 or 20 agents in which the problem occurs after 5 minutes of gameplay. Another option that can be used, rather than creating a small example, is stripping down a level that demonstrates the problem by removing extraneous parts. So once again, the result is a smaller test case that the programmer can then debug.

A senior designer, either the game designer or a senior AI designer, works with the AI programmer to define what the expected AI behaviors are that would be supported in the gameplay. So one of the activities that is performed early on is coming up with the set of AI behaviors that are required for the game.

Another area where the designer can spend a lot of time is the creation and tuning of a virtual player. One option that has been used for creating the virtual player is to create a rules-based system that specifies under which conditions the virtual player performs various actions. In several real-time strategy projects it was the AI designer who was responsible for creating the rule set that drove the behavior of the virtual player.

This rule set specifies various activities, such as the order of building structures in the AI's base or cities, when to build units to defend the structures, when to attack the opposing player, how to allocate resources between buildings and units, and other game related activities. So the game designer spends time creating and tuning the behavior of the virtual player to produce a good gameplay experience.

The last area that the AI designer spends time in is scripting the game levels for custom behaviors. This starts with simple trigger-based scripting so that certain events happen when the player enters certain areas or at certain times in the game. This can include more sophisticated scripting where the agents respond to certain events passed to them through the scripting system, and the designer modifies their behaviors based on the actions of the player in the vicinity.

Education

Unlike the programmer, there is not a specific college degree that will start you on the road to becoming a video game designer. Video game designers come from varied backgrounds, from math to computer science to literature. Rather than a specific degree, there are certain areas of expertise that are useful in becoming a game designer.

Experience with board, card, and role-playing games is beneficial. Studying game mechanics for games like *Magic: The Gathering* or *Axis and Allies* will help develop an understanding of how numbers can be used to control player behavior and, as a result, how numbers can be used dictate AI behavior.

Game theory is also useful. Video games are not often built directly on game theory, because it is somewhat abstract and dry. However, the concepts in game theory are often applicable to areas of video games. Understanding the background can be helpful when designing and putting together the gameplay of a video game.

A background in literature is helpful. Frequently the game design that is done, both for the AI and for the flow of the game, is narrative oriented. Familiarity with the makings of a good narrative and how to put one together can be used to improve the quality of the narrative in a game.

Most video games are built in a 3D environment, so a designer should have knowledge of 3D modeling packages for games, such as Maya or 3D Studio Max. The tools that are used to build those environments are either the 3D modeling packages or tools very similar in function and concept to the 3D modeling packages. Designers are able to create level layouts and environments for their AI agents much more rapidly if they understand the concepts of using a 3D modeling package.

AI designers require more programming skills than most game designers. The AI designer is often responsible for creating and modifying the agents' behaviors. Training in general programming and languages such as Python, Java, and Lua will provide the necessary concepts. What is more, these languages are used in a number of video games.

Experience

The most important experience, as with the programmer, is actually building a game. In the case of a designer, the best choice is to start with a mod. Mods allow designers to quickly create and modify gameplay, rather than having to spend a lot of time on programming details. This allows them to focus on designing gameplay and creating behaviors for agents.

Modding: A Powerful Form of Training

Starting with a mod can be an extremely powerful form of training. Several of the guys I work with now began in a modding community, and I am seeing this more often as a way to get into game design. As the player community gets more access to better tools (because we are shipping better tools as an industry), we are able to better judge the quality of potential game designers based on their mods. *Warcraft III* currently has a thriving mod community that in its own small way rivals that creative enthusiasm we find in the *Half-Life* community.

—*Dustin Browder (Lead Designer, Blizzard Entertainment)*

AI designers create behaviors that make games entertaining and believable. They need to have an understanding of human psychology and how people play, as well as good computer skills. They often work with scripted systems, so programming skills are helpful. Creating games, either paper or modified computer games, is one of the best ways to learn game design.

AI programmers and designers work together to create compelling, detailed AI behaviors in modern video games. The task requires creativity, as well as technical skills and attention to detail. Both programmers and designers can get experience by working with game mods. Great game AI is often the result of collaboration between talented individuals who bring different skill sets to the process of AI development.

Future of Game AI

Video game AI will continue to evolve in complexity and sophistication. Third party AI packages are available with sophisticated AI systems. Game AI programmers and designers will be able to focus on behaviors rather than the AI systems, and thus create more complex behaviors and interactions. The AI programmers for *Half Life 2: Episode One* indicated that the challenge in that game was the creation of artificial personality rather than artificial intelligence, as one of the goals was to express the personality of the AI characters, rather than just having them shoot back and use cover properly.

The next-generation consoles have enough graphic and computing power to support real-time facial expressions on characters. This will require the creation of systems to allow designers to script expressions and use facial animations as cues. This will create a desire for automatic systems to manage facial expression and emotion—a complex area indeed.

Another interesting technology is AI that can be trained by example. Rather than coding scripts or rules, the AI character is played by a human player. The system captures the behaviors and automatically creates an AI controller that mimics the human player's behaviors. At this time the technology is unproven, but it has potential to speed the development of AI characters in games and to allow players to create multiple AI personalities in a game.

The requirements for game AI vary from game to game, and from genre to genre. In some cases, individual characters with complex autonomous behaviors are created. In other cases a virtual player is created with control over a number of simple agents. The production of a game's AI systems involves designing the systems to meet a game's needs, then creating the systems and revising them. While a good initial design is important, the needs of the game always evolve as the game is developed, so it is important to quickly prototype AI behaviors and be able to improve them. Once the game is running and the AI agents are working in the game, a number of improvements become obvious. It is important to plan the development process so that these improvements can be made, resulting in a high quality, entertaining game.

> Artificial intelligence has helped to provide a robust solo play experience—one that we need to continue to offer. We need to continue to develop AI so that we emphasize re-playability and fun for our games. AI that can substitute for human players to "fill in" a multiplayer experience is also very necessary.
>
> —*Frank T. Gilson*
> *(Senior Developer, Wizards of the Coast)*

Game artificial intelligence is a fascinating field that combines complex technical algorithms with theatrical sleight of hand to produce behaviors that are fun and engaging for the player. AI programmers combine state machines, search algorithms, scripts, code, and data to produce sophisticated behavior on the part of agents in the games. Designers specify, trigger, and tune behaviors in the game. A great deal of work goes into each game, resulting in a compelling, satisfying, and rich gameplay.

:::CHAPTER REVIEW:::

1. Consider various video game genres and specific games in each genre. What AI systems or techniques would be applicable to a wide variety of games? Which would be specific to a single genre or game type?

2. Consider the design for a new game. How would you go about determining which existing features in the genre (or previous version if a sequel) should be kept? How would you decide which features should be improved or discarded?

3. Several new features are under consideration for this game. How would you evaluate whether the new features enhanced gameplay or are distracting and irritating?

4. A video game is being developed using an iterative development process. Think of some specific measurements that would indicate that it is time to move from development iterations to production iterations.

5. What are some less specific qualitative aspects of the game that would indicate that it is time to move from development iterations to production?

6. Consider two people: one who wants to become an AI programmer, and a second who wants to become an AI designer. Develop a plan for each person to gain education and experience relevant to achieve these goals.

Resources

There's a wealth of information on game development and related topics discussed in this book. Here is just a sample list of books, news sites, organizations, and events you should definitely explore!

News

Blues News—www.bluesnews.com

Computer Games Magazine—www.cgonline.com

Game Daily Newsletter—www.gamedaily.com

Game Developer Magazine—www.gdmag.com

Gamers Hell—www.gamershell.com

Game Music Revolution (GMR)—www.gmronline.com

Game Rankings—www.gamerankings.com

GamesIndustry.biz—www.gamesindustry.biz

GameSlice Weekly—www.gameslice.com

GameSpot—www.gamespot.com

GameSpy—www.gamespy.com

Game Industry News—www.gameindustry.com

GIGnews.com—www.gignews.com

Internet Gaming Network (IGN)—www.ign.com

Machinima.com—www.machinima.com

Music4Games.net—www.music4games.net

Next Generation—www.next-gen.biz

1UP—www.1up.com

PC Gamer—www.pcgamer.com

Star Tech Journal [technical side of the coin-op industry]—www.startechjournal.com

UGO Networks (Underground Online)—www.ugo.com

Video Game Music Archive—www.vgmusic.com

Wired Magazine—www.wired.com

Directories & Communities

Apple Developer Connection—developer.apple.com

Betawatcher.com—www.betawatcher.com

Fat Babies.com [game industry gossip]—www.fatbabies.com

Gamasutra—www.gamasutra.com

GameDev.net—www.gamedev.net

Game Development Search Engine—www.gdse.com

GameFAQs—www.gamefaqs.com

Game Music.com—www.gamemusic.com

Game Rankings—www.gamerankings.com

Games Tester—www.gamestester.com

GarageGames—www.garagegames.com

Moby Games—www.mobygames.com

Overclocked Remix—www.overclocked.org

PS3—www.ps3.net

Wii-Play—www.wii-play.com

Xbox.com—www.xbox.com

XBOX 360 Homebrew—www.xbox360homebrew.com [includes XNA developer community]

Organizations

Academy of Interactive Arts & Sciences (AIAS)—www.interactive.org

Academy of Machinima Arts & Sciences—www.machinima.org

Association of Computing Machinery (ACM)—www.acm.org

Business Software Alliance (BSA)—www.bsa.org

Digital Games Research Association (DiGRA)—www.digra.org

Entertainment Software Association (ESA)—www.theesa.com

Entertainment Software Ratings Board (ESRB)—www.esrb.org

Game Audio Network Guild (GANG)—www.audiogang.org

International Computer Games Association (ICGA)—www.cs.unimaas.nl/icga

International Game Developers Association (IGDA)—www.igda.org

SIGGRAPH—www.siggraph.org

Events

Consumer Electronics Show (CES)
January—Las Vegas, NV
www.cesweb.org

Game Developers Conference (GDC)
March—San Francisco, CA
www.gdconf.com

Serious Games Summit (SGS)
March (San Francisco, CA at GDC) & October (Washington, DC)
www.seriousgamessummit.com

D.I.C.E. Summit (AIAS)
March—Las Vegas, NV
www.dicesummit.org

SIGGRAPH (ACM)
Summer—Los Angeles, CA; San Diego, CA; Boston, MA (location varies)
www.siggraph.org

Tokyo Game Show (TGS)
Fall—Japan
tgs.cesa.or.jp/english/

E3 Business & Media Summit
July—Santa Monica, CA
www.e3expo.com

Austin Game Developers Conference
September—Austin, TX
www.gameconference.com

E for All Expo
October—Los Angeles, CA
www.eforallexpo.com

Colleges & Universities

Here is a list of schools that have strong game degree or certificate programs:

Academy of Art University—www.academyart.edu

Arizona State University—www.asu.edu

Art Center College of Design—www.artcenter.edu

Art Institute Online—www.aionline.edu

The Art Institutes—www.artinstitutes.edu

Carnegie Mellon University—www.cmu.edu

DeVry University—www.devry.edu

DigiPen Institute of Technology—www.digipen.edu

Expression College for Digital Arts—www.expression.edu

Full Sail Real World Education—www.fullsail.edu

Guildhall at SMU—guildhall.smu.edu

Indiana University - MIME Program—www.mime.indiana.edu

Iowa State University—www.iastate.edu

ITT Technical Institute—www.itt-tech.edu

Massachusetts Institute of Technology (MIT)—media.mit.edu

Rensselaer Polytechnic Institute—www.rpi.edu

Ringling College of Art & Design—www.ringling.edu

Santa Monica College Academy of Entertainment & Technology—academy.smc.edu

Savannah College of Art & Design—www.scad.edu

Tomball College—www.tomballcollege.com

University of California, Los Angeles (UCLA) - Extension—www.uclaextension.edu

University of Central Florida - Florida Interactive Entertainment Academy—fiea.ucf.edu

University of Southern California (USC) - Information Technology Program—itp.usc.edu

University of Southern California (USC) School of Cinematic Arts—interactive.usc.edu

Vancouver Film School—www.vfs.com

Westwood College—www.westwood.edu

Books & Articles

Object-oriented programming is a large topic and is only lightly covered in this book. Those who wish to practice AI programming should study objected-oriented design, Java, and C++ programming:

Gamma, E., Helm, R., Johnson, R. & Vlissides, J. (1995). *Design patterns: Elements of reusable object-oriented software.* Addison-Wesley.

Meyers, S. (2005). *Effective C++: 55 specific ways to improve your programs and designs (3rd ed).* Addison-Wesley.

Schildt, H. (2006). *Java: A beginner's guide (4th ed).* McGraw-Hill Osborne Media.

Stroustrup, B. (2000). *The C++ programming language (3rd ed).* Addison-Wesley.

The following is a list of references and suggested reading associated with game artificial intelligence and other game development topics:

Adams, E. (2003). *Break into the game industry.* McGraw-Hill Osborne Media.

Adams, E. & Rollings, A. (2006). *Fundamentals of game design.* Prentice Hall.

Ahearn, L. & Crooks II, C.E. (2002). *Awesome game creation: No programming required. (2nd ed).* Charles River Media.

Aldrich, C. (2003). *Simulations and the future of learning.* Pfeiffer.

Aldrich, C. (2005). *Learning by doing.* Jossey-Bass.

Atkin, M. & Abercrombie, J. (2005). "Using a goal/action architecture to integrate modularity and long-term memory into AI behaviors." Game Developers Conference.

Axelrod, R. (1985). *The evolution of cooperation.* Basic Books.

Bates, B. (2002). *Game design: The art & business of creating games.* Premier Press.

Beck, J.C. & Wade, M. (2004). *Got game: How the gamer generation is reshaping business forever.* Harvard Business School Press.

Bethke, E. (2003). *Game development and production.* Wordware.

Brandon, A. (2004). *Audio for games: Planning, process, and production.* New Riders.

Brin, D. (1998). *The transparent society.* Addison-Wesley.

Broderick, D. (2001). *The spike: How our lives are being transformed by rapidly advancing technologies.* Forge.

Brooks, D. (2001). *Bobos in paradise: The new upper class and how they got there.* Simon & Schuster.

Business Software Alliance. (May 2005). "Second annual BSA and IDC global software piracy study." www.bsa.org/globalstudy

Campbell, J. (1972). *The hero with a thousand faces.* Princeton University Press.

Campbell, J. & Moyers, B. (1991). *The power of myth.* Anchor.

Castells, M. (2001). *The Internet galaxy: Reflections on the Internet, business, and society.* Oxford University Press.

Castronova, E. (2005). *Synthetic worlds: The business and culture of online games.* University of Chicago Press.

Chase, R.B., Aquilano, N.J. & Jacobs, R. (2001). *Operations management for competitive advantage (9th ed).* McGraw-Hill/Irwin

Cheeseman, H.R. (2004). *Business law (5th ed).* Pearson Education, Inc.

Chiarella, T. (1998). *Writing dialogue.* Story Press.

Cooper, A., & Reimann, R. (2003). *About face 2.0: The essentials of interaction design.* Wiley.

Crawford, C. (2003). *Chris Crawford on game design.* New Riders.

Csikszentmihalyi, M. (1991). *Flow: The psychology of optimal experience.* Perennial.

DeMaria, R. & Wilson, J.L. (2003). *High score!: The illustrated history of electronic games.* McGraw-Hill.

Egri, L. (1946). *The art of dramatic writing: Its basis in the creative interpretation of human motives.* Simon and Schuster.

Erikson, E.H. (1994). *Identity and the life cycle.* W.W. Norton & Company.

Erikson, E.H. (1995). *Childhood and society.* Vintage.

Evans, A. (2001). *This virtual life: Escapism and simulation in our media world.* Fusion Press.

Friedl, M. (2002). *Online game interactivity theory.* Charles River Media.

Fruin, N. & Harringan, P. (Eds.) (2004). *First person: New media as story, performance and game.* MIT Press.

Fullerton, T., Swain, C. & Hoffman, S. (2004). *Game design workshop: Designing, prototyping & playtesting games.* CMP Books.

Galitz, W.O. (2002). *The essential guide to user interface design: An introduction to GUI design principles and techniques.* (2nd ed.). Wiley.

Gardner, J. (1991). *The art of fiction: Notes on craft for young writers.* Vintage Books.

Gee, J.P. (2003). *What video games have to teach us about learning and literacy.* Palgrave Macmillan.

Gershenfeld, A., Loparco, M. & Barajas, C. (2003). *Game plan: The insiders guide to breaking in and succeeding in the computer and video game business.* Griffin Trade Paperback.

Giarratano, J.C. & Riley, G.D. (1998). *Expert systems: Principles & programming (4th ed).* Course Technology.

Gibson, D., Aldrich, C. & Prensky, M. (Eds.) (2006). *Games and simulations in online learning.* IGI Global.

Gladwell, M. (2000). *The tipping point: How little things can make a big difference.* New York, NY: Little Brown & Company.

Gladwell, M. (2007). *Blink: The power of thinking without thinking.* Back Bay Books.

Gleick, J. (1987). *Chaos: Making a new science.* Viking.

Gleick, J. (1999). *Faster: The acceleration of just about everything.* Vintage Books.

Gleick, J. (2003). *What just happened: A chronicle from the information frontier.* Vintage.

Godin, S. (2003). *Purple cow: Transform your business by being remarkable.* Portfolio.

Godin, S. (2005). *The big moo: Stop trying to be perfect and start being remarkable.* Portfolio.

Goldratt, E.M. & Cox, J. (2004). *The goal: A process of ongoing improvement (3rd ed).* North River Press.

Gordon, T. (2000). *P.E.T.: Parent effectiveness training.* Three Rivers Press.

Hamilton, E. (1940). *Mythology: Timeless tales of gods and heroes.* Mentor.

Heim, M. (1993). *The metaphysics of virtual reality.* Oxford University Press.

Hight, J. & Novak, J. (2007). *Game development essentials: Game project management.* Thomson Delmar.

Hsu, F. (2004). *Behind Deep Blue: Building the computer that defeated the world chess champion.* Princeton University Press.

Jensen, E. (2006). *Enriching the brain: How to maximize every learner's potential.* John Wiley & Sons.

Isla, D. (2005). "Handling complexity in the *Halo 2* AI." Game Developers Conference.

Johnson, S. (1997). *Interface culture: How new technology transforms the way we create & communicate.* Basic Books.

Johnson, S. (2006). *Everything bad is good for you.* Riverhead.

Jung, C.G. (1969). *Man and his symbols.* Dell Publishing.

Kent, S.L. (2001). *The ultimate history of video games.* Prima.

King, S. (2000). *On writing.* Scribner.

Knoke, W. (1997). *Bold new world: The essential road map to the twenty-first century.* Kodansha International.

Koster, R. (2005). *Theory of fun for game design.* Paraglyph Press.

Krawczyk, M. & Novak, J. (2006). *Game development essentials: Game story & character development.* Thomson Delmar.

Kurzweil, R. (2000). *The age of spiritual machines: When computers exceed human intelligence.* Penguin.

Laramee, F.D. (Ed.) (2002). *Game design perspectives.* Charles River Media.

Laramee, F.D. (Ed.) (2005). *Secrets of the game business. (3rd ed).* Charles River Media.

Levy, P. (2001). *Cyberculture.* University of Minnesota Press.

Lewis, M. (2001). *Next: The future just happened.* W.W.Norton & Company.

Mackay, C. (1841). *Extraordinary popular delusions & the madness of crowds.* Three Rivers Press.

McConnell, S. (1996). *Rapid development.* Microsoft Press.

McCorduck, P. (2004). *Machines who think: A personal inquiry into the history and prospects of artificial intelligence (2nd ed).* AK Peters.

Mencher, M. (2002). *Get in the game: Careers in the game industry.* New Riders.

Michael, D. (2003). *The indie game development survival guide.* Charles River Media.

Montfort, N. (2003). *Twisty little passages: An approach to interactive fiction.* MIT Press.

Moravec, H. (2000). *Robot.* Oxford University Press.

Morris, D. & Hartas, L. (2003). *Game art: The graphic art of computer games.* Watson-Guptill Publications.

Mulligan, J. & Patrovsky, B. (2003). *Developing online games: An insider's guide.* New Riders.

Murray, J. (2001). *Hamlet on the holodeck: The future of narrative in cyberspace.* MIT Press.

Negroponte, N. (1996). *Being digital.* Vintage Books.

Nielsen, J. (1999). *Designing web usability: The practice of simplicity.* New Riders.

Novak. J. (2007). *Game development essentials: An introduction. (2nd ed.).* Thomson Delmar.

Novak, J. & Levy, L. (2007). *Play the game: The parents guide to video games.* Thomson Course Technology PTR.

Novak, J. (2003). "MMOGs as online distance learning applications." University of Southern California.

Oram, A. (Ed.) (2001). *Peer-to-peer.* O'Reilly & Associates.

Piaget, J. (2000). *The psychology of the child.* Basic Books.

Piaget, J. (2007). *The child's conception of the world.* Jason Aronson.

Rheingold, H. (1991). *Virtual reality.* Touchstone.

Rheingold, H. (2000). *Tools for thought: The history and future of mind-expanding technology.* MIT Press.

Robbins, S.P. (2001). *Organizational behavior (9th ed).* Prentice-Hall, Inc.

Rogers, E.M. (1995). *Diffusion of innovations.* Free Press.

Rollings, A. & Morris, D. (2003). *Game architecture & design: A new edition.* New Riders.

Rollings, A. & Adams, E. (2003). *Andrew Rollings & Ernest Adams on game design.* New Riders.

Rouse, R. (2001) *Game design: Theory & practice (2nd ed).* Wordware Publishing.

Salen, K. & Zimmerman, E. (2003). *Rules of play.* MIT Press.

Sanger, G.A. [a.k.a. "The Fat Man"]. (2003). *The Fat Man on game audio.* New Riders.

Saunders, K. & Novak, J. (2007). *Game development essentials: Game interface design.* Thomson Delmar.

Sellers, J. (2001). *Arcade fever.* Running Press.

Shaffer, D.W. (2006). *How computer games help children learn.* Palgrave Macmillan.

Standage, T. (1999). *The Victorian Internet.* New York: Berkley Publishing Group.

Strauss, W. & Howe, N. (1992). *Generations.* Perennial.

Strauss, W. & Howe, N. (1993). *13th gen: Abort, retry, ignore, fail?* Vintage Books.

Strauss, W. & Howe, N. (1998). *The fourth turning.* Broadway Books.

Strauss, W. & Howe, N. (2000). *Millennials rising: The next great generation.* Vintage Books.

Strauss, W., Howe, N. & Markiewicz, P. (2006). *Millennials & the pop culture.* LifeCourse Associates.

Tufte, E.R. (1983). *The visual display of quantitative information.* Graphics Press.

Tufte, E.R. (1990). *Envisioning information.* Graphics Press.

Tufte, E.R. (1997). *Visual explanations.* Graphics Press.

Tufte, E.R. (2006). *Beautiful evidence.* Graphics Press.

Turkle, S. (1997). *Life on the screen: Identity in the age of the Internet.* Touchstone.

Van Duyne, D.K. et al. (2003). *The design of sites.* Addison-Wesley.

Vogler, C. (1998). *The writer's journey: Mythic structure for writers. (2nd ed).* Michael Wiese Productions.

Welch, J. & Welch, S. (2005). *Winning.* HarperCollins Publishers.

Weizenbaum, J. (1984). *Computer power and human reason.* Penguin Books.

Williams, J.D. (1954). *The compleat strategyst: Being a primer on the theory of the games of strategy.* McGraw-Hill.

Wolf, J.P. & Perron, B. (Eds.). (2003). *Video game theory reader.* Routledge.

Wysocki, R.K. (2006). *Effective project management (4th ed).* John Wiley & Sons.

Index

IMPORTANT-READ CAREFULLY: This End User License Agreement ("Agreement") sets forth the conditions by which Delmar Learning, a division of Thomson Learning Inc. ("Thomson") will make electronic access to the Thomson Delmar Learning-owned licensed content and associated media, software, documentation, printed materials and electronic documentation contained in this package and/or made available to you via this product (the "Licensed Content"), available to you (the "End User"). BY CLICKING THE "I ACCEPT" BUTTON AND/OR OPENING THIS PACKAGE, YOU ACKNOWLEDGE THAT YOU HAVE READ ALL OF THE TERMS AND CONDITIONS, AND THAT YOU AGREE TO BE BOUND BY ITS TERMS CONDITIONS AND ALL APPLICABLE LAWS AND REGULATIONS GOVERNING THE USE OF THE LICENSED CONTENT.

1.0   SCOPE OF LICENSE

1.1   <u>Licensed Content</u>. The Licensed Content may contain portions of modifiable content ("Modifiable Content") and content which may not be modified or otherwise altered by the End User ("Non-Modifiable Content"). For purposes of this Agreement, Modifiable Content and Non-Modifiable Content may be collectively referred to herein as the "Licensed Content." All Licensed Content shall be considered Non-Modifiable Content, unless such Licensed Content is presented to the End User in a modifiable format and it is clearly indicated that modification of the Licensed Content is permitted.

1.2   Subject to the End User's compliance with the terms and conditions of this Agreement, Thomson Delmar Learning hereby grants the End User, a nontransferable, non-exclusive, limited right to access and view a single copy of the Licensed Content on a single personal computer system for noncommercial, internal, personal use only. The End User shall not (i) reproduce, copy, modify (except in the case of Modifiable Content), distribute, display, transfer, sublicense, prepare derivative work(s) based on, sell, exchange, barter or transfer, rent, lease, loan, resell, or in any other manner exploit the Licensed Content; (ii) remove, obscure or alter any notice of Thomson Delmar Learning's intellectual property rights present on or in the License Content, including, but not limited to, copyright, trademark and/or patent notices; or (iii) disassemble, decompile, translate, reverse engineer or otherwise reduce the Licensed Content.

2.0   TERMINATION

2.1   Thomson Delmar Learning may at any time (without prejudice to its other rights or remedies) immediately terminate this Agreement and/or suspend access to some or all of the Licensed Content, in the event that the End User does not comply with any of the terms and conditions of this Agreement. In the event of such termination by Thomson Delmar Learning, the End User shall immediately return any and all copies of the Licensed Content to Thomson Delmar Learning.

3.0   PROPRIETARY RIGHTS

3.1   The End User acknowledges that Thomson Delmar Learning owns all right, title and interest, including, but not limited to all copyright rights therein, in and to the Licensed Content, and that the End User shall not take any action inconsistent with such ownership. The Licensed Content is protected by U.S., Canadian and other applicable copyright laws and by international treaties, including the Berne Convention and the Universal Copyright Convention. Nothing contained in this Agreement shall be construed as granting the End User any ownership rights in or to the Licensed Content.

3.2   Thomson Delmar Learning reserves the right at any time to withdraw from the Licensed Content any item or part of an item for which it no longer retains the right to publish, or which it has reasonable grounds to believe infringes copyright or is defamatory, unlawful or otherwise objectionable.

4.0   PROTECTION AND SECURITY

4.1   The End User shall use its best efforts and take all reasonable steps to safeguard its copy of the Licensed Content to ensure that no unauthorized reproduction, publication, disclosure, modification or distribution of the Licensed Content, in whole or in part, is made. To the extent that the End User becomes aware of any such unauthorized use of the Licensed Content, the End User shall immediately notify Delmar Learning. Notification of such violations may be made by sending an Email to delmarhelp@thomson.com.

5.0   MISUSE OF THE LICENSED PRODUCT

5.1   In the event that the End User uses the Licensed Content in violation of this Agreement, Thomson Delmar Learning shall have the option of electing liquidated damages, which shall include all profits generated by the End User's use of the Licensed Content plus interest computed at the maximum rate permitted by law and all legal fees and other expenses incurred by Thomson Delmar Learning in enforcing its rights, plus penalties.

6.0   FEDERAL GOVERNMENT CLIENTS

6.1   Except as expressly authorized by Delmar Learning, Federal Government clients obtain only the rights specified in this Agreement and no other rights. The Government acknowledges that (i) all software and related documentation incorporated in the Licensed Content is existing commercial computer software within the meaning of FAR 27.405(b)(2); and (2) all other data delivered in whatever form, is limited rights data within the meaning of FAR 27.401. The restrictions in this section are acceptable as consistent with the Government's need for software and other data under this Agreement.

7.0   DISCLAIMER OF WARRANTIES AND LIABILITIES

7.1   Although Thomson Delmar Learning believes the Licensed Content to be reliable, Thomson Delmar Learning does not guarantee or warrant (i) any information or materials contained in or produced by the Licensed Content, (ii) the accuracy, completeness or reliability of the Licensed Content, or (iii) that the Licensed Content is free from errors or other material defects. THE LICENSED PRODUCT IS PROVIDED "AS IS," WITHOUT ANY WARRANTY OF ANY KIND AND THOMSON DELMAR LEARNING DISCLAIMS ANY AND ALL WARRANTIES, EXPRESSED OR IMPLIED, INCLUDING, WITHOUT LIMITATION, WARRANTIES OF MERCHANTABILITY OR FITNESS OR A PARTICULAR PURPOSE. IN NO EVENT SHALL THOMSON DELMAR LEARNING BE LIABLE FOR: INDIRECT, SPECIAL, PUNITIVE OR CONSEQUENTIAL DAMAGES INCLUDING FOR LOST PROFITS, LOST DATA, OR OTHERWISE. IN NO EVENT SHALL DELMAR LEARNING'S AGGREGATE LIABILITY HEREUNDER, WHETHER ARISING IN CONTRACT, TORT, STRICT LIABILITY OR OTHERWISE, EXCEED THE AMOUNT OF FEES PAID BY THE END USER HEREUNDER FOR THE LICENSE OF THE LICENSED CONTENT.

8.0   GENERAL

8.1   <u>Entire Agreement</u>. This Agreement shall constitute the entire Agreement between the Parties and supercedes all prior Agreements and understandings oral or written relating to the subject matter hereof.

8.2   <u>Enhancements/Modifications of Licensed Content</u>. From time to time, and in Delmar Learning's sole discretion, Thomson Thomson Delmar Learning may advise the End User of updates, upgrades, enhancements and/or improvements to the Licensed Content, and may permit the End User to access and use, subject to the terms and conditions of this Agreement, such modifications, upon payment of prices as may be established by Delmar Learning.

8.3   <u>No Export</u>. The End User shall use the Licensed Content solely in the United States and shall not transfer or export, directly or indirectly, the Licensed Content outside the United States.

8.4   <u>Severability</u>. If any provision of this Agreement is invalid, illegal, or unenforceable under any applicable statute or rule of law, the provision shall be deemed omitted to the extent that it is invalid, illegal, or unenforceable. In such a case, the remainder of the Agreement shall be construed in a manner as to give greatest effect to the original intention of the parties hereto.

8.5   <u>Waiver</u>. The waiver of any right or failure of either party to exercise in any respect any right provided in this Agreement in any instance shall not be deemed to be a waiver of such right in the future or a waiver of any other right under this Agreement.

8.6   <u>Choice of Law/Venue</u>. This Agreement shall be interpreted, construed, and governed by and in accordance with the laws of the State of New York, applicable to contracts executed and to be wholly preformed therein, without regard to its principles governing conflicts of law. Each party agrees that any proceeding arising out of or relating to this Agreement or the breach or threatened breach of this Agreement may be commenced and prosecuted in a court in the State and County of New York. Each party consents and submits to the non-exclusive personal jurisdiction of any court in the State and County of New York in respect of any such proceeding.

8.7   <u>Acknowledgment</u>. By opening this package and/or by accessing the Licensed Content on this Website, THE END USER ACKNOWLEDGES THAT IT HAS READ THIS AGREEMENT, UNDERSTANDS IT, AND AGREES TO BE BOUND BY ITS TERMS AND CONDITIONS. IF YOU DO NOT ACCEPT THESE TERMS AND CONDITIONS, YOU MUST NOT ACCESS THE LICENSED CONTENT AND RETURN THE LICENSED PRODUCT TO THOMSON DELMAR LEARNING (WITHIN 30 CALENDAR DAYS OF THE END USER'S PURCHASE) WITH PROOF OF PAYMENT ACCEPTABLE TO DELMAR LEARNING, FOR A CREDIT OR A REFUND. Should the End User have any questions/comments regarding this Agreement, please contact Thomson Delmar Learning at delmarhelp@thomson.com.